More Praise for *Taking Charge*

"In one concise and enjoyable volume, Joan Lester has given women what we always thought the 'old boys network' gave to men: She offers women of all backgrounds personalized feminist strategies for clearing away internalized baggage and finding the power within. Her book not only provides many examples of how the personal is political, it is a step-by-step guide to making the personal powerful."

—Helen Zia, contributing editor, *Ms.*

"*Taking Charge* is more than a 'how to' book—it is a 'why to' book. It should be required reading for all women entering the business world or professions—and don't be surprised if your male friends want to borrow it."

—Erica Garay, senior partner, Radler & Kremer; recipient 1993 Achiever in Law, Long Island Center for Business & Professional Women

"*Taking Charge* teaches self-reliance, networking, alliance building, and imagining—invaluable tools in an increasingly entrepreneurial planet."

—Vicki Torres, small-business reporter for the *Los Angeles Times* and columnist for *Lesbian News*

"Dr. Lester provides an authoritative, practical guide to success for women of all ages, classes, ethnicities, races, and sexual orientations. I highly recommend this book to anyone who has not yet actualized her dreams."

—Nanette K. Gartrell, M.D., associate clinical professor of psychiatry, UCSF

"A must read for every woman and girl!"

—Betsy Koffman, business developer, investor, and entrepreneur

"Every woman is in this book—find yourself . . . Buy it for the Action Guidelines alone—it's practical, powerful, accessible, and personalized."

—Maureen Phillips, founding member and past president of the Massachusetts Women's Bar Association

"Through warm and insightful examples from her own and other women's lives, Dr. Lester deftly teaches women how to own their own excellence, move past the shackles of 'over-nice' imposed by our society, and create the vision of a better future for all humanity."

—Sue Patton Thoele, author of *The Woman's Book of Courage* and *The Courage to Be Yourself*

"How wonderful that women have a book like this one to encourage our power and potential!

"I read Joan Lester's book hungrily, looking for encouragement and instruction. I got both. Dr. Lester understands that women must take charge of our lives. Her objective is strength, not selfishness. She does not see women as isolated strugglers, but as connected seekers of a healthy and rewarding future.

"*Taking Charge* gives us a base from which to develop our power and the power of women we reach out to in our personal and public lives.

"I have made *Taking Charge* a 'must read' for the Women Working with Women workshops I present across the country. Thank you, Dr. Lester!"

—**Carolyn S. Duff, author of** *When Women*
Work Together

Taking Charge grounds in the deep yearning so many women feel to connect the human family across the divides of gender, race, age, ethnic background, sexual orientation and ability. In *Taking Charge,* we discover or remember that we cannot be empowered apart from this yearning fulfilled, through mutual support across the differences. Joan provides hands-on robust tools to guide us through the fear, self-doubt, and unconciousness that block the new and powerful connections required for diversity to liberate rather than divide us, as individuals, companies and communities.

—**Barbara Waugh, Personnel Manager, Hewlett-Packard**
Company

Taking Charge

Also by Joan Steinau Lester

The Future of White Men and Other Diversity Dilemmas

Taking Charge

*Every Woman's Action Guide
to Personal, Political and
Professional Success*

Joan Steinau Lester

*Foreword by Eleanor Holmes Norton,
Washington, D.C. delegate to Congress*

CONARI PRESS
Berkeley, CA

Grateful acknowledgment is made for a quotation from *The Women and the Men* by Nikki Giovanni, copyright © 1970, 1974, 1975, by Nikki Giovanni, by permission of William Morrow & Co., Inc.

Conari Press books are distributed by Publishers Group West.

Cover design: Kathy Warriner
Cover photo credit: Bob Aufuldish
Author photo: Irene Young

ISBN 1-57324-052-4

Library of Congress Cataloging-in-Publication Data

Lester, Joan Steinau, 1940-
    Taking charge : every woman's action guide to personal, political & professional success / by Joan Steinau Lester; foreword by Eleanor Holmes Norton.
        p.   cm.
Includes bibliographical references and index.
ISBN 1-57324-052-4
    1. Women–United States–Life skills guides.   2. Success–United States.
3. Leadership–United States.   I. Title.   II. Title: Every woman's action guide to personal, political & professional success
HQ1221.L64   1996   96-24101
46.7′0082–dc20   CIP

Printed in the United States of America on recycled paper.

10 9 8 7 6 5 4 3 2 1

for *Carole*
and
for *Barbara* and *Morton Steinau*

I used to want the words "She tried" on my tombstone. Now I want "She did it."

—Katherine Dunham

CONTENTS

FOREWORD

By Congresswoman Eleanor Holmes Norton

In this country, virtually every generation has marveled at the rapid change of its period and the extraordinary challenge that this change presents. Surely, however, no change has been as cosmic in its implications nor as sweeping in its effects as the extraordinary change associated with a revision of the role of women in American society. *Taking Charge* will help women to navigate the change.

Change in who women are and in who they can become has no antecedents. The civil rights movement, which helped blacks redefine and empower themselves, was an immediate and immensely influential precedent, but blacks are only a small part of the population, not half or more, as women are. When women decide to move in any direction, their numbers alone can transform everything and everyone.

In the United States, women's change has been largely unaccompanied by societal intervention, except for the law. This legal engine, initially created by activists and lawyers in the civil rights movement, was to drive the entire equality revolution for all who were unequal before the law. For women, though, more will be required than the daunting and effective power of the law. When women, the indispensable partners in human existence, redefine themselves, sometimes gently, sometimes with determined willfulness, they force change everywhere.

No change this fundamental is seamless or effortless, as many in this country are pretending. Women's change is being accomplished with little help except from their own families. Often there is little visible dislocation, but there is a lot more to this picture. Most of what is necessary for women to make the journey to a new status and a new self-awareness has not been available. American women, who have made greater strides than most, often have done it without such basics as maternity leave and child care. They have done it well enough to have created antifeminism, an unmistakable sign of the success of the new woman. Yet the joy of self-discovery has often obscured doubt and self-doubt, disappointment and disillusion, and pain and suffering. Joan Lester's "action guide" unapologetically discusses the barriers and the problems wherever she finds them, whether in women themselves or in others they must confront. She then helps chart a course as practical as it is sensitive.

Joan Lester manages the unlikely task of creating a guidebook for women to personal, societal, and occupational success all at once. She does this by exposing inner demons and societal barriers alike and then systematically suggesting pathways around the obstacles. Using her guidebook approach, she urges women to believe that, like anything else, there are practical ways to confront even the most stubborn roadblocks. Her real-world anecdotes and vignettes will connect women to real people and thus heighten the sense of the possible. (A few sentences capturing Joan's memories of the college days that she and I shared reminded me that I was more brassy and confident than I had any right to be.)

This book gets its memorable insights and its best reality check, however, from Joan's fifteen years' experience traveling the country with workshops, lectures, and training sessions on the many and varied issues of equality. Joan has been in the vineyards, making equality more than rhetoric and more than law. She has been making equality work. In this book, she goes wholesale, sharing what works on the broader scale that a thirsty reading public increasingly welcomes.

Taking Charge makes the case that women can overcome if they stop suffering through and start doing something about it. The second feminist generation has accepted the gains for themselves. Now they must begin new quests to conquer new problems that progress always brings. The heady experience of inventing modern feminism continues, but the inevitable mixture of success and failure requires continuous self-criticism and rethinking.

To realize that there is no turning back is not the same thing as knowing how to move forward. Unlike the feminist vanguard of the 1960s, today's women live with two kinds of consciousness: a joyful awareness of opportunity, but also an intelligent skepticism about the burdens that inevitably come with opportunity. In the beginning, the search was for feminist consciousness. The search today is likely to be for feminist coping strategies. "There is no 'right way' to live a woman's life," Joan Lester says. For many women, the question has become, Is there a way at all?

This book affirms that there certainly are many ways to live a full and happy life as a feminist, but Joan Lester accepts the reality that how to live the life of a modern woman may not be obvious to many captured in today's transition. With women still defining womanhood as they go along, roles and expectations are still often unassimilated. *Taking Charge* will be a helpful compass not only for its usefulness, but also because it conveys a shared sense that there are many women who are rowing in the same waters.

User's Guide

Taking Charge is a multi-layered book, with several possible uses.

1. You can choose to read this like any non-fiction. You may be the kind of reader who skips over the "Tool Kit" at the end of chapters, preferring to stick with the narrative, letting the process of osmosis work its subtle magic.

2. You may want to read the text and then try out strategies in the Tool Kits. Each Tool Kit includes suggestions for specific interventions, bringing to ground ideas described within the chapter.

3. The book is also structured for use as a ten-step course. There are ten chapters ("Milemarkers"), sequenced to take you from the best starting point for any journey—yourself—to the place where you act to influence your whole environment.

   If you choose to use the book as a course, read one chapter a week (or at another interval that suits you), and practice implementing the strategies in the Tool Kit as part of your week's "lesson."

4. If you use *Taking Charge* as a course, you may take it alone, or with others. The exercises are designed to be effective either way. If you use the book with others, it could become the agenda for the first ten meetings of a support group, your Action Team.

5. There is information about how to form, develop, and use an Action Team, a women's support group focused on women taking charge of their lives and acting more effectively as a result. The Action Team material is boxed at the end of each chapter, after the Tool Kit.

   The Action Team segments may be utilized independently as a handbook to form a women's leadership support group. I recommend, however, that even if the development of such a group is your main focus, you at least skim the rest of the text. Reading it will help your group be more successful.

6. And then, there are the marginal quotations. Copy them, post them, use them as affirmations. Gifts from our sister-mothers, these bits of wisdom are our women's encyclopedia, and the taillights we follow to freedom.

7. The bibliography offers an extensive and unusual reading list of diverse women's perspectives on the issues we face. The books and articles cited are not meant to be exhaustive, but are some of my personal favorites, read or reread during the research for *Taking Charge*. Choose a few unfamiliar texts for an exploration into new viewpoints.

One stylistic note: As I collected biographical data on the women whose quotes I placed in the margins and whose stories I cite in the text, I debated whether to include ethnic and sexual orientation descriptors. My desire to incorporate such data was strong, generated by my understanding that women are so often silenced, and, when their voices are heard, they may not be identifiable as women of color or lesbians. Knowing these aspects of a woman may open a door to deeper understanding. Pulling against that understanding was the realization that identifying women with these labels may also pigeonhole them. New dilemmas open: do I risk "outing" some women whose lesbianism is not widely known? And sexual orientation or preference is fluid, while print in a book is fixed. What about those whose partnering habits—or ethnicity—I don't know? Do I, in the interest of parity, then include everyone's sexual preference or ethnicity—not just those who are in numerical minorities?

Ethnic or racial assignments are not so simple either, as I well know, being the mother of biracial adult children. In the space of a short phrase, would the risk of caricature or misrepresentation be greater than the educational value? "Such

My wish is to tell stories about women, historical or contemporary, who walk through fire and come out standing.

**—Linda Lavin,
actor and director**

categories are dynamic ones, based not on transcendental truths, but on the cultural forces of a particular place and time," in the words of writer mocha jean herrup.

I decided the damages of labeling, in these thumbnail portraits, outweighed the advantages of providing visibility, so I include such social data only when it is directly relevant and organic to the quotation or story cited. For example, when ethnicity is a key aspect of an anecdote—as in one I cite by Patricia J. Williams—I include it. When a woman is a "first," and that is a significant aspect of her achievement, I sometimes incorporate that information.

Because of power inequities, there is a convention in the United States that the lack of racial or sexual orientation identification means a person is white or straight (just as the lack of a female designation often implies maleness, as in "lawyer" and "woman lawyer.") In this book, however, that is not the case. Part of *Taking Charge* is getting in the habit of constructing environments that reflect the true diversity around us. So I ask you to make the assumption, as you read about the Sonias, Rosies, Kalimas, Bettys, and Jocelyns herein, that they represent the variety of women who really exist. They do.

Each of the anecdotes I describe is based on an incident I observed or heard from clients or friends, or have experienced directly. Several of the stories about others are composites, and in some descriptions of people and their environments, details have been changed to protect confidentiality.

Enjoy the ride.

Setting Out on the Road to Success

Assessing where women are today on the road to power is difficult—for sexism, like air pollution, looks so normal that we usually notice it only when the occasional danger-level alert is called. Otherwise, our little compromises, the ways we "give up" in portions of our daily lives, fade into the haze. Taking charge means we start conducting regular smog checks, life-scans as regular as our pap smears. Even if we think we don't need to. Like I did.

Two years ago, during my fifteen minutes of fame after my first book was published, a UPI photographer came to shoot a photo for a feature story. He directed me to assume several uncomfortable poses, with my head and body turned this way and that. He posed me, in other words, like a model. The shot his editor finally selected had me seated on a railing with my knees drawn up, arms girlishly around them, while I smiled coyly over one shoulder. A fifty-three-year-old co-ed seated on the railing of a building. (Imagine a middle-aged male executive posed that way.)

The photographer directed. And, equally strangely, I complied.

When I saw that photo, reproduced across the country in sixty-five newspapers, I was humiliated. I was furious at him, and at myself. How could I, a feminist down to my DNA, have allowed such an image to accompany my life story—which described a woman who would never let this happen?

Then I understood: Female amnesia. We so easily forget who we are and what we've done. We forget our miracles as soon as we make them. We don't know how to loop them back to ourselves so we can see the impact and know, I caused that.

When I did a bookstore reading shortly thereafter in an unfamiliar mall, a friend and I drove around looking for the store. Suddenly, we saw a giant marquee, with my name in

It is hard to fight an enemy who has outposts in your head.

—Sally Kempton, writer

Men are taught to apologize for their weaknesses, women for their strengths.

—Lois Wyse, photographer, journalist

lights. The bookstore had a quote from then-Governor Ann Richards ("Terrific Writer!") along with my name and book title. In this extraordinary moment I became real to myself through the novelty of seeing "my name in lights."

Often, however, I forget. So, like many of us, I automatically defer. The photographer was a professional, and knew his business, I thought. (Even those of us who never saw *Father Knows Best* got its message.) I gave away my judgment, and let this man, whom I had never met, control my image. I assumed he knew what he was doing. And he did, from his perspective. He put me in the "female poses" of his repertoire. It was shocking, but informative, to see how he saw me.

A man in my position would be asked to adopt quite a difference stance and project a different persona. In fact, just after my photo appeared, I happened to notice a man exactly my age, a leader of the militia movement, described in *The New York Times Magazine* as being put through a series of "male poses" to accompany the feature story. "Gritz does what the photographers want him to do: he props one of his black cowboy boots on a barbed-wire fence and stares off squinting . . ." Not quite the co-ed look, though perhaps fueling an equally disastrous stereotype.

Because of this photographic convention, in which women sit coyly and men straddle fences, Gloria Steinem's cover photograph by Sigrid Estrada on *Moving Beyond Words* was astonishing. She is shown propped against the side of a house, dressed in black boots and black jeans, with her legs spread wide open, taking up space and putting herself in a public pose typically denied to women—except when nude. A few years later, Alice Walker's cover photo by Jean Weisinger on *The Same River Twice* compelled me the same way. I sat staring at this woman looking boldly and happily at the camera, legs spread "unfemininely" apart.

To those who call us bean counters for demanding parity in every profession, my retort is these photos. I now call mine "cheesecake with clothes." A woman seen through a man's eyes.

Yes, the mind behind the camera—or the pen or gavel—does matter; it comes with a history.

And when I look at that photo now with some chagrin, it's a reminder: Never again will I give up and hope for the best, simply because it seems easiest at the time. Now I ask myself, as often as I can remember: Am I going on automatic, saying Yes when I have a feeling, however vague, of No? Is this an area where I should be taking charge, making the decisions? Rather than leave everything to the "experts."

Over the last fifteen years, I've coached scores of dynamic female leaders—business owners, corporate vice presidents, college administrators and professors, executive directors of non-profit agencies, national change agents. All powerful and accomplished women with whom I've worked behind the scenes, helping them assert power. I've also assisted women in junior positions struggle to take leadership, in all the ways they define it. I've worked with women on the line, with secretaries and teachers, women who are active participants in their own lives. And during this time I've observed myself grow as well, as an author, speaker, syndicated commentator, and executive director of a national agency.

One startling thing we all have in common: none of us realize how good we are. And we each think this is our unique flaw. Women act powerfully in the world—women are powerful—but our actions have a nasty habit of disappearing from view before we fully take in who we are and what we've done. Thus we are always on edge, over-preparing, waiting for the other shoe to drop. We hardly notice the subtle ways we still defer, handing out bits of our power like lifesavers.

Why do so many women not realize their impact, and thereby their power? Why is it that Jean, for example, a woman who makes major decisions all day long, defers so utterly in the evening to her male dates, listening patiently over dinner to long stories in which she lacks interest? Or Mickey, who runs a five-million-dollar business, still thinks of herself as heading a small start-up? And Sharon, a lawyer internationally renowned

Dr. Kissinger was surprised that I knew where Ghana was.

—Shirley Temple Black, former Ambassador to Ghana

xix

as an expert on domestic violence, a woman who writes legislation for state governments and keynotes conferences, sometimes finds herself looking idly in the paper at want ads, scanning jobs for "legal secretary." "That's a job," she told me, "I'm sure I could do—and get."

Moving Forward

This is a remarkable era. Over these last few decades, women have opened ourselves, as never before, to the possibility of fully taking charge of our lives. We have demanded, and accomplished, massive change in every sphere of U.S. life, crashing through barriers to greater choices. We've summoned the courage to speak truth to power—and to each other, talking of bitterness, disappointments, and dreams that lay curled in our hearts. We've made our agenda central to the nation, educating legislators and families about our issues.

Women are taking leadership in ever new arenas, exploring new careers, demanding reproductive control and equal pay, claiming flexible work options, same-sex partner benefits, and child care on the job. Women are consciously networking as never before. We're even being reminded to toot our own horns, after centuries of silence in the brass section.

We've flooded out of kitchens, forcing entry to jobs closed to us for centuries. We've secured those jobs using the teeth in the 1964 Civil Rights Act, requiring nondiscrimination to women in hiring and promotion. As we've expanded our horizons in the generation since this remarkable legislation, women have created an international movement, with dramatic results. In the past twenty years, the worldwide "gender-related development index" almost doubled, rising to .6 on a U.N. scale where 1 equals equality.

The 1995 U.N. Beijing conference on women, reflecting the sophistication we've developed over the last few decades of organizing, issued an unprecedented statement affirming women's right to control our sexuality, free from coercion,

It wasn't just a song for us, "We Shall Overcome." It was our strength. When I see people heading up organizations and doing all these things, it didn't come about overnight and it didn't come without pain . . . Now, I am the law. I am over the slave owners that used to be over me.

—Unita Blackwell, mayor, Mayersville, Mississippi

discrimination, or violence. And under pressure from the conference, the U.S. government made a commitment to establish some major "firsts," including a White House Council on Women, a Justice Department domestic violence campaign, and a Labor Department program to improve workplaces for women.

In the last thirty years women accomplished all this—while we transformed North America's workplaces. Not bad for a generation's work.

Now, as we approach the millennium, it's time to take off with renewed vigor. We are well positioned to blast forward. We have the experience, with a generation's victories under our collective belt, and we have the technology, reproductive devices, and machinery—like computers and cranes—that equalize differences in the statistically "average" male and female body sizes and strengths.

Taking the Driver's Seat

Today, we ourselves hold the key to moving forward. For now that women have opened at least partial access to every arena, our next step is to learn how we compromise our power. And how to take charge in every setting, taking action to grab hold of the equality that still seems to elude us.

We are, as women, on a road marked for power. But it's been a route with unexpected detours and forced turns. Some years we found unexpected energy; adrenaline burst through our veins like high octane-gas exploding in an engine. Those years we've shot ahead, no matter the rough terrain. At other times we find the road littered with yesterday's scraps, remnants we thought had long ago been cleaned up.

The pressures to return to the old ways—to defer—are particularly intense today, with a growing backward-looking movement. We face a complicated climate for women that is at once hostile and hospitable, with budget cutbacks dismantling social supports to women's independence: subsidized day care,

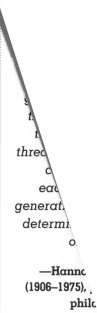

three

ea

generat

determi

o

—Hann
(1906–1975),
phil

welfare, and affirmative action. Simultaneously we have a flowering of women's networks and literature, legislation like the Family Leave Act, a new judicial willingness to punish sexual harassment, and a movement of young women re-inventing feminism for a complex era.

How, in this confusing climate, one that says Yes but may mean No, do we get to the point where we decide to take the risk and hop in the driver's seat of our lives? And then, once in, how do we pass up the many detours that lure us with nostalgic images? Maybe, those detours promise, we don't have to be in that uncomfortable driver's seat after all. Wouldn't it be nicer just to sit back in the passenger seat and let someone else steer around those hard bumps in the road? It's tempting to think that someone else might take care of our troubles. However, those of us who have taken routes to the past find that the fantasy rarely delivers. Despite the appeal of the promise that someone will "take care of us," in this life we usually have to climb the rough side of the mountain ourselves.

This isn't to say we have to go it alone. On the contrary, women in every setting do better with the aid of others. Recent studies of breast cancer patients find we even live longer in support groups. Creating such collaborative networks is something we, as women, are well poised to do. But the assistance we get needs to be grounded in respect. Our allies must cheer us on, rather than grab the wheel.

Many of us find it hard to claim our power, including insisting on allies who support our leadership and encourage our decision-making capabilities. Too often, internally, we still let others describe and define us in one way or another. How do we, unwittingly and unnervingly, still allow ourselves to be so often maneuvered by others' expectations? And, specifically, what can we do about it, alone and in concert with other women?

How, we wonder, can we finally put to rest that Cinderella brain cell that keeps popping up, replaying the old story: "If I

Roseanne is an example of how hard it is to separate victimization from empowerment today. On the one hand, she is one of the ones who've "made it," a "powerbabe" if ever there was one. . . . (But) her success hasn't kept her from being endlessly exploited and humiliated by the very media through which she has gained so much "power."

—**Elayne Rapping,** professor of communications

am very, very good, someone will come to save me, and take care of me forever." (And put me in the passenger seat of the pumpkin, of course.)

Women have developed a literature explaining the persistence of this maverick brain cell which dictates to women: Yield! Concede power! Feminist scholars like Jean Shinoda Bolen, Carol Gilligan, Matina Horner, Rosabeth Moss Kanter, Audre Lorde, Jean Baker Miller, and Alice Walker, among many others, have examined how women sabotage ourselves on the way to power, sometimes just as we're accomplishing major life achievements. The world can be so inhospitable to our success that occasionally, as law professor Patricia J. Williams writes about one woman, a judge, who split at the seams, "Knowing she was to be devoured by life, she made herself inedible, full of thorns and sharp edges."

When we do succeed, the cognitive dissonance can be massive. Who am I now? we wonder. Am I still a woman, am I still loyal to "my people" (whoever they are) if I triumph, when so many of my sisters don't?

At the same time, these scholars analyzed our tendencies to self-destruct when faced with impossible expectations—do succeed/don't succeed—they noticed how poorly women fit existing models of success. When norms are based on the typical life cycle of men (and whites), scales defining success don't fit the breadth or depth, the very shape, of our lives. Feminist investigators found that we are often considered failures when we aren't, because the assessment norms aren't appropriate.

We now have an illuminating body of research describing the problems. Women in business, women in academia, women in leadership anywhere—are stretching, breaking barriers, and having trouble. The practical discussion of how to address these challenges—the self-sabotage, the poor fit—has just begun. Precisely how, after being socialized to throw away success, do we claim it? How do we remember to shift to drive when our tendency, as we are threatened, is to go into reverse? What will help us stand firm when all our training is

Thoughts have power. Thoughts are energy. And you can make your world or break your world by your thinking.

**—Susan L. Taylor,
Editor-in-chief,
Essence**

Implicitly adopting the male life as the norm, they have tried to fashion women out of a masculine cloth. It all goes back, of course, to Adam and Eve—a story which shows, among other things, that if you make a woman out of a man, you are bound to get into trouble.

—Carol Gilligan, scholar, author

whispering, "Make nice?" Or "Assimilate. Fit in." Exactly how do we move out of the passenger seat over to the driver's side and steer our lives? Where are our guides as we make this shift, in power and in self-perception?

And how do we change the norms by which performance is assessed, in a climate where we often hear the concern that our presence will lower standards? Given that women's sense of self is, as Jean Baker Miller says, "very much organized around being able to make, and then to maintain, affiliations and relationships," how do we use that skill to advantage in today's workplace? Can we proudly claim our "feminine" strengths, using them to move forward, without giving anything up, and create groups of women who advance together, rather than compete for the few spots we think are available?

Recent writing by Sally Helgesen, Felice Schwartz, Carolyn S. Duff, Alice Walker, and Judith B. Rosener, among others, describes the unique nature and contribution of female work styles, forming what Helgesen terms "the female advantage." This advantage is an expertise that comes easily to many women, resulting from our training to nurture and value relationships—skills much needed in today's work world. Managerial methods now viewed as female-pioneered are newly "discovered" inclusive forms of organization. Communication, for instance, is now encouraged among people from all levels and specializations. Such reorganization and reengineering, along what we might call feminist principles (less hierarchy, greater input in decision making, flexibility, good communications) is helpful news to many organizations.

How do we claim these historically female strengths and skills, without being type-cast as Earth Mothers? And how do we acknowledge some of the down-sides of these styles (such as feeling we have to get everyone's approval before we move ahead), without reverting to self-condemnation? It's time to assert the worth of "female" attributes we've devalued, like expertise with relationships; and it's time to expand our repertoires to include the strengths men have claimed as their unique territory—like assuming they'll be in charge wherever they go, setting self-oriented goals, and habitually choosing options that benefit themselves. Now is the moment to expand our visions so we can select our actions from the full spectrum of possibilities. And we need to claim this territory together.

Taking Charge offers a helping hand on the journey. It is an action guide for women at any stage of self-understanding and self-development who need help finding within themselves the assurance to succeed, and are looking for specific ideas about how to do this. Depending on where you are in your life's journey, you will draw different strengths and skills from *Taking Charge*. If you're just starting out in the work world, you'll see that whether you're making computer chips or designing fabrics, teaching elementary math or becoming a free-lance journalist, you face a set of internal and external injunctions similar to those confronted by women around you. You'll discover a range of tactics to help you move forward at the speed you choose. *Taking Charge* provides an unusual multidimensional perspective, noting both the similarities of our challenges, and differing limitations faced by each woman, depending on her age, class, and ethnic background. The stereotypes imposed on each of us reflect the culture's idea of our expected role, and thus our boundaries.

If you're a young woman who grew up as part of the feminist movement, and you carry the burden of high expectations—"we gave you the moon, now jump over it"—this book may help you relax into yourself. It can give you the encouragement you need to follow your dreams, set goals and make the choices that make your heart sing, rather than having to prove your exemplary status—a new twist on the old theme of female self-sacrifice.

If you're a woman who supervises people at work or at home—setting rules and giving instructions—you can learn from successful strategies employed by other women in similar situations. And if you've been thinking about questions of equality for decades, *Taking Charge* provides inspiration and a

It is always a magnificent sight when great masses of people are able to collectively harmonize on extremely high moral frequencies. It is comparable to a sunrise.

—Alice Walker, Pulitzer Prize-winning author

It is time to apply in the arena of the world the wisdom and experience that women have gained over so many thousands of years.

—Aung San Suu Kyi, Nobel laureate

framework for joining two strands of feminist thought: the external backlash, and our own unwitting self-sabotage. *Taking Charge* links strategies for dismantling both barriers.

This book, like women's lives, is about our insides and our outsides, and how they relate. As a multi-faceted woman myself—mother, mate, administrator, commentator, author, artist, friend, and women's support group member—I have drawn from many aspects of my own experience to create *Taking Charge*.

I started the project excited about its uniqueness. It melds, as my own life does, several issues crucial for women: our personal empowerment; effective outward strategies as we increasingly take charge of our lives; and our ability to support each other in groups. Many books have concentrated on one or the other of these topics. I combined them. As I was close to finishing, I worried that the book was too complex. "Oh, this is what I always do," I groaned one evening to my Women, Money and Power support group. "Why can't I just write a book about one topic? This is so complicated. Too broad. What's wrong with me?" One of the women in the group looked at me in astonishment. "Joan, the breadth is one of your—and the book's—greatest assets. Start thinking about it as a great quality. You're taking a comprehensive look at women's lives rather than a narrow one. Right now you're doing just what you write about, self-deprecating, not even seeing what this book is!" She smiled at me in that friendly, quizzical way we each do when we can so clearly see another woman's accomplishment, and are puzzled that she can't see it herself. With her words, I got an exciting glimpse of my work, and saw, for that moment, how I eclipsed myself.

I also suddenly realized that I was doing something so early ingrained it's unconscious: comparing myself to a male, linear "one right way" and "one thing at a time" model. Women's lives aren't like that. We talk to each other about our periods or lack of them, seamlessly move to international policy or our latest work projects, then back to our day, our families, or a recent movie or TV program we saw. "What's happening with Oprah?" we ask, and then it's on to an analysis of the politics of talk shows, sliding effortlessly back to our bodies, or the babies in our families.

Women are also used to doing several things at once: vacuuming while tending a child or two, folding laundry while we return phone calls and simultaneously jot down a shopping list or "To Dos" for our job, or notes for a song we're writing. We live on many levels, combining attention to work with deep commitments to family and home—often adding community, friendship, and spiritual interests to the mix. We live broadly. And, to cope with the immensity of our challenges, we improvise. There is no one "right way" to live a woman's life... but there are travel tips from those who have gone this way before.

If I actually ran the world, I'd do it from the kitchen. It's not anything deliberate or a statement or anything, that's just how I understand things.

—Jamaica Kincaid, novelist

The Map

I set out, with this book, to answer the question: How can women—all women—become empowered enough to act as forcefully and effectively as we need to, to succeed in the roles we're winning our way into?

I discovered three paths, each of which takes courage to follow:

- Becoming central beings in our own universes.

- Deciding to take charge in every aspect of our lives.

- Creating alliances where we support each other's leadership and also deliberately develop male allies.

This book is dedicated to the proposition that we get to travel all three roads; we can embrace the breadth of our resplendently complex potential. None of us has to settle for half-lives, where we act powerfully and then snatch our victories away—or allow them to be stolen—before we even notice what has happened. It is possible to transform ourselves, and simultaneously, society.

Taking Charge is a map breaking the trip into four

It is the easiest thing in the world to say every broad for herself—saying it and acting that way is one thing that's kept some of us behind the eight ball where we've been living for a hundred years.

—Billie Holiday (1915–1959), musician

highways: Getting Centered, Taking Action, Building Alliances, and Creating a Vision. Following this route, women will be able to get all the way home, in company with other women (and our male allies), confident that we have a place in this society as shapers and definers—rather than being molded and defined by others.

Many women have pioneered this road. Each one of us who travels it, a pilgrim, wears a deeper track. My own journey began with a consciousness-raising group I led in New York City in 1968. That same year I was a delegate to the first National Women's Liberation Conference, held in Chicago. We dashed into every taboo topic: The family, reproduction, space of our own, sexuality.

During those years, we studied, wrote, talked, marched, changed laws and policies. And our lives exploded. The women's movement tore through our lives, uprooting universes and reorienting perspectives. (Before 1968, I took it as a compliment when men told me I "thought like a man.")

Our realities ruptured. I was angry for the next ten years.

When the hurricane passed, a decade later, I was a single mom, working one and sometimes two jobs, taking classes at night. I was struggling. In 1981, I got my doctorate in multicultural education. That same year, as the white parent of African American children, I recommitted myself to making a safer world for them by conducting seminars on Unlearning Racism in my living room. And that year I came out. Soon, my new life-mate (a civil rights lawyer) and I co-founded Equity Institute, a national think tank and consulting agency on diversity strategies.

Over the fifteen years since then, as we've conducted programs and provided executive coaching to leaders, I've been struck by the tenacity of the women I encounter. So many persevere in the face of seemingly impossible obstacles. Women manage dazzlingly complex lives, with mind-boggling schedules of parent/teacher meetings, shopping, meal preparation, and jobs. Some endure closeted work lives, solo parenting, or indifferent spouses, whose own careers flourish with the home-support they enjoy. At work, women too often find colleagues habituated to women in subservient or sexual roles.

Yet even with the weights dragging women down, we continue to deliver miracles: Getting that college degree, making supervisor on the job, publishing five scientific papers in a year, starting a contracting business, becoming the night manager of a grocery store, raising wonderful children, taking leadership in communities, organizing women's groups at work, nurturing friendships.

And sometimes, our miracle is simply that we survive—no small victory.

Opening the Roads

Women, pouring into the U.S. workforce, are now almost half of all paid workers. Partly as a result of the backlash we face inside established companies, we're starting our own new businesses five times faster than men—a rate sure to increase even more with a new Treasury Department Program (announced at the 1995 Beijing Conference) to give start-up resources to women. As these new companies mature, they become significant employers. Women-owned firms currently hire eleven million people, more than the Fortune 500 combined.

Women now provide about half of families' financial support, nationally. (Yet employed outside the home or not, nine out of ten of us remain responsible for taking care of the people in our families.)

Women have also penetrated formerly all-male networks in politics. Female senators like Carol Moseley-Braun are changing the old-boy Senate routines in which women's concerns were given perfunctory attention. According to Congresswoman Marge Roukema, "There are some matters that have received attention only because of the presence of senior women in positions of power." For the first time, we

I have met brave women who are exploring the outer edge of human possibility, with no history to guide them, and with a courage to make themselves vulnerable that I find moving beyond words.

—Gloria Steinem, co-founder, *Ms.*

I make a choice between career and lifestyle daily, hourly, by the minute. . . . If I need to leave a meeting to do something for my son Jason, I do, and if I need to be working at 10 at night I bring my kids in. My kids would probably tell you they work at Intel, too.

—Carlene Ellis, Vice President, Intel Corp.

have a few. While a few tokens don't completely alter a patriarchal picture, as commentator Mary Zepernick says, women in Congress are raising new issues. In other political arenas, we are beginning to get leaders as well: Laura D'Andrea Tyson, for instance, who chairs the President's Council of Economic Advisers.

With our new clout in business and politics, we're forcing recognition of the realities of women at work. We're making noise about the precarious balancing acts women attempt without the luxury of "wives" who devote themselves to our careers and our laundry. (Several recent studies found, not surprisingly, that fathers whose wives stay home earn more and get higher raises than those whose partners work.) Women en masse are demanding public conversations about the difficulties of juggling family, household, community or religious life, and work, and the challenge of trying to keep all the balls up in the air while remaining half-way lucid. In response to these demands, policies and laws are changing. Workplaces must now give Family Leave, some companies offer child care at work, flex time, job-sharing, and day-care stipends. Yet the "second shift" women still work at home adds an estimated additional fifteen hours to our work weeks, compared to men's. Researcher Arlie Hochschild calculated that over a year, women work an extra month of twenty-four hour days.

And, adding insult to injury, in spite of our new clout, women still have a tough time being taken seriously. Historically, even our time has been disrespected, as any woman knows who has ever gnashed her teeth waiting for a repair person or telephone installer. Since it was only women at home awaiting these heroes, corporations saw no need to commit to appointments more specific than a four hour time block, giving us a clear message about the low value of home labor. And the laborers. (This glass is, however, also half full. Twenty years ago, the industry standard was full-day appointment spans. So our social value doubled in a generation!) Having to "prove" ourselves at work is a carry-over of the low regard we've suffered at home, and remains an obstruction for women in every occupation, at every level. Female entrepreneurs, for example, find that lenders still look at women-owned businesses as part-time activities run out of the home. Women of color who present business plans to banks face double hurdles: racial lending discrimination coupled with the stereotype of women as homemakers rather than executives. Proving capability and establishing the credibility of their businesses are the biggest problems facing almost half the women who responded to a 1995 survey by the National Foundation for Women Business Owners.

So, while we're moving forward, women continue to face roadblocks: not being taken seriously, expectations of dual roles, harassment, lack of mentoring and support networks. And lower pay. Despite a concerted women's movement, and despite progress in pay, women still make only 74% of male wages, on average. Even in traditionally female fields, women earn less than men for the same job. A male elementary school teacher, for example, averages a $34,000 salary while a female in the same job makes $24,000. For lawyers and psychologists, the pay differential is the same, at every level. It's hard to live on less money. It also lessens ability to accumulate assets. Ultimately, lower pay today means smaller social security and pension checks tomorrow.

In this environment—where women have made giant gains, yet still face entrenched obstacles—we need to figure out how to accelerate our movement. We have opened the roads, legally, and gotten past some of the roadblocks. We attend many of the meetings that used to be men-only. Now we need to know how to be taken seriously once we get there, and we need to figure out how to get critical masses of women there alongside us.

We're having trouble cracking the usually better paid "male" jobs. Ninety-eight percent of all secretaries, for instance, are women, but fewer than one of fifty carpenters or auto mechanics is female. Only 9% of all female job-holders

White men, 33% of the U.S. population, remain in firm control of over 90% of the senior ranks of virtually every occupation.

—"Glass Ceiling" Commission Report, 1995.

> *I have no modesty,*
> *none. It's a waste of*
> *time. It's a learned*
> *affectation . . . If*
> *life slams the mod-*
> *est person against*
> *the wall, he or she*
> *will drop that mod-*
> *esty quicker than a*
> *stripper will drop*
> *her G-string. What I*
> *hope I have and*
> *what I pray for is*
> *humility. Humility*
> *comes from within.*
> *Humility says there*
> *were people before*
> *me who found*
> *the path.*
>
> **—Maya Angelou,**
> **writer**

work outside the traditional female spheres. The last twenty-five years have, however, made a difference. Women are now almost 50% of all economists—up from 14% a generation ago; 23% of lawyers and judges (up from 6%) and 25% of doctors (up from 11%).

Yet even when women get into these skilled occupations, careers stagnate. Women make up 50% of entry-level accountants but under 20% of accounting firm partners; 74% of teachers but only 6% of school superintendents. For too many decision makers, the workplace is not the place we are meant to be, at least not as peers. This attitude was poignantly (and pathetically) expressed by Presidential contender Senator Phil Gramm in his response to a question about whether he might share his ticket with a female running mate. "No," he said. "Sophia Loren is not a citizen."

That perception by gate-keepers to power is one reason women constitute less than five percent of senior executives. We're making some headway in prestigious Boards of Directors—a third of Fortune 500 companies now have more than one female director. But they still employ no female CEOs. (Among Fortune 1000 firms there are only two female chief executive officers: Linda Wachner of Warnaco, a New York apparel maker, and Marion Sandler is co-CEO and co-chairman, with her husband, of Golden West Financial in Oakland, California, which she cofounded.)

The complexity of our lives is reflected in the struggles of our public women. "If life is a three-legged stool—work, family and personal life—" says one senior executive, Barbara Otto of Bank-America, "I gave up the third leg." Even those few women who have "made it" seem to be having difficulty.

"In the big picture of gender battles in public life," notes social critic Elayne Rapping, "there aren't clear winners and losers. Not yet... Madonna and Amy Fisher, Anita Hill and Lani Guinier—they're all in the same game. So, too, are Tonya and Nancy. And Lorena Bobbitt and Thelma and Louise. Even Zoë Baird and her au pair girl. And none of them, from Zoë to

Anita, has totally escaped the bonds of sexism. The truth is that there are no individual winners."

Given these challenges, how do we resist the pressure to settle for crumbs—because they're so delicious after the starvation diet we've been on? How do we find the determination to hang tough in a negotiation, when our male counterpart expects us to back off? How do we get our voices heard when men take disproportionate air time, and they're louder anyway? How do we break into the loop, when the guys go out after-hours for beer or golf with the boss? How do we consciously develop male allies—and simultaneously form our own networks? How do we bring other women along with us?

We have come a long way, but the variety of new barriers is endless. How do we supervise or manage other people, when our training is urging us to take care of them—and to make sure they like us? What do we do when we're working on a construction site (we finally got the training, and the job) and the men lift the port-a-potty we're occupying off the ground with a crane—as happened to a union carpenter in California? Or when we find graffiti on our locker at work, as one New York woman did, that says, "If women listened to five little words there would be no domestic violence: Shut the fuck up, bitch!"

And what do we say when we get home after work, and our partner, who has been there for two hours, asks, "What's for dinner, honey?"

To continue our progress without getting derailed by these predicaments, we need new strategies, expansive images, and a renewed understanding that to move ahead in any lasting way, we need to band together.

This wave of the women's movement began with women coming together to investigate our common dilemmas. We probed the patriarchy, we analyzed and marched, we spoke truth to power. After a decade of such scrutiny and mutual support, many women went off on the road alone: to focus on families, make it financially, go into therapy, or otherwise

Why should I feel threatened? There'll never be another me.

—Leontyne Price, operatic soprano, winner of eighteen Grammy Awards

The quantum world has demolished the concept of the unconnected individual.

—Margaret Wheatley, author.

rummage through our individual psyches, go back to school or develop careers. Now, using the insights from both sets of experiences, and fortified by a new generation of women who have grown up with expanded expectations, we are coming back together to figure out how to claim all our power—external and internal. Emerging in new forms to accommodate an old need, we are today witnessing a surge of Women's Power Groups, Leadership Teams, Mentoring Programs, Sister Circles, Female Networks, and Wise Women Gatherings.

Now, we realize, it's time to mobilize our interior strengths and use them to leverage the force we generate in groups, so we can move ahead together with maximum effect. That is why this book contains both strategies for personal development and, at the end of every chapter, a discussion of how to form a group and how powerful it can be.

It's hard to reach for the strongest essence of ourselves when we lack support from the women around us. Yet accessing that support isn't always easy. One barrier to forming powerful teams is that many of us imagine that other women, who we see accomplishing big things, have a secret ingredient we were born without. It's difficult to rejoice in other women's successes—and thereby truly give or get support—as long as we're in a competitive mode. How can we form effective support groups if we feel insecure and inadequate when someone else gets attention? Or, if we put ourselves at the other end of the spectrum, the "up side," we may feel better, but our task of making common cause with those to whom we now feel superior is no easier.

Women who do maintain a strong sense of self, women who are able to remember most of the time, even under attack, that they're smart and tough, often face another hurdle: They wonder if they're selfish, because they're devoting themselves wholeheartedly to work—or play—and enjoying it so much. If they were "feminine enough," they wonder, wouldn't they be thinking more about others' needs?

Many powerful women are like the child beaten up in the

school yard, who goes home after school to a whipping for having been in a fight. Women who are criticized—by coworkers, friends, or community colleagues—then often suffer an internal interrogation: Who do you think you are? Don't you want anyone to like you? And the most damning condemnation of all, the self-directed one: I'm selfish, mean—an ogre!

Offered the terrible choice between love and respect, we, unlike men, have been programmed to choose love. When we make the conscious decision to go for respect, we're suddenly on a road we've never seen before. The scenery may look beautiful, but we're in strange country. How are we supposed to act here?

Today, women are ready to tackle the complexity of these topics. This is a moment when we have the experience and the momentum of our multi-faceted movement. We have a string of victories behind us. Could we have imagined just a decade ago that sexual harassment would take center stage as a workplace issue of stunning proportion? Could we have foreseen the bravery of Anita Hill as she battled the "world's most exclusive men's club"? Did we dream that both senators from California would be female—and Jewish? And that one of them, Barbara Boxer, would lead the fight to expose another senator's lechery to public scrutiny, forcing him to resign?

Little did we imagine that "firsts" would be tumbling at us every week: the first woman entering The Citadel or serving on an aircraft carrier; the first female Native American chief; the first critical masses of women forming in police departments; college after college finally inaugurating women at the top; and ivy-covered, New England, old-line Smith College selecting its first African American female president. Now we're entering an era where we're beginning to get "seconds," like the two women on the Supreme Court.

The list goes on. We've been widely successful. And, as we move along, we continue to encounter speed-bumps, obstacles to our rapid progress. At this moment, when we have a wealth of insights gained over the last three decades, it's time to focus

For women to put our hopes and desires into words is still a magical and rebellious thing in spite of how common it may seem to be.

—Jewelle Gomez, writer, activist

You don't get to choose how you're going to die. Or when. You can decide how you're going to live now.

—Joan Baez, folksinger

our energies into practical strategies.

My goal for you, the reader, is to make your journey along the road to your empowerment—whatever it is—an easier one, and to give you practical tools to help you get farther than you ever thought you could go.

My goal for myself is to fully live the precepts I so boldly set out. The concepts underlying *Taking Charge* were developed with hundreds of thousands of participants in Equity Institute programs, conducted over the last fifteen years by myself and my training staff. The exact configuration of words and thoughts in this book have been piloted on a sample of one—the author. And it's working.

During the writing of *Taking Charge,* as I created sentences that hammered themselves into my brain, my leadership became noticeably more effective. I retrained myself to monitor, in difficult situations, my internal responses. I now notice, for example, what internally "giving up" looks like for me, as when I deferred to the photographer who posed me like a pin-up girl. I realize this "giving up" brain cell activates when the pressures of leadership become too great; I feel the urge to abdicate, rather than think about how to get support or take charge. As I wrote the book and further explored my own responses I came to more deeply understand how common, how tempting—and how disastrous—such avoidance is. Now, when I feel the desire to flee (and conjure up the fantasy-life du jour) I ask myself, How can I take charge here? Where is my power in this situation?

And then I tell myself: Exert it!

Reflecting on my life and how "giving up" has manifested at various times, I realize that I literally did intend to give up everything, including my life, in two suicide attempts I made as a teenager. Looking back to those years, I have often wondered what could have made me want to flee so much that I would put my head in an oven, turn on the gas without lighting the pilot, and wait, with my head on a pillow, for death. Fortunately, I was an impatient teen. After half an hour, when nothing happened, I gave it up. Another time I took an entire bottle of aspirin, causing me only a night of vomiting and a two-day hangover. But what could have been that hard? I had loving parents, friends, was bright and acknowledged as such, and was attractive in the conventional way of the times. My teen-age years came just a little after Sylvia Plath's suicide, and before this wave of the women's movement. Though talented and "looking good," I was utterly lost. Where was my road to power? I couldn't see one, so I gave up.

With today's perspective, I understand why I couldn't see a place for myself anywhere. Not a place that I wanted. I had not one tail light to follow—no woman's life that looked like the one I wanted—until, in college, where I had no female professors, I met the wife of my English teacher. She, an intellectual herself, was very kind to me, as was he. No wonder I shortly thereafter married a writer, since that's what I wanted to be. I had no idea how to actualize this potential in myself, but editing my husband's work and socializing with his friends got me closer to what I then saw as the way to create ideas.

Today, I feel lucky to be alive, and to have survived to ride this wave of the women's movement. It was just in time. Today, in tough situations, I consciously survey possible sources of support, and make sure to utilize them. When I'm setting out in a new direction, I look for examples of women who have taken the road before me. If I can't find any taillights to follow, I surround myself with other resources as I plunge ahead into the fertile, but sometimes bewildering, darkness.

And this time, as I set out to take even greater charge of my life, I wrote the book I needed to read. My hope is that it proves as helpful to you as writing it has been for me. May we all provide taillights for other women to follow as they take their own journeys to power, however that pilgrimage looks for each woman.

The universe is made of stories, not of atoms.

—Muriel Rukeyser (1913–1979), poet and teacher

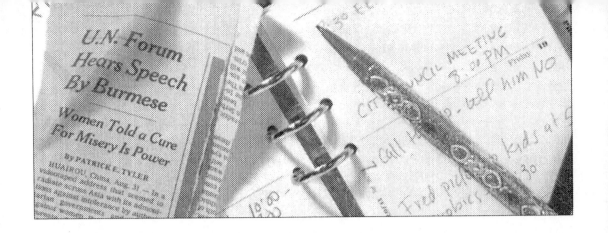

Highway One:
Getting Centered

●

Mile Marker One:
Remember Who We Are

The foundation chapter for the book
explains pressures on women to "forget"
who we are and suggests strategies
for remembering the infinite
possibilities open to us.

Mile Marker One:
Remember Who We Are

All my life I've wanted to be somebody. But I see now I should have been more specific.

—Jane Wagner, Lily Tomlin's collaborator

It's a challenge to create fully realized lives without road maps. What women have taken the road to power before us and how did they do it? We hardly know, since the few markers they left have been demolished or overtaken with weeds. During the last generation, we've unearthed some of the signs and learned to read symbols previously misunderstood—or erased. But these precious guides to diverse life scripts continue to be few. Growing up in "a man's world" has created voids that we fill with imagination, if we follow an impulse to escape the one narrow route that is visible. We are constantly creating something (our lives) from nothing.

Just like God did, but we don't get near the credit.

With no good map in hand, imagining that we are capable, that we make great engineers or heads of state, is still unthinkable for most women. Our mental map is dated; it comes from the old world and gives us an image of a universe in which we aren't the heads of anything. We're usually the hands—and the heart.

This outdated map is still being re-issued. For instance, when a would-be senator from California was recently found to have an undocumented nanny in his past, his first comment was that his wife had made the decision but he, "as head of the family, should have vetoed it." (Uh oh, Father didn't know best.)

The reality is that women, as heads, have created a powerful global movement, opening many new roads. To continue traveling, we have to keep expanding our picture of what our lives could look like.

It's hard to remember our capabilities when we have so few accurate mirrors: powerful, public women whose presence reminds us, "I can do that too!" We've never had a woman visibly and openly orchestrating national policy. When Hillary Rodham Clinton tried to lead the national health plan, she was widely vilified as a power-monger only too eager to step in and make decisions abdicated by her hen-pecked husband. (All strong Presidential wives, like Rodham Clinton, Nancy Reagan or Eleanor Roosevelt, have been accused of usurping power.) We've learned that we can influence policy so long as we settle for the back seat, the "power behind the throne." Too often our brain is the stealth brain, remaining safely under cover, running no risk of igniting other female intellects. Thus we remain invisible to each other, and even to ourselves. So we "forget," or never notice, how often we actually lead the organization, generate the strategy, or write the books, so pleased are we to have any role at all.

We still aren't used to seeing anyone other than men—usually tall white men—be in charge of the really big things. Even our money, that paper that makes the world go round, is imprinted only with that one visage. Everyone else is seen as incompetent or, if too clearly capable to be so easily dismissed, overreaching.

With this kind of distorted road map, leading to constant dead-ends, how do women get an accurate sense of their capabilities?

We need new maps. And there are many ways to create them.

Some of us paper our walls with markers. When put together, they lead us in a new direction. In my study, for example, I look at a page torn from a newspaper, picturing all the women in Congress. I see a collage I made in a seminar, magazine headlines pasted on bright red paper:

THAT'S WHEN I DECIDED THAT MY NEXT HERO WOULD BE ME, AN ENGINE MOVING 79 MPH, THE FAST TRACK.

I have a poster entitled, "Sanctuary: The Spirit of Harriet Tubman." Remembering Tubman, a woman who was definitely on the fast track—as she not only rode, but created an underground railroad to free enslaved African Americans before the Civil War—keeps me moving along on my own journey. On

Remember, Ginger Rogers did everything Fred Astaire did, but she did it backwards and in high heels.

—Ann Richards, former Texas governor

my study wall I also see a "Women and Physical Power" calendar, with its photo of a focused teen winding up for a pitch, and am reminded that reclaiming physical power is part of remembering ourselves. I see an envelope from my son addressed to Joan Lester, Author, sent when I first began to realize I was one. I have poems and notes from friends, letters from women I admire, publicity posters from my bookstore readings.

I also look at images of Aunt Jemima as even she has changed. Seeing the shift from plantation cook to professional woman reminds me that our work has made a difference—and that we're only halfway there, for she's still somebody's aunt, with no last name. (Can we envision a CEO called Aunt Jemima?)

Over my printer I've posted a collage of old women, mounted on neon pink paper showered with sparkling stars. A drawing shows one gray-haired woman with arms thrown back, standing tall beneath the words "I Survived 5000 Years of Patriarchy." There are newspaper photos of several blooming hundred year olds. One, Audrey Stubbart, is a full-time columnist. And there's a radiant hiker, seventy-five-year-old Cecilia Hurwich.

My walls give me constant, subliminal support. They become the bread crumbs showing me the way.

Some women personalize computer screen savers, putting on variants of I AM THE GREATEST to remind them of who they are. Others post notes in their cars, bathrooms, or on refrigerators: I AM SMART. I AM STRONG. Stitched in blankets, on pillows or wall hangings—we have found endless ways to affirm ourselves with positive statements.

At first the reclamations may feel fake. But stating our capacities—to think, play sports, make money—is simply a reminder of abilities in eclipse. They are there; we only need to make them visible.

Many women find sustenance in stories about those who preceded us, women who survived and, sometimes, thrived. We look to biographies or autobiographies of historical women who took transformative journeys, or to contemporaries and peers. We watch these women, looking for clues. How did each of them find the strength to become leaders in difficult circumstances? What decisions did they make that might help us?

We need this outer reflection of our possibilities because our self-esteem has typically been so eroded. (Research in the last twenty years shows girls' confidence as high as boys' until the pre-teen years, when it begins to dramatically decrease—if not collapse altogether.) Some female actors seek out strong roles to provide those reflections. As Geena Davis says in a *Vogue* article—whose title, "The Brainy Bombshell," reflects our dilemma and our parameters—" It's my responsibility as a human being, a woman and an actor," to choose roles that "women can appreciate and relate to," or that "at least don't denigrate women and make you feel cheapened and sickened for having watched the movie." Some women, like Barbra Streisand, Julie Dash, Penny Marshall, Maria Maggenti, and Jodie Foster, become directors and producers to make sure such roles exist. And fortunately, we have at least a few women out there writing them. Callie Khouri, the screenwriter for *Thelma and Louise,* said, "I just got fed up with the passive role of women. They were never driving the story because they were never driving the car."

When we do see women driving the story—and the car— we are riveted. According to Geena Davis, Thelma and Louise were never meant to be role models. "No one was saying, 'Go hold up liquor stores and drive off a cliff.' They were only examples of women who, for better or worse, took control. I think that's why women liked that movie so much," Davis says. "We fucked up a lot, we made some really bad choices, but the exhilarating thing was that we were in charge of our own destiny."

Some women find current real-life women for inspiration, women leading the kind of lives we'd like to construct. We watch the power and self-assurance of Maya Angelou as she speaks, we find role models in the few public women in office.

I could not help noticing the great role women played in Pueblo society. Women owned the houses and actually built them. Children often got their mother's last name . . . It made me a little jealous. Of course, the Pueblos were lucky. Unlike us poor Sioux who were driven into fenced-in reservations, they still live in their ancient villages, which had already been old when the Spaniards came.

—Mary Crow Dog, activist, author

We observed Enid Greene Waldholtz from Utah—before she was brought down by a classic "he done me wrong" scenario. She was only the second House of Representatives member ever to be pregnant, and the first in two decades. The transformation of the House culture (with a membership still nearly 90 percent male) is slow but, as Waldholtz said, "It won't be another twenty years before we have the next pregnant member."

In the work world, we are beginning to get a critical mass of women mixing pregnancy and power, thanks to the many bold women not scuttling out of sight to hide their expanding bodies. "It's kind of a humanizing element when I'm meeting with other representatives on the Rules Committee," Waldholtz told a *San Francisco Chronicle* interviewer. "I just use it as a way to get into discussions about other issues."

Apparently the pregnancy hasn't affected her brain. "You'd never know she was pregnant except from looking at her," said Rules Committee Chairman Gerald Solomon, in a comment he intended as a compliment.

Anchor Katie Couric is another woman who used her visibility as a pregnant woman to model someone using her uterus and her brain simultaneously. Couric also features family/work issues, showcasing working mothers.

Some women, not seeing around them real-life images representing futures they want, look to fiction. Charlayne Hunter-Gault, the Peabody award-winning journalist (and a role model herself as the first African American woman admitted to the University of Georgia) discovered a possible future in an unlikely place: a comic-strip. Brenda Starr was a fictional character, but she was the only female journalist Hunter-Gault saw when she was growing up.

"Brenda Starr, a beautiful white woman with red hair and blue eyes, was my fantasy role model," she recalls. "I loved this life of hers and thought it was very exciting. If I had not been given to fantasy, I never could have imagined myself doing something like that because there were roles set up for us, women like me, we knew 'our place.' That's where the title of my book comes from: *In My Place*. Our place was teaching or nursing—nothing wrong with that; it just wasn't what I wanted to do. Fantasizing enabled me to see beyond the limits of Jim Crow, and, while I didn't know how I was going to get there, I felt that I could get there and I fantasized about getting there, and the way was made. I partly made it, but it got made."

For some women, the best device for understanding our true capabilities is turning inward to filter out the world's "shoulds" and "shouldn'ts," the world's description of our "places," through meditation or journal-writing. Writing and sketching myself in my journal is a device I stumbled on years ago, a fail-proof method for bringing me back to myself when I've lost my center. As soon as I've written a page or two, or drawn a sketch of who I am today—oh, that's me!—I breathe more deeply, confusion evaporates, and I begin to smile.

Your instrument of remembrance can also be an Appreciation Book to write in when people express admiration for something you have done. Like pennies for a rainy day, such a book is there to shine out who we are when we most need it.

Another mechanism for remembering ourselves can be words that spur us on. Mercedes, a friend who is a politician, uses Eleanor Roosevelt's advice to women in politics: "Every political woman needs to develop skin as tough as rhinoceros hide!" Each time Mercedes reads this statement, which she has posted on her wall, she remembers that being attacked doesn't necessarily mean she is doing anything wrong. She just looks at the quote, adds another layer of skin, and pulls herself up again to go on out there. She relies on the saying, also framed on her wall, "It isn't the water under a boat which sinks it. It's the water a boat takes in." She vows to keep on floating, no matter who's trying to pour water on her career.

It also helps to have strong role models for inspiration. One of mine is a colleague and mentor whose progress down the road to power looks effortless, although I know it isn't. Like every other woman, Barbara has had plenty of reasons to give

For each of us as women, there is a dark place within, where hidden and growing our true spirit rises.

—Audre Lorde (1934–1992), New York state poet laureate

9

Power is the ability to get things done, to mobilize resources, to get and use whatever it is that a person needs for the goals she is attempting to meet.

—Rosabeth Moss Kanter, professor, Harvard Business School

up and take a back seat. She is a solo working mother who contributes heavily to the expenses—college included—of many people in her extended family. And she is a dark-skinned woman in a country where "fair" means both light-complexioned and beautiful.

But Barbara never ceases to expand her vision of what is possible. Even when disaster hits. A few years ago her house burned to the ground while she was on one of her periodic business trips to South Africa. Everything she had gathered in her forty-four years was gone: gifts from friends all over the world, the only copy of computer disks holding her half-finished book, thousands of books, journals, notes for courses she teaches, never-to-be-replaced photos of her cherished niece who has passed on, and other irreplaceable objects representing an unusually full life.

After the first shock, and many tears, Barbara laughed, "I wanted a new house anyway. Been saying it for years." Then she focused on an outpouring of community love that surprised and delighted her, and on designing her dream house. Now, three years later, she is living in that house, high on a hill. It's a house with a view, brand-new, full of light, built exactly to her design. The old house was too dark, she always said, shaded in a pine grove.

How did she do it? Barbara found her way by setting up mini-support groups. Since she travels frequently, they are all over the world. Wherever she goes, she has someone to call for a few minutes, with whom she can be open about her fears—or her anger, so often prohibited to women. (Men got anger. We got crying.) Remembering our full selves means we get to do it all: scream and cry. And after rage or sorrow, surprisingly, there is often laughter.

In these support groups, Barbara gets reminders of who she is from people who understand that her feelings are just that. When she lapses into believing she "can't" or she "isn't," they understand that is sexism—or racism—talking. "Oh, that's just I.S.—internalized sexism," they say. "That's worse than P.M.S. Let it go."

And she does.

Another mode of self-remembrance was demonstrated to me this year by a new friend, Sam, a white woman in her early thirties who had never left Oklahoma until a few days before I met her in California. In fact, she hadn't left her county until the day she got in her car with her three daughters and drove to California.

For sixteen years, Sam had been a battered wife trying unsuccessfully to get law-enforcement help. It never came, so one day she simply drove away—from her husband, her parents, and the town where she had lived all her life.

When I met Sam, shortly after her arrival in California, and she told me a little of her story, I asked her how she had gotten the inspiration to finally leave. She thought for a few minutes and then said, "One day, I just looked in the mirror and saw who I was. God didn't want me to settle for this awful life. I had to get out. I didn't deserve this torture."

That glimpse of her real self—a moment of grace—was the thread she turned into a rope. Two weeks later she had an apartment, a job, and a brand-new life in a brand-new state.

One sunny spring day a few months later, my partner and I took Sam, her children, and her new boyfriend to an ocean-side park for an afternoon of kite flying. At the end of the day, Sam began to cry as she thanked us. "We've never had a day like this before. Ever. To just be outside and play, without fear." I was stunned to get a glimpse of how un-free she had been, and to see what getting in the driver's seat was doing for her life.

Still another source of self-memory for women is the legacy we each carry. Even when our personal histories are full of limitation, there is always some nurturance we can find. Col. Margarethe Cammermeyer, for instance, the highest-ranking U.S. officer to challenge the military's anti-gay policy, describes a Norwegian childhood in which her mother passed on "in daily homespun doses, the unspoken rule of our house that women could not expect to compete with men." Yet she also

I think if women would indulge more freely in vituperation, they would enjoy ten times the health they do.

—**Elizabeth Cady Stanton (1815–1902), suffragist leader**

We need not repeat our past histories; my daughters and I need not merely survive with strength and determination. We can live fuller and richer lives. My politics as a woman are deeply rooted in my immigrant parents' and my own past.

—Mitsuye Yamada, writer, professor

recalls being riveted to stories of the courageous Norwegian resistance—especially those of heroic women—during World War II.

"Movies and books about their struggle made a powerful impression. I was shown the prison in Oslo where the Norwegian freedom fighters had been tortured and killed. I envisioned myself there—in fact, these fantasies were so compelling they became as real as my own experiences.

"I learned women could be partners in the daily struggle for freedom. I saw them risk their lives and save others by feeding those in need, sheltering those who were hunted, strolling with the baby and the guns under the blankets, past the Nazis. Those images shaped me throughout my life. And they inspired my attraction to the military.

"For me, being a soldier meant more than merely firing a gun or flying on a bombing raid. Would I be woman enough, as the models I revered from childhood were, to do the hard job of fighting for country and freedom?"

There are as many ways to remember who we really are as there are women. Margarethe found her rock in childhood heroines, Sam relies on her faith in God, Barbara uses her worldwide support web, Mercedes finds inspiration in the writings of political women who have preceded her, and I depend on journal writing and the power map I've created on my walls. Other women rely on models found in real life, in print or on the screen.

And some of us use humor.

Kathleen, the most senior female vice president in her entire industry, told an Equity Institute seminar for women that she still sometimes feels like a little girl when she sits in the board room with her male colleagues talking about football and million-dollar deals. At those moments, she employs her well-honed wit to lob jokes into the conversation. She gets a great response, and in the process of group laughter is able to get the distance from her discomfort that enables her to remember what a powerhouse she is.

In San Francisco, a group of women found another way to use humor to empower themselves and make a point about discrimination. One day, the local chapter of the Lesbian Avengers stormed the offices of Exodus International, a religious organization dedicated to "curing" lesbians of their "affliction"—and released one thousand crickets with the statement: "If anyone deserves a plague of Biblical proportions now, you do."

Most of us aren't corporate VPs or as openly defiant as the Avengers, but we can still find ways to remember our possibilities for powerful action. Tasha, who came from a prison-release program to an Equity Institute Leadership Development seminar, described herself to the group. A former prostitute and check forger, she had been in and out of prison for fifteen years. Yet standing there in her green prison uniform, Tasha radiated personal power and was clearly a leader in the room. Later she told us that she had kept alive her sense of who she was through meditation, love, and grit.

Six months after the seminar, Tasha left prison. Determined to stay out this time, she chose not to return to the city where she grew up—in spite of the urgings of friends and family—but remained in the rural area around the prison, continuing the work she began in the prison-release program, running groups for women with HIV. Today Tasha is a successful counselor, planning her dream: a future as a dairy farmer.

These are women who live all around us. Tasha, Kathleen, Margarethe, Sam, Barbara, Mercedes. We need to notice and cherish them, models who remind us that taking charge of our lives is always possible, no matter what the circumstances.

Each of us is also a model. When we're posting those notes—our emergency self-repair kits—around the house, creating our own power maps, let's remember that some day we too could be subjects for biography and role models for others. The women we look to are actually a lot like us.

As we seek to remember ourselves, there are constant

The Ashanti of Ghana and other people in West Africa have an icon. It is the image of a bird that looks backward and the feet of the bird are pointing forward. This symbolizes that a people must be rooted in their past if they are to move forward.

—Niara Sudarkasa, first female President of Lincoln University

challenges, stop signs on the road to power. As I was recently reminded.

Dave, an associate producer from a national talk show, called one day, inviting me to be a guest. The topic was "angry white men," my subject. The format he outlined was that several white men would give their views on welfare, affirmative action, immigration and gays, countered by a few female and gay advocates. Then, I, the "expert," would come on and dispassionately cover all the issues.

I told Dave I wasn't sure I could drop everything to fly to New York in three days, but I'd let him know in the morning.

"Great," he said, when I called back the next day with a "Yes."

"Is this definite?" I asked, knowing how fast media plans change.

"Yes," he replied. "I have confirmation and authorization from my producer to go ahead. We're all set. You'll be hearing from our travel department in a few hours. Okay, I just have to do a pre-interview, a formality. If you don't mind my asking, what is your age?"

"Fifty-four."

"And, just for our records, your social security number? Address, home phone, work phone?"

Then he asked a few questions about the content of what I might say about "angry white men."

"Fantastic," he enthused to my answers. "You're just what we need for the show. Level headed, articulate. My producer wants to talk to you. She'll call you right back and I'll see you Monday for taping. Bye. Thanks again."

Ten minutes later, the phone rang.

"Hello, is this Joan?"

"Yes."

"This is Brenda, the producer of the show. I'm canceling you."

Pause.

"Why?"

"I won't bullshit you. I could, and make up something, but I'll give it to you straight. It's the demos. It's our policy."

My brain was working fast. I hadn't sent her my demo tape of clips from appearances on other talk shows. What was she talking about? Did she mean they never had guests who had been on other shows?

No. "We never have anyone over thirty-five on the show." she said. "I'm afraid you couldn't keep the interest of the younger viewers." Pause. "I'm an old woman too. You wouldn't want to be on this show anyway. You'd say, 'These are a bunch of jerks.' This show is like Ricki, not like Donahue. You don't want to do it."

My brain was whirring. Dave had assured me that "this show is not like Ricki, it's more like Donahue." His exact words. At Dave's suggestion I had watched the show and found the host likable and respectful to the guests.

I muttered something about Dave.

"Oh," Brenda said, "He doesn't know anything. He's young, he's new. But he did do a great job finding you. Your book is perfect. You're the perfect person for the show. And he found you. But we can't have you on because of your age."

I was in shock. Wasn't this arbitrary, not to mention illegal? Are younger people never interested in the words of a fifty-four year old? And how are young people going to realize they can develop into interesting older people if they never get a chance to see any on TV?

When I came to, I wondered how many "perfect people" we've lost for all sorts of jobs. Because political leaders don't consider women electable to the White House, for instance, we may have overlooked many perfect presidents.

I thought of the old "race records," racially segregated phonograph records sold separately in the 1920s on the assumption that white people wouldn't be interested in Ma Rainey and Bessie Smith. What a joke that turned out to be.

And for me, how to not take in the slur?

I thought about my friend Barbara and all the women I

*Speak your mind—
even if your voice
shakes. Well-aimed
slingshots can
topple giants.*

**—Maggie Kuhn
(1905–1995), author,
founder, the Gray
Panthers**

know who refuse to accept the limitations put on them, women who went down into mines when men said they couldn't, women who work on aircraft carriers, female criminal attorneys who face down their male counterparts in life-and-death confrontations, women who have survived harassment of every conceivable nature. And I remembered who I am and what I am capable of.

I turned to my Appreciation Books, wrote in my journal, looked at the heroes on my wall, and read my positive screensavers. And I responded.

My reply was in the form of a syndicated newspaper and radio commentary about the incident. I used it to raise awareness—and got many wonderful letters as a result.

How strange that the reality of who I am is so at odds with the stereotypes. But then, isn't that just the way with rigid classification systems? One of Brenda's more stunning comments, given the context, was to dismiss Dave with, "He doesn't know anything. He's new, he's young."

Jocelyn, a twenty-nine-year-old development associate for a college, also frequently gets this response. She described to an Equity Institute seminar how often she is discounted as inconsequential or inexperienced because of her age, her sex, and her height. A Filipina, Jocelyn is short by U.S. standards, and has to work three times as hard as most people to get noticed at corporate meetings or community forums, where she is networking or doing political work. Once Jocelyn gets attention, she said, her social profile is usually forgotten, because she is so knowledgeable. But she has to work extra hard to compel that attention.

She has developed several strategies that work for her. Whenever possible, she makes a first contact with a foundation or potential donor by telephone. She is so articulate and business-like that people on the telephone don't tend to dismiss her. Once her credibility is built, she schedules in-person meetings. They may be surprised at how young she is, but they already respect her. Other young women I know have taken

I am grateful and blessed because those women whose names made the history books, and a lot who did not, are all bridges that I've crossed over to get to this side.

—Oprah Winfrey, talk show host

voice lessons to learn to carry more authority in their voices.

Jocelyn also has adopted the tactic of taking a more senior member of her staff, a white lawyer, to important meetings. This too serves to enhance her credibility. Jocelyn still takes the lead in the presentation, but the solidity of her organization is established through the presence of her teammate, Susan, a woman who acts strongly as her ally. Susan deliberately defers to Jocelyn and uses any other opportunity she notices to help establish Jocelyn's trustworthiness. At first, Jocelyn resisted this tactic, because it seemed to play right into all the "isms" she confronts every day. But she eventually decided that, in the same way corporate training teams often use male/female pairs to establish rapport and credibility—since some men will only hear information from another male—she would use the technique that yielded success. Once her rapport is built with the assistance of her senior partner, Jocelyn takes over the contact herself.

Many women report using male colleagues similarly, to establish initial credibility. They make sure they take charge, however, in any presentation, so they are not viewed as "sidekicks" to power.

Jocelyn's other tactic, commonly adopted by many women of color, is to dress beautifully, in up-to-the-minute fashions. This highly professional appearance gives her another step up in gaining the confidence of the clients with whom she works. Deploying clothing in yet another way, an African American friend who is a trainer tells me she intentionally "dresses very African" in some settings. In addition to being enjoyable, this conveys an additional type of authority.

Jocelyn works hard not only externally, but internally, to not absorb the indifference she sometimes inspires. How to hold on to ourselves in the face of discounting is a common dilemma. Even those few women in top corporate positions, the forty-two year olds making $500,000, are still often viewed by male colleagues in ways that inhibit their ability to influence policy. If too "feminine," they are unleaderlike. If too "masculine," they

There are and will be those who think I have gone overboard. Let them rest assured that this assessment is correct, probably beyond their wildest imagination, and that I will continue to do so.

—Mary Daly, theologian

are too strict or considered "too tough on their people" to be effective leaders. The thin middle line is sometimes very thin indeed; positively invisible at moments. When these high-powered women find themselves still peripheral in team meetings—and wonder if it was something they said or the way they said it—they, like the rest of us, have to do the vital work of maintaining strong interior selves, devising strategies for remembering themselves. Is it fair? Should it be that way? Of course not, but many women find that they can use the opportunity to strengthen themselves. They adopt the "If life hands you a lemon, make lemonade" philosophy, and, rather than spending a lot of energy bemoaning their fates, enjoy their drinks instead.

The Tool Kit: Strategies for Remembering Who We Are

The following strategies are tools that Equity Institute developed and teaches in leadership programs. They are effective interventions for individual women or those in groups who seek to develop strong foundations for Taking Charge.

 Put yourself in surroundings that reflect your strengths. Be with people who expand your ideas of what is possible, people who mirror the best in you. Be with women doing what you think you'd like to do, living as you imagine you'd want to live. It does rub off. You get stretched by new ideas, possibilities, and images of strong women.

 Plaster your walls with heroes, including yourself. Read books by and about women you admire, go to hear and see music made by women. See women's art. Immerse yourself, soak up creative energies expressed by women. You have to make an effort to find this inspiration, since it's not primarily what we learn in history, literature, music, or art courses. But women's culture and women's achievements exist all around us.

☉ *Do positive power assertions. Repeat them, post them, surround yourself.* Stretch yourself with statements such as I AM SMART, or I AM STRONG, or I AM A LEADER. Or simply, I AM GOOD. As you begin to layer these thoughts into your brain, they snag on to the part in you that truly is smart, strong, a leader. And good, even when you're not thinking of others.

As power assertions take hold, we realize that what may have sounded ridiculous at first actually has some validity. We build on that truth and soon crowd out the old messages of limitation. Thus, we remember who we really are.

🔩 *Find an internal anchor, a catch phrase or some other way to ground you, to remind you of your authentic self.* Develop your personal counter to the invalidation the world sometimes offers, a personal statement that affirms "I am" and "I can" when the world says you aren't and you can't. Create your own version of "I am somebody." An Equity Institute exercise is to focus on that place in you that has never been hurt, never damaged, never told you are "less than."

Try on: "I am brilliant." "I am successful in everything I do." "I am _____."

☉ *Construct a daily practice for centering.* Some women find writing in a journal brings them right back to center; others get the same result from meditating. Walking or jogging can provide a similar sense of balance, well-being, and the sense of being in touch with your vital center of self.

What all of these methods have in common is that each

I love myself when I am laughing . . . and then again when I am looking mean and impressive.

—Zora Neale Hurston (1891–1960), writer, folklorist

requires time devoted to self, time just for you. There, freed from the pull of others' needs, you can best recall the essence of who you are.

 Keep "Appreciation/Accomplishment Books." In order to know ourselves, we have to be able to connect actions with impact: I caused that to happen. The day care center didn't emerge on its own, the report didn't just write itself, this year's graduating class didn't grow unguided, the company didn't double its revenues by itself. I did that.

When people compliment you on a success or express appreciation for your hard work, write the comments down in a book. It's like a family photo album, but it's all about you. And instead of photos, it carries words: the qualities that others admire about you.

So the next time someone says, "You are wonderful!" and goes on to elaborate, you aren't going to let that gem of your soon-to-be-past pass you by. You're going to record it.

Everyone gets praise to include in Appreciation books. It's simply a matter of getting in the habit of noticing when recognition comes your way, realizing that's you they're talking about—you did it—and holding on to the acknowledgment.

Doing this is crucial because many women hear compliments in a fog and get embarrassed at the attention. The words wisp away before we fully absorb them, so busy are we nodding, smiling, and thanking (and hardly able to believe this could be true about us). Also, we're often thinking about sending the compliment right back where it came from—a female twist on the childhood taunt, "My words are jelly, your words are glue. Everything you say sticks back to you." We fall all over ourselves telling the other person how truly she or he is the amazing one.

Being humble doesn't mean one has to be a mat. In fact, just the opposite. What it means is, I will make myself so fine that I will be of use to you, make myself useful, do what I can do, and be an instrument of God.

—Maya Angelou, writer

When you get really bold, you'll add in pages generated solely by yourself: "What I Achieved This Year (or This Month)." Making these entries, and then reading them back, can provide the same rush as writing a resumé or looking back at a completed project. "I did that? I can't believe it!" Or, "I'd never seen it quite that way. I was so mired in daily hassles I lost sight of the bigger picture."

Appreciation Books provide that bigger picture, full of our strengths, a book to stack next to the mental one we are all used to keeping, the one full of our "mistakes," which seems easier to remember.

Draw knowledge of who you are from your heritage. Find out about the women who preceded you, in your family and your culture. We aren't the first generation of women to know that we can "be somebody." We're doing it in our unique way, with unprecedented opportunities, but every culture and every family has spawned extraordinary women who pushed the limits of the boundaries imposed upon them—some of them breaking right through.

Women who have gone before us are our own past stories, with a wonderful breadth of lives to emulate. Find out about the Ida B. Wellses, the Emma Goldmans, the Mother Joneses, and the La Pasionarias in your background ("La Pasionaria" was the name given to Dolores Gomez Ibarruri, a Spanish journalist and political leader whose life spanned most of this century). Claim them as living, breathing sisters. They were real women who had struggles and overcame, women who suffered just as we suffer, even though much detail is lost to us, and we may only read today, "Mother Jones' five children died in the cholera epidemic. Then she became a labor organizer and became the most famous and feared woman of her day."

> *We have created a room of our own, and it is gorgeous.*
>
> —Rebecca Carroll, **writer**

> *A circle of women is a place where you listen to another woman's truth, and it mirrors back who you are; it's a place where women find their own voice and courage; where true emotion expressed by one, facilitates access for others; a safe place for repressed and undeveloped selves to emerge.*
>
> —Jean Shinoda Bolen, author, psychiatrist

These women's lives, originating as they did in a variety of constrained conditions—for none of them was born into perfect circumstances—remind us that we each have almost infinite possibilities available to us as life scripts. We simply have to remember that and choose the one we want, tailored to our unique self.

 Join or start a support group, your own Action Team. Find people who will be there to remind you that you are fine and that you can—women who will help you act more effectively in your own life.

We each need at least one group of women with whom we can be totally honest and open about our challenges and triumphs. We need a group—no matter how small—that meets regularly, even if only once a month, with whom we can reveal our strengths and our struggles, who will help us clear away the obstacles that impede our movement.

Remembering ourselves is easier if we're not isolated. In fact, paradoxically, it's easier to know who we are when we do part of our work in concert with others, when we're not holding "secrets," keeping up the front. Watching other women change and grow helps us understand more about common challenges, even as they manifest uniquely in our own lives. In a group, we also get inspired by other women's perseverance and creativity in meeting life's dilemmas. There is a remarkable synergy that often occurs in such teams, so that our concerted efforts yield surprising results.

It's helpful to have other women there to be mirrors for us too. "Does it make sense for you to have a baby—or move—when I just heard you say, 'I can't deal with anything else. I need a month of rest'?"

Connecting with other women in a regular way is so crucial that I include an explanation of how to form

Action Teams that runs throughout the book. There is specific information about the formation and maintenance of such groups in a box at the end of each chapter, implementing ideas discussed in the chapter.

Forming an Action Team

An Action Team can be as small as three women or as large as fifteen. The form can be variable too: evening meetings, brunch, or occasional weekend retreats. Whatever schedule suits your life is fine. The keys to success are regularity of meetings and commitment to each other.

You may want to organize the team around a theme, such as occupation, health, age, or family status. It can be a group of women from your office or your neighborhood—or friends. There are an infinite number of possible organizing topics. Being a woman itself is one. And there are lots of possible subdivisions, as outlined by several contemporary authors:

Gail Sheehy proposes Wise Women in Training (WWIT)—groups for women over fifty.

bell hooks describes Sisters of the Yam support groups she created to assist African American women in their transformative process as they recover from sexism, racism, and the combined effects. "Everywhere black women live in the world," she says, "we eat yam. It is a symbol of our diasporic connections. Yams provide nourishment for the body as food, yet they are also used medicinally—to heal the body."

Julia Boyd, author of "Girlfriend to Girlfriend: Affirmations from the Sister Circle," says her own sister circle consists of seven friends who get together at least once a month. "I would define my sister circle as that validation and celebration of who I am as a black woman," she says. "It's my family of choice."

Merris Obie, youth coordinator for a program serving

Two or three things I know for sure, and one of them is how long it takes to learn to love yourself, how long it took me, how much love I need now.

—Dorothy Allison, Lambda Literary Award Winner

Native Americans from the Hoopa, Yurok, and Karok tribes in California, created "Talking Circles" at Hoopa High School, safety groups allowing young women to share experiences in a protected environment.

Naomi Wolf suggests power groups in which women network about careers, exchanging resources.

An Equity Institute Dismantling Classism seminar organized "troikas," groups of three people, each from a different background: poor or working-class, middle-class, and wealthy. They meet three times a year for weekend retreats to talk about their backgrounds, learn more about how class affected each of them, get closer, and learn to support each other across that historic division. One such multiclass (and multiracial) troika has met for five years. The women stay connected between retreats, helping each other in a variety of ways. When one of its members suffered a breakdown, the other two helped her get into a good hospital program and nurtured her back to health. This troika has evolved into a lifelong commitment.

Whatever they are called, each of these groups for women serves a common purpose: generating support, skills, and ultimately, power.

I have been in many women's groups over the last twenty-five years. The first, in the late 1960s, was made up of ten young women. We called ourselves New Women, and our goal was to be just that. We selected a subject each week—bodies, mothers, children, work, sex, relationships, health—and discussed our feelings and thoughts on the topic. It was extraordinary to discover how similar our private lives were. Together we brainstormed goals that seemed outrageous and remarkable then: A women's library, a resource center, a women's building. Such significant institutions grew out of those early women's support groups, when we dared to dream together of things we could hardly imagine individually.

Some years later I led a support group for white women in interracial families. Still later, when my son was a young teen, I formed a group of three: feminist mothers of teen-age sons. How could we raise these young men, empowering

Our primary need is a support system for women, which means that they have to establish that support system for each other.

—**Dolores Huerta, co-founder, United Farm Workers Union**

them to be all they could be, at the same time assisting their escape from the most difficult parts of male conditioning: objectification of women, silencing of their own emotions, arrogance? During the three years we met weekly, this group was a vital part of my ever-increasing closeness with my wonderful son. (And all of our sons grew up to be the men we had hoped they'd become.)

I have also been in several writers' networks, exchanging news of agents, publishers, contracts, book promotions. These gatherings remind me of the first women's group meetings: breaking long isolation, relief at getting news of others.

I am currently in a Women, Money, and Power support group with twelve members—half white women, half heterosexual women spanning thirty-five years in our ages, women from every class background and three continents. Our original goal was to become fully empowered about money. Now, in our second year of monthly meetings, we've expanded to support each other's total growth, while continuing to focus on money and power.

Every group I have been in has moved me along the road more easily. Each one gave me information when I needed it, insights into women's common lives, and a crucial connectedness that allowed me to leap forward in my growth.

To start an Action Team, one that will help you to make more effective movement in your life, think about who you'd like to get closer to and who might stretch you. Then notice who is missing: younger or older women, women of different sexual preferences, cultures, classes, or religions. You want to strike a balance between enough similarity to enable you to feel comfortable and enough difference to stretch you. The wider the stretch the more complete picture you will get of women's experiences. And the larger the picture, the more you will come to understand your own place in it.

To find women outside your circle to include in the group, push yourself to participate in activities that tend to

I say that if each person in this world will simply take a small piece of this huge thing, this tablecloth, bedspread, whatever, and work it regardless of the color of the yarn, we will have harmony on this planet.

—Cicely Tyson, actor

Power, like love, grows stronger when it is shared.

—Anon.
(Often a woman)

draw women different from yourself. You'll make new friends. Check your local newspaper for listings. Pick something of interest that you normally wouldn't attend. You'll enlarge your circle, and maybe even find an existing group.

Or think about women you know but perhaps not well. Neighbors, women you've met professionally, women from your workplace. There may be women in your life who are already acquaintances, who would love to be in a group with you.

The Action Team will take a while to gel. Give it time. There is a saying that a healthy group goes through four stages: *Forming, Storming, Norming,* and *Performing.*

Forming (electing to come together)

Storming (hashing out goals and ground rules)

Norming (establishing group norms)

Performing (actually carrying out the group function)

Not all groups go through such clearly defined stages. Sometimes they overlap, and the stages are often subtle, but their functions need to be accomplished. Don't worry then, when your group has some storming. It's healthy and necessary to sort out your purpose and norms.

Hang in there. An Action Team can change your life. You'll create visions of yourselves that would be impossible to generate on your own, and access abilities, strengths, and capacities you didn't know you had.

Mile Marker Two: Be Central

This chapter contradicts the
peripheral image of females we grew up
with, and dares us to become central
in our own lives.

Mile Marker Two:
Be Central

Being alone and liking it is, for a woman, an act of treachery, an infidelity far more threatening than adultery.

—Molly Haskell, film critic

"Give a group of women money and power and ask what they want to do with it," says women's workshop leader Diane Balser. "Most likely they want to build a school, hospital or day care center, not buy up multinational corporations or start a world bank."

Women's compassion is laudable—but our scopes are limited.

We have been so trained to think of others before ourselves that the most subversive thing a woman can do is to put herself first, at the center of her own life. And then think big. If we do manage to outwit our conditioning enough to make ourselves central, and significant, we often feel terrible.

"Was I a bad person?"

"Am I mean or selfish?"

"Will anyone still like me?"

The message that it's best to be peripheral comes early and often. When I was eight, my mother told me she wished I could be more like my friend's older sister, Suzette. When she spoke of Suzette, my mother's face shone. Suzette (whom I quickly grew to hate) always thought of others first. She seemed perpetually out doing good, never, ever thinking of what she wanted. Unlike myself, it seemed. Then Mummy said, in a worried way that scared me, "You're too often in charge when you play with your friends. Ask them what they want to play, or pretty soon, nobody will want to play with you."

And here I thought my friends and I had been having a wonderful time, exploring the mysterious "mushroom house" in the woods, playing tether ball, cutting out paper dolls. This criticism, meant to assure my place among the well-loved, was one I pretended to take in stride. But inside my embarrassment was born the suspicion that I was selfish and self-centered. I spent decades making sure this self was buried deep under mountains of goodness—goodness on behalf of everyone but myself. Now I finally understand that what my mother noticed was what might be called, in a boy, leadership. Worried about my survival, she reined me in.

Women have heard it all our lives: don't be first. We've lived in these cramped mental quarters so long it feels like home. Existing at the side of other lives, we even tend to write in the margins, those little spaces we can find, scrawling poetry on the back of an envelope while wiping tears from a child's eyes. We put journals away in drawers, not out in public space. For the most part, women still create art or generate visions in found slices of time, temporary places of privacy into which we can crawl for a moment.

It's amazing any women have published at all. Fortunately, women are living longer now. As we grow, some of us begin to force those margins open. And younger women are starting out lives with different expectations.

Great rivers have been dammed up, and the dam is finally bursting. It was those margins and the habits they engendered of making ourselves small, of caring for others, until there are so many "others" that the quiet space in which ideas can form and flow never appears, and dreams deferred eventually wither into wisps of regret. "Thought interruptus," I described my mental process in a poem when my children were small. I was honestly afraid I had brain damage, until I realized that my head held grocery lists and other details of daily life quite well. But the constant interruptions of that life did not allow me to formulate abstractions or major concepts, as female artists have discovered for generations. It's not true that "cream always rises to the top," as a caller once told me on a radio talk show, explaining why we have so few prominent or accomplished women. (And I was too kind to retort, "Well, so does fat, but we skim that off and throw it out. So let's not play analogies.") I'm convinced that great rivers of women's creativity still lie dammed up by piles of laundry and extravagant pride in others' accomplishments.

Becoming central in our universes—insisting, for example,

We need to begin treating ourselves as well as we treat other people. That would be an enormous revolution.

—Gloria Steinem,
writer, co-founder, Ms.

It is not easy to learn to cherish oneself when one's life has been organized around cherishing others.

—Mary Catherine Bateson, writer, professor

that our need for uninterrupted time must somehow be met—is the only reasonable way to be centered, as so many women long to be. Trying not to occupy our own cores, for fear of being called selfish, throws everything off balance. We need to be like those pop-up clown dolls, so heavily anchored that no matter what force pushes us down, we keep coming up, internally balanced.

Our anchor is our sense of self. We may fear that if we tend to it we'll never come back and care about anyone else. We needn't worry; as humans, we have an innate sense of compassion and connectedness. But we can't be fully balanced and access that compassion in its entirety—including consideration for ourselves—until we are centered. When we are, we will have enough self-respect that it will spill over into care for others. And our connections will be clearer, because they are not being made at our own expense.

The antidote to the conditioned "taking care of" is not to think only about ourselves—or to insist that others never care for us. The solution is for all of us to think clearly about the whole picture. The same is true for caretaking of all sorts; it goes better when it is shared. When one driver has been driving for many hours, for example, it makes sense to switch positions. As we learn to share power in women's groups, we might remember the metaphor, and recall a time when we've been driving over-long. How good it feels to turn the wheel over to another. Yet this doesn't mean we relinquish power permanently. And it doesn't mean that we can't still think with the new driver about optional routes. It simply means we no longer bear the sole, or main, responsibility, for this period of time.

There is a distinction between caring for others and "taking care of," as there is a difference between being cared for and "being taken care of." In the former cases (caring for others or being cared for), we are still the suns around which our own lives rotate. We are centered and central. Our connections to others are clear, unentangled by resentment, over-nurturance, guilt, or passivity. But when we take care of others excessively, or when we ourselves fall into a passive "being taken care of" stance with regularity, our links to others become confused. Figuring out how to recognize the difference between rational caring and over-responsibility is one of the biggest challenges for many of us.

The challenge of centrality is geometrically compounded for women who become mothers. Too often, the mother part of us swells like a grow-toy, one of those little creatures you put in water that magically expands, eclipsing all else. This idealized "good mother" of our imaginations hovers tirelessly around the edges of her universe, making sure everything runs smoothly in the center, where she's put her children and partners, while who she is and what she needs is hopelessly blurred. Our devotion to this kind of mothering is spurred on by headlines like HEROIC MOM, SHE LIVED ONLY FOR HER KIDS. Those women who don't have children, or are "empty nesters," may replicate these heroic, peripheral lives with causes for which they work tirelessly and "selflessly," pouring everything they have into others.

Yet, when we relinquish our center, we start to wobble, and it's hard to keep our judgment intact. Julienne Busic, for example, a convicted hijacker, wrote from prison that she had been overwhelmed by her husband, Zvonko, who organized the hijacking. "He was in control, nothing could go wrong if I trusted in him." She described how she had surrendered her interests "to his goals, which I felt were more noble and worthier than mine." His goals, unfortunately, resulted in joint convictions for air piracy and murder.

While it may seem easier at any given moment to go with someone else's program—it isn't nice to make a fuss—in the long run, as Busic's story demonstrates, it's often simpler to take the time, and maybe make the trouble, that listening deeply to our own needs entails. It takes a lot of energy to continually vacate that center and "forget" that, for my universe, I am the sun.

The poet Nikki Giovanni was heretical enough to write a

Women have served all these centuries as looking glasses, possessing the power of reflecting the picture of man at twice its natural size.

—Virginia Woolf (1882–1941), writer

*Besides
Shakespeare and
me, who do you
think there is?*

—Gertrude Stein
(1874–1946), author
and life-partner of
Alice B. Toklas

poem, entitled "Ego Tripping," in which she exults and exag-
gerates ("I walked to the fertile crescent and built/the sphinx")
to remind us of our significance. She asserts, "I caught a cold
and blew/My nose giving oil to the arab world." And, my
favorite line: "I am so hip even my errors are correct."

The image of self in this poem is so expansive, so joyful, it
counters every bite of limitation we've ever ingested. Yet it takes
an act of will for most of us to make ourselves central, and keep
ourselves in that spot, when so much pulls us away. As the
writer Pamela Haines explains, "It wasn't long ago that the idea
of me being at the center of my universe seemed pretty outrageous. After all, I was just one of billions of people on this earth
and not a very important one at that . . .

"I can't remember when I realized that such a 'humble'
assumption about my role was in basic conflict with the forces
of physics (or at least physics as is makes sense to me). My universe must, of necessity, be centered in me. It expands out from
me endlessly in all directions. Where else could its center possibly be located? This must logically be true for me, as it must
logically be true for everyone else. We will have common interests, overlapping boundaries, deep connections, but each of us
belongs at the center of our universe.

"The implications are staggering. . . . In my universe, I am
the central character. I am the only one who can make a difference from this particular point. There's no use sitting around
waiting for somebody else—more experienced, more qualified,
more daring—to do it for me, because they can't. For my universe, I am the one."

We have to give up waiting for someone else to make everything all right, to save or validate us, someone to guide us
through the maze of life. No one else can give us the ultimate
report cards. As the centers of our own lives, we may look to
others for support, but not for rescue. Ultimately, it's our show.

This comes as a shocking, and, at first, painful recognition
for many women, bred as we are on fantasies of Mr. Right, the
handsome prince arriving on the scene, discovering that the

glass slipper fits ("I'm popular!"), happiness forever. And the scene fades to black. In the real world, the scene doesn't fade. We're still living the story, and while there is abundant love available all around us, it usually doesn't come in Disney form. Happiness rarely flows from a life of marginality, however pampered it may be.

With, on the one hand, the seductions of media and myth pulling us to await "rescue," and, on the other, the sanctions we face for "self-centeredness," how do women find the strength to assert our centrality?

Some women find it as a result of adversity. Mary Cantwell, a member of *The New York Times'* editorial board, describes herself as a young editor at a fashion magazine twenty years ago. "I was one of those underpaid editors, though perhaps a little less underpaid than most. But if I was nervy enough to demand the occasional raise, it was not because I believed I deserved one. It was because I had responsibilities in the shape of two children, and their needs made me brave. Never did I feel entitled to more money, nor did most of my colleagues. We were grateful for any pittance, and amused rather than angered that the pensions we might one day receive would not buy us a room in an S.R.O. hotel. . . . It is because of such memories," Cantwell writes, "that I am enamored of Oprah Winfrey and Linda Wachner, two of the very few women who have become multimillionaires not by marrying money, not by inheriting it, but by earning it."

Other women come to conscious decision. Rose Kennedy, for instance, once commented, "I just made up my mind that I wasn't going to be vanquished by anything. I refuse to be daunted." Another example of such disciplined decision is the President of Maxwell House Coffee Company: Ann M. Fudge, one of the fifteen most powerful women in American industry. Breaking through not only the glass ceiling but also the brick wall—the one that blocks people of color from the upper ranks—she cites the riots she lived through after the assassination of Rev. Martin Luther King Jr. as formative. While painful,

One of the things about equality is not just that you be treated equally to a man, but that you treat yourself equally to the way you treat a man.

—Marlo Thomas, actor

"they made me incredibly determined," she told *New York Times* reporter Judith H. Dobrzynski. "I wanted to do something that black people hadn't done before. When I hit roadblocks, that was what kept me going." Now, she said in a *Glamour* interview, "When people tell me, 'You can't grow this business,' that's when it gets fun."

Yet even this woman, who must have made herself central in so many ways to arrive at this extraordinary position in corporate America—even this woman spends the Sundays before business trips cooking meals for the next three days for her family. "And my husband helped," she told Dobrzynski, implying that the provision of meals is still her responsibility.

Simone de Beauvoir, author of the ground-breaking classic, *The Second Sex,* refused to be "second" when she saw what happened to virtually all the women of her era. To secure the role of "first" in her own life, she decided in the 1930s not to marry or mother. For many of us who learned of her in the 1960s and '70s, this decision—strange though it seemed—was a beacon, simply because de Beauvoir was the first self-centered woman we ever heard of.

Many women today refuse to choose between self or life-companion. In spite of the difficulties in negotiating two equal, and sometimes competing sets of needs, some young women now expect they will be able to have it all: family, work, and autonomy. (The difficulty of maintaining the double workload of family and work life continues to challenge those who attempt to "do it all;" observing this, some young women still opt not to have children if they want to dedicate themselves to careers, while others make the choice to devote themselves solely to nurturing family.) The majority of women who do, through necessity or choice, undertake both family and paid work, understand that economic independence gives them clout at home. They look to "an income of their own" as one basis for establishing centrality in the family.

More and more, women are keeping separate bank accounts even when they are in couples, to establish their own credit and control their resources. One young woman, Sonia, who conducted all financial business in her husband's name, told me after an Equity Institute seminar that she went and opened her own bank account. As she related the story, she was radiant. "It was a great sense of accomplishment!" she beamed. "I don't think anything will happen with Alberto and me. But just in case, for myself, it felt wonderful. I feel stronger all around, just knowing the bank balance is there, in my own name." Many couples today keep three bank accounts: one for each partner and a joint fund for shared expenses.

Having one "head of the family" is like being on a one-way street. Everything goes one person's way. Having two centers is a two-lane road: We have to watch out for each other coming and going, we might have to install some traffic lights and make some rules, maybe even put in a rotary or two. Our lives become more complex. But when we set off in the mornings, we each get to go out in the main traffic flow, full speed ahead.

Trying to do anything besides be the center of our universes is almost impossible when women are so squeezed between home and work. "We have to be a wife, a mother and a professional, and to be ourselves, which usually takes last place," a thirty-seven-year-old intensive-care nurse told Hillary Rodham Clinton in Santa Fe. However, giving ourselves last place, when we are so central to the whole plan—at home or on the job—is a recipe for disaster.

Today, the Labor Department reports, three out of four working women have school-age children, and half of all married women who work outside the home for pay contribute half or more of household income. Over twenty per cent of women with paid employment are their household's sole provider. This pivotal economic role is a trend that is here to stay—and we are going to have to learn to be central if we're going to survive.

Hurrying from home to work, rushing home from work (as I used to do, literally running the five blocks from the subway in order to be at home when the children arrived from school)

There is a necessity to be selfish at the point of trying to save a little bit of yourself for yourself . . . even if nobody else agrees, and if it looks as if you're being hard-hearted, take a little time to restore your own soul.

—Muriel S. Snowden, founder, Freedom House in Roxbury, Mass.

is a stress-filled way to spend our days. Not to mention the guilt that clings to this way of life. There's remorse if we're not with our children full time or if they are latch-key kids. Distress that we're not achieving more on our jobs, or fulfilling our creative potential. Chagrin that we don't provide home-cooked meals or spend the kind of time together as a family that we'd like.

The only way out of this is to give up judging yourself altogether. Go cold turkey, remember you're doing the best you can. You're part of an exciting (and challenging) transition era. And since we are all connected, what is good for each of us is ultimately going to be productive for all the systems we are part of: family, work, community, and friends.

Women today are able to be more pivotal than they've been for hundreds of years, in most cultures. But because centrality is such a novelty, it's hard to use our feelings as a guide to what is appropriate and what isn't. We are going to feel selfish even if by some "objective" standard we're not. It's similar to the way it's difficult to tell when we're full—or if we're fat or thin—if we've been dieting/binging/dieting for years. Our thermostat for fullness is "off," and so are our mirrors.

Many women in our seminars say that when they think about putting themselves in the middle of their lives, they feel selfish—the one thing they were taught not to be. So it's confusing if we use feelings as our guide.

Women have been so squeezed to the side of most pictures that it sometimes feels "unnatural" to be right in the center. And in fact, some people consider a self-centered female an abnormal being—which may be why single women or lesbians are so frightening. Throwing off the conditioning to defer to a male mate, they more easily have attention to make themselves central. And, in fact, some lesbians are called "selfish" by their parents when they come out, suspected of choosing to live at the center of their own lives.

Fortunately, many women in their teens and twenties don't experience the discomfort of centrality as much as women who had already lived through girlhoods or early adulthoods when

I suppose I think that the highest gift that man has is art, and I am audacious enough to think of myself as an artist.

—Lorraine Hansberry (1931–1965), playwright

the women's movement cut a new expressway through the land. These younger women, inspired and coached by their big sisters to demand parity, are now opening their own new freeways—on which older women too are driving. Together, we are creating visions of female possibility new to this time. And those potentialities include being centered—and central.

 The Tool Kit: Strategies for Becoming Central

 Make a Murphy Brown or Khadijah "Me-First" commitment to watch these shows. What is so delightful about Murphy and Khadijah (Queen Latifah on Living Single)—and makes them so "unladylike" and popular—is that they unabashedly think about themselves first, and usually last too. They're "me, me, me" kind of women. This might not be appealing in daily doses, but seen weekly, they pull us toward centrality. Since most women are so unbalanced, we can use that tug. They are metaphors, exaggerating a role which helps us move in that direction.

The two women also present rare models of independence, making deliberate choices about career, parenting, relationships. It is their ability to make themselves central in their own lives, sometimes making untraditional choices, that makes them so threatening to those who struggle to maintain a lost way of life, where women had only forced turn signals.

 Look in the mirror and say, "You are the most important person in my life." Even though it feels strange to do this, it's true. Looking yourself in the eye is a powerful reminder that you are the center of your own life, and that you are the only one living that life.

Take your life in your own hands, and what happens? A terrible thing: no one to blame.

—Erica Jong, novelist

Then treat yourself as if you believe it. We provide a service for others, as well as ourselves, by modeling this self-respect. A woman battered for fourteen years later told her minister, "I stayed with him because I thought the good in me would rub off on him."

When she finally realized that her heroic efforts were not saving her husband but were endangering her own life, she put herself first and left. This created such shock for her (now ex-) husband that he entered a recovery program for batterers.

 To help you remember that you are the most important person in your own life, do for yourself all the things you typically do for someone else. Pick or buy flowers. Cook a special dinner for—YOU. Make yourself a present. One thirty-something woman I know does this regularly. She lives alone and likes it that way. And she always has candlelight dinners.

 Make a list of entitlements. If you have children, think about what you (and they) feel they are entitled to. If you don't have children, reflect on young people you know. What do they deserve?

Then list your own entitlements. Be sure to include everything you put on the young peoples' list: loving attention, a good education, a safe home. And everything else you imagine others merit.

 Practice saying out loud: "I am entitled to _____" *(fill in the blank).* Repeat this exercise for ten days. The phrase enters your subconscious and you'll begin to act as if, yes, you are entitled: to good treatment, respect, privacy, decision-making, happiness, or specific material comfort and assistance, like being cooked for.

 Ask for appreciation at work. Suggest how to give it: sincerely, about behaviors or actions others really appreciate, and without containing any hidden jabs. Then practice receiving it openly, with no apologies.

At Equity Institute biweekly staff meetings, the last agenda item is always "Appreciations." Each person in turn receives a minute or two of attention from coworkers who take the opportunity to thank the staff member for particular leadership, specific cooperation on a project, a good idea, keeping a sense of humor when the stress level is rising, doing the final edit (or draft) of a report, or any other concrete contribution the individual has made during the last few weeks.

The benefit of this regular exercise can hardly be over-stated. New workers are typically embarrassed the first time. By the second or third staff meeting they're adept, and soon leading the process.

Not only does conducting "Appreciations" keep morale high, it speeds and enhances growth as we hear about attributes we may never have noticed. (For women, it's a good guess that we haven't been aware of many of our strengths.) "Oh," we think in a pleased sort of way, when we hear the specific recognition, "I guess I do have a pretty light and expert way of giving thoughtful, and sometimes difficult, feedback." The next time we set out to repeat that job, we'll have a little memory of how well we did the first time. And it will go better.

Once this kind of acknowledgment becomes ritualized as a regular part of meetings, it begins to spread through the work day. And even beyond.

Equity Institute has introduced this technique to thousands of client groups. After an initial flirt with discomfort, the unease evaporates and everyone beams. Many clients now successfully incorporate this exercise as part of their meeting structure.

Power is strength and the ability to see yourself through your own eyes and not through the eyes of another. It is being able to place a circle of power at your own feet and not take power from someone else's circle.

—Lynn V. Andrews, author

No one can make
you feel inferior
without your
consent.

—Eleanor Roosevelt
(1884–1962), journalist,
U.N. delegate,
First Lady

 Eliminate self-criticism for even one day, or one hour. Take a small chunk of time to start with, during which you determine you will remain conscious of your thoughts about yourself. Notice when and how you begin to critique your own actions; monitor your response as you interrupt that habitual mental flow.

 Determine "appropriate" self-centeredness by imagining a friend. How would you counsel her, as she struggled with centrality and guilt? Apply the same reasoning to yourself.

 Be visible, even when it feels uncomfortable. Part of the fear of centrality is the visibility it brings. At the periphery, we can hide. Perhaps we feel safe there from criticism or attack. But, at the margins of life, neither can we shine.

In order to become visible, we may need to unearth humiliation we've experienced—as women, as Jews, Latinas, Asian, African, or Native Americans, as people with disabilities, raised poor or wealthy, or women larger or smaller than the average size—as females who felt uncomfortable because we were different from the illusory "normal middle" we suspected everyone else belonged to.

How many of us were ashamed as children because our parents spoke "too loudly," or in a language other than English? Or we squirmed from something else they did which made us unpleasantly aware of being different. Many of us longed, as the writer Sigrid Nunez says, "to be an all-American girl with a name like Sue Brown." Perhaps we felt unwelcome as immigrants or young lesbians.

So first the work is internal, identifying what keeps us fearful of stepping out in front. Then move forward into your "positively selfish center." We can move into the central spots in our own lives, with other women and men (occupying their own centers) by our sides.

Action Team Ground Rules

Modern-day Action Teams are recasting ancient women's circles, allowing a unique type of shared learning as we access the experience and wisdom of each member.

It's a good idea to formulate one or two questions to address each time you meet. They provide the skeletons around which each woman frames her story. And it is in the telling and hearing stories—even short ones—that we are transformed. As the poet Muriel Rukeyser wrote thirty years ago, "What would happen if one woman told the truth about her life? The world would split open." Today we are telling those stories, and the globe is indeed splitting open.

In order to provide an environment where you can tell your truth, establish some ground rules. They help provide norms and safety, as women know what to expect. Your guidelines will depend on your goals, how well you know each other, and your comfort level with different cultural styles, e.g., more or less formal. But there are a few suggested basics:

Focused Listening is essential, since part of the function of the gathering is to hear from each other. And simply being heard—especially for those whose voices have traditionally been ignored—is powerful for the speaker.

You may want to take turns in some way. A check-in at the beginning, for instance, is a good way to get started, hearing from each team member. Some groups choose an object to pass to someone who wants to speak, marking the moment so there will be an awareness of sharing the floor. Most groups don't do anything this ritualized, but acknowledge the issue, thereby fostering awareness of apportioning time.

I have, for too long a period of time, accepted the opinion of others (even though they were directly affecting my life) as if they were objective events totally out of my control.

—Mitsuye Yamada, author, professor

41

When women work on reclaiming the lost parts of themselves, they're also working on reclaiming the lost soul of the culture as well.

—Maureen Murdock, author

The check-in might have a theme, in which each team member speaks for a minute or two in response to a question, such as:

What are you particularly proud of, since we last met?
How are you displaying leadership?
What actions have you taken that meet your goals?

Speaking this way doesn't come easily to many women, whose rules taught us that "bragging" is bad. (Consultants who mentor women agree that the biggest problem for most is learning to self-promote.) Don't worry, you're not likely to become an egomaniac. You may just end up with a healthier sense of self. And you'll be inspired by other women as you hear about their accomplishments.

You might tag another question to the check-in: *What is going well in your life? What's new and good?*

(Later, provide space for what's old and still terrible! Couple this "problem" and problem-solving time with an opportunity to release feelings associated with the struggles. Working in pairs is good for this. Each woman takes a designated period of time—anywhere from five to fifteen minutes—to listen to the other. This one-way care, in which we get to bask as we tell our woes, is powerful. Naming and feeling our complaints in the presence of loving and confidential attention provides a surprising release, enhancing our ability to think clearly.)

After the check-in, provide some mechanism for rotating speakers. The time doesn't have to be equally shared to have a good support group, but there needs to be some parity and a sense that every woman's voice is necessary to the whole.

You might choose a theme for discussion, related to the purpose of the team (for example: career advancement, parenting, health, making the decision about whether to have children, lesbian-networking, or women in publishing). Or you may prefer less formal discussion, especially during the early meetings, as you are getting to know each other. Then, team building may take a higher priority than the substance of conversation.

Confidentiality is another basic ground rule, providing an atmosphere in which women can be genuinely open. To create this safe environment, women need to know this is protected space where there is an assumption that women are figuring out life together—not issuing press releases (at least, not yet).

Commitment to each other and to attending meetings is a ground rule whose specifics need to be determined during the early months of the group, as part of the *Forming*, *Storming*, and *Norming* process.

Leadership. Decide how the group is to be structured. Is there a designated leader, or will leadership functions rotate or otherwise be shared? Who takes responsibility for starting things off, keeping track of an agenda if there is one, getting a membership list out, calling around when a meeting changes, organizing the questions to start the meeting?

A woman doesn't have to know everything in order to be a leader; she doesn't have to be "perfect" or have everything in her life already worked out. A leader is someone who commits to thinking about the group. She agrees to put aside her own feelings and agendas for some time period, so she can clearly plan and conduct meetings with everyone's growth in mind. She'll incorporate her own needs as one of the members. It's important that the group recognize this is who she is—and what her function is—so they don't get disappointed when she shows her own struggles.

Discuss how you will support your leaders. Those who take on responsibilities need group sustenance. If your leaders are not performing as you think they should (or if you yourself, in leadership, notice areas in which you are unsure), these are perfect opportunities for growth. You can do self-estimation sessions in which leaders discuss their goals, how they think they are doing, and what support they'd like. Action Teams are wonderful training grounds for leaders, if they are valued and respected. Make sure you cherish your leaders, assisting them when they stumble.

I've been married to one Marxist and one Fascist, and neither one would take the garbage out.

—Lee Grant, actor

43

One of the difficulties female leaders confront is the conditioning to think only of others; being in leadership can enforce this pattern. So make sure your leaders are getting their needs met in the group. This is a great chance for women to establish healthy and balanced leadership styles.

Each of these suggested ground rules will need to be tailored to fit your group. The process of such custom-designing will in itself get the group going and help form its culture.

I think, until I got older, I had never believed in my own reality. I believed that I was what I did for other people, or that I was only alive if I was being useful.

—**Gloria Steinem,** author, co-founder, *Ms.*

Mile Marker Three:
Get Over "Nice"

Contrary to our training, "nice"
doesn't always get us what we want—
although sometimes it's a useful tactic.
This chapter continues the theme of
overcoming women's conditioning
to subordinate ourselves.

Mile Marker Three:
Get Over "Nice"

Each of us, as a woman, confronts a limitation—the stereotype that exists about us. As long as we conform to it, we will be treated the way the image demands: for many of us, the stereotype is that no matter how invisible we are made or how poorly we are treated, we'll be "nice."

Being "nice" is so expected, as a predominant cultural image, that even my trusty thesaurus lists, as synonyms for "female:" soft, gentle, docile, submissive, delicate, and deferential. "Womanly" gives me ladylike, while "manly" is brave, two-fisted, strong, bold, forceful, resolute, and virile, with the antonyms: cowardly, effeminate, faint-hearted, and hesitant.

The message is clear about who we are supposed to be. So it comes as a shock to discover that being "nice" often doesn't get us where we want or need. Many woman have discovered, after years of trial and error, that being "nice" didn't get them anywhere, whereas being firm commanded respect and got them exactly what they wanted.

Kalima is the twenty-five year old secretary to the director of a large non-profit agency. After she'd been working there for just a few days, she was stunned to hear her boss reprimand her with, "Naughty, naughty," when she made a mistake in her typing. And then say, "Good girl," when she handed him a perfect letter. At first, she says, "I decided I wouldn't give these comments life by even attending to them. I just left them alone, and went on with my work."

After a few months of being courteous and professional in response to her employer's comments, she realized they were bothering her. So she waited for an opportunity to speak to him. "After he had used one of those terms again, I decided this was the perfect opportunity. So I sat him down and talked to him."

"What did you say?" I asked.

"'Jim, I have something I want to talk to you about,' I told him. 'I'm having a problem with the way you're addressing me as to whether you approve of my work or not. Originally I pushed this aside and considered it something I didn't need to give life to. But I'm really uncomfortable with the way you're addressing me pertaining to my performance.'

"'What are you talking about?' he asked me. I gave him some examples. In fact, he had just said 'naughty, naughty' so that was right there.

"'It makes me feel condescended to,' I told him, 'that I'm beneath you and there's a caste system. I understand I'm your subordinate but I don't find the way you're talking to me appropriate and it makes me uncomfortable.'

"His response was, 'A subordinate? No. I think of us more as a team.' And that's the way you address a team member? I thought, but I said, 'I am your subordinate, even though we work as a team. It's not appropriate language.'

"'OK, so you feel that I'm speaking to you in too familiar a tone?'

"'No,' I told him. 'It's not a matter of familiarity. That might be acceptable with a parent speaking to a child, but I'd prefer you say 'I'm not happy with your work in this area,' and give me specifics about improvement. Or tell me specifically about my good performance, what it is you're commending me on.' From your background it may be comfortable for you to speak this way, but it's not that it seems too familiar to me; it's condescending. It can be interpreted as patronizing.'

"He said, 'OK.' Then his response was, 'I'm happy you felt you could talk to me. Do you feel our relationship is better now? I do understand what you're saying.'

"'Yes,' I told him, 'I feel relieved.' He just thanked me and asked me to close the door for him on the way out, which he always does.

"I felt I was being strong and assertive. I presented the problem and I already had a solution for it, telling him how I wanted him to address my performance. I sensed uneasiness and insecurity on his part. After that, for three months it never

> *A man has to be Joe McCarthy to be called ruthless. All a woman has to do is put you on hold.*
>
> —Marlo Thomas, actor

*The thing women
have got to learn
is that nobody
gives you power.
You just take it.*

—Roseanne,
comedian

came up, and he never reverted to his old way of talking. Today I was able to reword a fundraising letter so it was a lot clearer. He started to say, 'Good girl,' but he corrected himself. Then we both acknowledged that he's not using that language anymore."

Kalima was definitely brave, strong, bold, forceful, and resolute—all qualities defined by my thesaurus as "male." She wasn't gentle, soft, docile, submissive, delicate or deferential—the "female" characteristics. When she was submissive, not commenting on her employer's unacceptable behavior, it continued unabated. But when she took hold and took charge, she had a wonderful outcome. She transformed her work environment, generated her boss' respect, and feels proud and more empowered to take on the next challenging situation in her life.

Being "nice" often means being passive, accepting without protest the limitations put on our lives. When we do object to being treated unfairly or in demeaning ways, as Kalima did, we may be attacked for stepping out of that "female" (i.e., acquiescent) role. Fortunately, her employer seems to have had an unusual ability to take criticism in stride, and to alter his behavior as she requested. If he hadn't, she told me, she had planned to maintain her detached and firm demeanor, continuing to insist with clear logic that she was entitled to professional, respectful treatment. By not personalizing the discussion, Kalima helped him keep it on the same professional level. She had also planned to talk to colleagues at the office, if necessary. But she was hoping to handle it herself, as she did, in order to keep it from becoming too charged.

Sometimes the "nicest" thing a woman can do is to stop being nice. My mother, for example, finally created a change in her marriage when she refused to continue accommodating my father's temper or his drinking. Married at nineteen, with three babies by twenty-five, my mother had been timid about ever speaking up, and she never confronted anyone directly. Yet one evening, when my dad was drunk and yelling, she somehow rolled him up in a blanket and sat on him so he was unable to move. And she got up the courage to tell him, "Don't ever act this way again. If you do, I'll leave you."

The next day, he was a changed man. They went to couples therapy and over several years made a series of new agreements about how to treat each other; he progressively stopped drinking, until he was finally done with it altogether. During this period they forged a remarkable partnership, which has flourished ever more each decade. He has become a terrific ally and champion of her autonomy; today they have an extraordinary relationship. He is truly a devoted partner, and it all began the day my mother "sat on my father."

We get double messages. We see women like Kalima and my mother, Barb, succeed when they act strong and bold. Yet we also observe women like Anita Hill, who blow the whistle and get attacked. Or we watch a Hillary Rodham Clinton—whose major policy initiative was denounced—pull back, or be reined in by others. We are caught in a transitional era, when most of our institutional leaders—and our thesauruses—haven't caught up to this generation of women, with our insistence on going way beyond nice. So we get a confusing mix of cultural imperatives: Be "nice!" Be "powerful!"

While we all receive a perplexing mixture of signals, they come at us differently, depending on who we are. African American women who step out of line (or are perceived to) fall into a well-worn groove. The supernaturally powerful and aggressive black image leaps forth: a woman of Herculean strength, who is then attacked for this exaggeration. The slur is applied in every context. As *New York Times* columnist Frank Rich pointed out, African American women leaders are routinely vilified with epithets spun off that popular Reagan-era racial code phrase, "Welfare Queen." Professor Lani Guinier was quickly labeled the "Quota Queen," in spite of her proposals to include majority and minority interests in voting outcomes, suggestions actually antithetical to quotas. Dr. Joycelyn Elders, a proselytizer for preventive measures in the age of AIDS, became, as she was taken down, the "Condom Queen."

Given this stereotype, moving out of niceness for some

Nobody objects to a woman being a good writer or sculptor or geneticist if at the same time she manages to be a good wife, good mother, good-looking, good-tempered, well-groomed, and unaggressive.

—Leslie M. McIntyre

I shall be an autocrat; that's my trade. And the good Lord will forgive me; that's His.

—Catherine the Great (1729–1796), Empress of Russia

women may bring difficult consequences. For me to walk into a store, or speak up at work and say, "Hey, this is what I want, and I want it now," can be powerful—and unexpected. Likewise for my friend Cindy, a thirty year old, average-sized African American woman with straightened hair. She initially gets little respect in stores or at jobs, and says, "To be effective is to be bold. If I don't display what I know and what I want, I get ignored or disrespected. I have to speak up. I get watched in stores, they shove you in a corner. I have to put myself out. Most women have the same story, and especially African American women. We have to be more aggressive and assertive to get what we want."

But my friend Akaya, who is six feet tall and wears dreads, says, "When I need something in the world, like this week when I bought a computer, I had to be nice in order to be taken seriously. People think I'm harsh and angry just by looking at me. I can't afford to 'get over nice' because the cost is too high. But," she laughs, "sometimes I play with the stereotype, and use it to my advantage. I can go into my 'don't mess with me' mode, and they don't! Our power is to exercise choice," Akaya reflects, "knowing what the images are of each of us. Our stereotype is our limit. When we jog that, we get people to look at it."

We are each hindered by the prevailing images of our particular group. They are our limitations. To the extent that we pay attention to and know what they are, we have a choice about how to react: to play against type, or use the image.

Jewish women of all ethnicities often find the "aggressive" label pasted on, sometimes even before they open their mouths. Both groups—African Americans and Jews—have pasts in which women had more economic responsibility and were more financially in charge than women from many other groups. Thus, when they demonstrate competence, or are authoritative, they often attract "unfeminine" and "power grabbing" reputations, sometimes encoded, interestingly enough, in the regal phrases, "Princess" and "Queen." (In 1995, a television movie on Leona Helmsley was entitled *The Mean Queen*.) So even the historical word for powerful women, our female leaders—queens—is distorted and tied to current cultural stereotypes.

"Aggressive" Latinas and Native Americans are often seen as "earthy," with eroticized overtones. Or as totally unmanageable. Emma, a Cuban American regional director of a large insurance company, was told by her European American supervisor, Sally, a national vice president of the corporation, that Emma was no longer wanted on the leadership team because she didn't really represent Hispanics. The Hispanics Sally knew in the past were, she told Emma with a laugh, all very maternal, submissive, quiet, and interested in family, "good team-members." Sally was dismayed to discover, once she brought Emma onto the management team, that she fit not one of these images. "Sally put me in a box," said Emma. "I'm not supposed to challenge authority, because that's my role as a woman of my background. In order to put together a team, Sally wants followers, so she's excluding me from decision making that needs to be made. She's forcing me off the team; I'm not what she expected from my name: Gomez. And she doesn't see that she's doing anything wrong because she's building a diverse work team. She brought me in as Hispanic. I just don't fit the image. I identify as Black Hispanic. So she says I can't be both. She's looking for another Hispanic."

"What are you going to do about it?" I asked.

"I'm out of there. I'm reverting to survival. It attacked my self-esteem, it put doubt on myself. But I joined a women's leadership group—outside of there. By joining the group it brings out my other qualities. The women in the group say, 'Don't let her run you out' because I love what I'm doing. But I'm leaving. The conflict is too bad." (Four months after this conversation, Emma was fired. With the support of her group, she used even that situation to empower herself. She negotiated a generous severance package and has started her own consulting business—which is what she had wanted to do for

Always it was a struggle to keep balance. Being Jewish but not "too Jewish." . . . It was all to be muted. Well-behaved. The rules were lengthy but consistent. Never to interrupt. Never to talk too loudly. Never to be too strident. Never to have a different opinion unless it was couched carefully in a warm, smiling voice.

—**Sandra Butler and Barbara Rosenblum (1944–1988), authors and partners** years—and is feeling confident about her future.)

Women of each ethnicity face different roadblocks. Asian American women who don't fit the meek mold suddenly flip into the Dragon Lady from hell. Every stereotype about the "mysterious" East flies up and attaches itself to the sexism, so this Dragon Lady holds unspeakable, unknowable, and therefore terrifying, powers. Karen, a young woman born in Thailand and raised in San Francisco, told an Equity Institute seminar how easily she gets office jobs, because whites assume she's efficient and docile: double nice. Another "good team member." Which she is. She's also a forceful and tough woman who grew up in a neighborhood where she had to speak up to get what she wanted. Once employers realize who she is, the flip side of the stereotype emerges: Karen is suddenly viewed as ruthless, devious, and even dangerous. Knowing how she may be perceived, Karen tries to put herself in situations where she can be open from the beginning about who she is. When she can't, she is aware of how easily her image, like Emma's, can flip; so she works to find allies, in and out of her workplace, to support her in being comfortably herself.

Outspoken European American women are often assumed to be working class—therefore doubly discounted by gender and class. Madonna is a perfect example. A woman in control of her art and her business, making money for herself rather than male managers (the characteristic female "star" pattern of the past), she is frequently disparaged as a maniacally ambitious woman, "driven by unceasing selfishness and ruthlessness," as one movie reviewer ranted.

White men who act similarly are considered success stories, powerfully in command of their fates.

For many women who have spoken out and spoken up— women with attitudes—there have been reprisals. We've watched many of our leaders get trivialized or slandered. And we've inherited some difficult legacies, not to be underestimated in their chilling effect: millions of women burned at the stake, over hundreds of years, in Europe. Other

We need to raise our voices a little more, even as they say to us, "This is so uncharacteristic of you." To finally recognize our own invisibility is to finally be on the path toward visibility. Invisibility is not a natural state for anyone.

—Mitsuye Yamada, professor, U.S. internment camp survivor

millions raped after their capture in Africa, or as Native American hostages in the "Wild West." It's easy to understand, with this history as a backdrop, why we might imagine that we better be nice and that super-goodness will protect us.

Yet it's confusing. Many of us have had experiences like Kamila's or my mother's, when stepping out of the compliant role won us respect, while quietly trying to please got no response. We want to act this way more, but are often afraid.

So we thrill to women who dare. We love to read about women like Amelia Earhart or Bessie Coleman—the first African American female pilot, who had to go to France to get her pilot's license, because she couldn't get it here—women who broke out of "nice" to follow their dreams, at the time considered male-only. We thrill when we hear about women who appear so unlike any female image we've grown up with. These are women not constantly saying "Yes," trying to appease, attempting to keep potential male anger under wraps.

Keeping our real angers under wraps often means turning them inward. No wonder women are being calmed down and perked up in record numbers with "mood sweeteners." A million prescriptions a month are written in the U.S. for Prozac; new antidepressants hit the market every year. A New York City pharmacist told a friend of mine that Klonopin, a calmative, was so hot he couldn't keep it in stock.

These drugs are a general anesthesia for women. We hardly know what rages or fears are pulling us down. Our rage is contained before it ever gets going, so well trained are we to be nice, to smooth things over.

I remember a time twenty-five years ago, when my husband had just left me with two young children, and I went to a therapist. At my first visit, I cried and cried. He prescribed Thorazine. I took one pill, got dizzy and threw the rest away. As I look back, drugs seem like a strange remedy for the state I was in, a young woman wondering where to go, how to make a living and how to shape my life. I was scared, and I was crying—why not? It took me years to construct the life I wanted and

I will make you shorter by a head.

—Queen Elizabeth I
(1533–1603)

become the woman I needed to be in order to live that life. It took all my strength and clarity. If I had been dazed by Thorazine or another "calmative," where might I be today? The possibilities are horrifying.

Fortunately the niceness compulsion has been wearing off lately, as we note the commercial success of movies with women "action heroes," such as Sigourney Weaver in the Alien series. Evidently millions of us thrill to the sight of women dishing it out as fast as it comes their way. We cheered when Thelma and Louise blew up the trucker's rig. This trucker was a man we have all encountered, and we loved watching because we realized: We don't have to take it anymore! Our unbelief matched his as the scene of harassment opened predictably, only to unfold to startling new consequences: women shooting his tires, then exploding his truck in flames. We saw women in control in a situation where we almost always feel helpless.

To counter this lack of control, our training has been to make nice, not to retaliate aggressively. Predators of women have been able to count on our thinking that if we are very, very quiet, maybe they'll go away.

But in actuality, "going quietly" rarely protects anyone, as Jews discovered so disastrously a generation ago in those European countries where they were most assimilated. (A history of pogroms having taught: Hide, be quiet, and you may be safe.) Today, we see women with various attitudes taking center stage, aggressively winning multi-million-dollar law suits against harassers, talking up and talking back, women dishing out more than the soup.

From the women who run with the wolves to those who jog with the poodles—not to mention those who would rather stroll with a basset hound—women are setting out to conquer the world. Our arena is no longer simply the home, our own or someone else's. Our bags are packed and we're ready to go, on bigger adventures, and in new capacities.

When we traveled in the past, it was rarely in the driver's seat. The famous North Pole expeditions, for example,

Life is either a daring adventure or nothing at all.

—Helen Keller (1880–1968), author

I suspect the problem is . . . the lingering sense most of us have that to crave money or power just isn't "nice."

—Mary Cantwell, editor and writer

regularly had one or two women living with the group as cooks and prostitutes. Often held captive, these Inuit (Eskimo) women were described in journals of the day as "seamstresses." One of them we know about seems to have had a definite attitude. An expedition organized by Vilhjalmur Stefansson in 1921 landed four white men (as the newspapers of the day said) and Ada Blackjack on Wrangel island, above the Arctic Circle. Two years later, when a resupply ship got to the island, only Ada Blackjack was still alive. According to her rescuer, Ada reported that she had requested that one of the men marry her. When they all refused, she stopped working. Three men left by foot for Siberia and died on the ice. After they didn't return, the fourth became ill with scurvy and could no longer hunt. Rather than give him the remaining small amount of food—and starve to death herself—Ada Blackjack kept it, and he died. According to newspaper accounts, she had undergone "a spell of considerable psychological disturbance." As indeed she might have, being "seamstress" to four strangers.

Women in many places and times have thrived without being boiler-plate nice. Josephine Baker, Roseanne, and Wilma Mankiller come easily to mind. A woman less known in the U.S. is Irma Serrano, a Mexican senator. She started with a successful singing career, where she became La Tigresa, singing bawdy ballads and leading a generally wild life. Using her celebrity status to business advantage, she made a fortune, ran for the Senate, and got elected. A familiar story—except for her gender.

Serrano is constantly attacked. "The male senators attack her for being vulgar or for having gained power through connections. Well, they've done exactly the same thing, and nobody says a word about it," commented a local reporter, Veronica Garcia, to a *San Francisco Chronicle* reporter.

Marta Lamas, a leading Mexican feminist, told the reporter she thinks it is Serrano's "scandalous past" and her willingness to talk about it that makes her political rise significant. "It demonstrates to the Mexican public that women are ambitious

When told about the inherent docility of female monkeys, ducks and bears, remember: it is the lioness who is the killer, not the king of the beasts. The ruler of the bees is female. It is the male seahorse who gives birth— the female deposits her fertilized eggs in him and swims blithely off.

—Robin Morgan, author, poet

I know a woman who was arrested in 1976 who was very brash and aggressive. Nine policemen interrogated her the first night, and they said, "If you don't talk, we're going to rape you, one after the other." She replied, "Oh great! The laws in this country never allowed me to have sex with a white guy. Who's going to be first?" And she started taking her clothes off, which totally shocked these guys, and they didn't do it.

—Elaine Mohamed,
South African
detainee in 1982

and not just self-sacrificing. I have disagreements with her, but if we want equality, we need people like her in power."

Serrano uses her position to raise unpopular issues. She talks about her own illegal abortions while advocating legalization, and criticizes the government's handling of the civil war in Chiapas, her home state.

Clara Brugada, one of the directors of Equipo Pueblo, a women's rights organization in Mexico City, told the *Chronicle*, "I think Serrano is extremely brave. Few women have the nerve to say what she does. When I visited Chiapas, I found . . . they have a lot of sympathy for her, because she says what she feels without worrying about who it offends."

We do have models out there, women who seem not to worry about "who they offend." For the rest of us, it's helpful to remember that when we stop being "nice" for a moment—or longer—and suddenly feel terrible about ourselves, this is a classic female syndrome. Notice when you act powerfully, taking leadership directly. Do you sabotage yourself afterward, wondering if you were mean or thoughtless? Do you ask your partner or Action Team, "Should I should have given her (or him) yet another chance? Do you think I'm bad?" We've so well absorbed the negative messages coming at us from the outside—in this case, the notion that we better be nice, or else!—that if there's nobody around to carry out the "or else" consequence, we do it to ourselves. It is helpful to note the syndrome, and then release it as quickly as possible. Realizing where it came from (media, family, teachers—the whole culture) sometimes makes it easier to pry out. It's just a lie about ourselves, a lie we've believed.

Being direct remains challenging for many women, who often deliberate for hours about how to deliver critical feedback on the job, agonizing over hurting someone's feelings or fearful of being disliked. Women at work typically feel responsible for nurturing relationships, just as at home, believing this will help them get what they want from colleagues. Men are more likely to tell a subordinate, "Get the data and get it right.

Now." Direct, critical instructions or feedback is the typical male M.O., with the key to relationships being: the best defense is a good offense.

For women, lacing our speech with honey and mulling over decisions—or consulting everyone—is the time-honored way to get what we want. "I've learned I get crushed when I go straight ahead," a friend confided to me, "so I use subterfuge, just as women always have." We didn't grow up watching *I Love Lucy,* or Wilma on the *Flintstones,* for nothing! It's not that good workplace relationships and getting input—our legacies—aren't important. Ironically, business leaders today are investing heavily in seminars that teach the very leadership skills women's training emphasizes: dialogue, networking, nurturance, and team-building. These cutting edge business practices are often described in professional literature in "I just discovered something amazing" theoretical terms—and rarely noticed to be common elements of female conditioning.

However, just as men are learning to cross over into hitherto "female" relationship territory, women need to claim both styles, appropriating the "male" one, too, for use as necessary. Expanding our repertoires is useful because while there are many situations in which our classic strengths—networking, collaborative leadership, and conditioning to not one-up our peers or subordinates—serve us well; at other times these habits thwart us. There are circumstances, typically old-line male environments, in which playing hardball achieves our goals. There are times when we have to engage directly in what business consultants Pat Heim and Susan K. Golant call "power-talk." In such circumstances, if we want to succeed, we must introduce ourselves in ways that establish influence and credibility; not relinquish the floor in a meeting even if we're being interrupted; present our ideas assertively, without hesitation or qualifications; get right to the point, being goal-rather than relationship-oriented; use direct approaches to conflict; and if we're in a situation where we can't be both liked and respected, choose respect.

Advances are made by those with at least a touch of irrational confidence in what they can do.

—Joan L. Curcio, **educator**

When such power-tactics are called for, needing to be nice can stand in our way. Being more aggressive can feel frightening. Competition. Conflict. Ouch! So we avoid it—to our detriment. Indeed, I believe women have no idea how much this gets in their way. Academic female scientists, for instance, don't reapply for research grants (the building blocks of science) nearly as often as men do, once they've been turned down. They give up more quickly, and therefore receive far fewer grants, proportionately, since many grants are funded on second or third tries. Without money, they can't do the research necessary to get tenure and thus, don't ever make full professor. It's a downward spiral, but it can be reversed. Networks of women in science are encouraging each other to be persistent, to keep going for funding, make connections in the granting world, serve on national boards, and to make the securing of grants a higher priority than service to students or the institution—something women tend to be asked to do more frequently than men (especially when there are fewer to "go around"), and to respond more positively.

Being aggressive can feel like grandiose self-promotion or terrifying confrontation. Yet it is often effective. As many women have learned, when they finally put the pedal to the metal, and say exactly what they want, they get it—and get it with respect.

Sandy, a part time law school lecturer, realized—after talking to other women in a support group on women and money—that she had been teaching a seminar and a clinical class at the same school for eight years without a raise. After one of the group's meetings she wrote a memo to her dean, asking for a raise of $3,000, to be added to the $6,000 she already received. She based her request on the lack of previous raises, a proposed increase in the units of her class from two to three, the number of students she supervised in the clinical course—six—and her supervision of ten students on their writing requirements. Much to Sandy's surprise, she got an immediate reply. "We would be pleased to raise your annual salary $3,000 this year, and $1,000 per year hereafter. We value your teaching and the contribution you are making to the school."

What surprised Sandy was that she had to make this request in order to get the raise. She wasn't used to "bragging," as she called what she had done in the memo, and was startled to see the positive result, with no negative repercussions.

Several months later, Sandy learned that two male part time lecturers—comparable in many ways to her in background, length of teaching experience, national reputation, and time with the school—both made a thousand dollars more than her new salary of $9,000! After much stress wondering how to handle this new information, and many conferences with friends, colleagues, and her support group, she again wrote to the dean, informing him of her discovery and her displeasure. In the letter she also proposed that she double the size of her clinical class from six to twelve, based on high student interest, and that her salary again be increased, this time by $1,000, to reflect both the greater responsibilities and to bring her salary in line with that of her male colleagues. She was afraid that this time she surely would get a reprimand, such as, "We've been good to you. Now what do you want, unreasonable woman? We are considering terminating you." She loved teaching, and this was her alma mater. It was near her home; her schedule allowed her time to do independent consulting and other legal and women's advocacy work. After Sandy wrote the letter and deposited it in the mailbox, she wished she could jump in and retrieve it. In fact, she briefly fantasized scenarios in which she used her legal status to intercept the letter, calling the postmaster with some bogus story.

She sweated out the next week. And once more, received a speedy reply. This time, the dean repeated that Sandy was a valued member of the faculty, and added a few sentences about the difficulty of comparing the unique contributions made by different faculty members. Then he accepted her proposal to increase the size of the clinical class and granted her an additional $1,000 raise for the current year, bringing her salary to

There's still this perception that women are not deal-makers, not tough enough to run major corporations. When I walk into a room, I assume I have to prove myself. But I also know I can prove myself.

—Yvonne Brathwaite Burke, Congress-woman

$10,000, with future annual raises of $1,000.

Sandy was stunned. She always assumed that merit would be rewarded, and that if she just did her work conscientiously she would be "noticed" and properly compensated. It turned out not to be that way in her environment. Simply by writing clear, cogent, and firm memos about why she deserved raises, she was successful in negotiating a two-stage raise, almost doubling her salary within a year!

Dr. William Du Bois once told me, "Never take a step backward or you never stop running." I never forgot it.

—Elizabeth Catlett, sculptor

We each need a few of these successes under our seatbelts to get over our fears of being considered "bitches," snarling meanies exiled from human friendship, if we dare to speak up for ourselves. We've absorbed the image subliminally, if not directly, all our lives. In our eagerness to put some distance between ourselves and that terrifying image, we smile extra hard, try to do everything others ask of us, and even anticipate all the things they don't ask for.

So part of getting over being boiler-plate nice is facing the fear of being thought of as mean. We don't always have to deliver service with a smile, or tuck our anger into a nicely folded napkin. We don't always have to understand how others feel, and ignore our own emotions. Sometimes, we get to be the sun and the moon, the stars, and the heavens.

Our very niceness has even been used against us. When unions were first being organized a hundred years ago, meetings were held in saloons where "nice girls" didn't go (especially since they should be rushing home to their "other" job). Female workers were thereby excluded. Many men viewed female factory workers as low-cost competitors who, desperate for jobs, usually accepted less pay than men, and terrible conditions. (Men of color were in a similar spot. Most of the unions also kept them out and, like women, they didn't usually earn enough anyway to pay the high union dues. Being barred from the unions, they were sometimes used as strikebreakers—a clear example of exclusion ending up hurting almost everyone.)

For women in workplaces, the one organization they would

expect to support their interests—unions—often didn't, but rather conspired to help them lose jobs. The differences in the lives of men and women outside the workplace were used to justify unequal treatment within it, much of it under cover of protecting "nice girls."

It's past time we laid that old image to rest. Women have a wide range of attitudes and behaviors—all of them appropriate, depending on circumstances.

> We have to "break silence" to come into our own and be visible.
>
> —Janice Mirikitani,
> writer, poet

The Tool Kit: Strategies for Getting Over "Nice"

 Just Say Maybe. Women are so used to bending to the demands of others that it can be useful to make a decision some mornings not to say "Yes" to anything that day. Say "Maybe" instead. Give yourself a chance to reflect on whether the request makes sense for you, without cutting off options as "No" would do.

 Stop apologizing. Count the number of times in a day that you, in some way, say, "I'm sorry." It may be that you introduce your ideas apologetically ("I might be wrong about this but I think . . ." or "This may be a silly idea, I don't know, but I thought that . . ."). Or you may be constantly excusing your presence: "Excuse me, I don't want to interrupt, but . . ."

Once you have identified ways that you are, however subtly, apologizing for your thinking or your presence, omit doing that for one day and see what happens.

 Notice how often you boost others' egos. Which is not a bad thing to do. It's great to be connected and to cheer others' growth. We need each other. It's simply that most females are terribly unbalanced: boosters for everyone else, but nowhere to be seen when it comes to tooting

Most white middle-class women I know, myself included, have been carefully taught to prefer being hit to having to hit.

—Phyllis Chesler, author

our own horns. We're striving for equity here, so for starters, count, in a day, how often you help empower another. Then:

 Talk about your accomplishments as frequently as you celebrate others. It feels artificial at first. Don't worry about it. As you integrate a strong sense of self, balance will come.

You might say, "I'm so proud and happy about_____ _____." (The way I went about getting this job, the book I am writing, my garden, the way I relate to my children, my parents, or my coworkers, the skill I've developed at work, the persistence I've shown in staying with something challenging). The list is as endless as your life's complexities.

 Brag. Note the details of your brilliance and talk about them to a friend. This isn't NICE! Keep bragging. And remember: Boasting about our children or partners' accomplishments is socially acceptable. (Though often tiring to listeners who are not blood relatives.) Let's include ourselves in this shower of attention.

 Take charge of some situation so that it can be just the way you want it to be, without apologies and without making sure first that it is acceptable to everyone involved. There are many circumstances where this is appropriate behavior, such as your birthday party or—sometimes—when you supervise people. Yes, you have the right to have the work you requested be done just as you need it.

 Practice laughing when someone slurs you for your take-charge attitude. It may seem strange to do this, but so will any new behavior, at first. We need to practice deliberately not taking in others' low expectations of us.

Moving your Action Team beyond "Nice"

In order to accomplish your mission of helping each other past roadblocks on the road to power, monitor the form your assistance takes.

Women's "support" sometimes colludes with feelings of victimization. We can commiserate overmuch. It's one of those thin-line places where you want to be empathetic but also encourage empowerment. Part of getting over "nice" is taking the risk of challenging another woman to grow, expecting greatness. Every woman is a work in progress, with leadership capacity beyond what most of us can envision.

It's sometimes a formidable task to know when to push for that vision, and when to simply nourish. Each team needs to find its unique balance.

The other aspect of "niceness" to monitor in support groups is the overly solicitous mask many of us wear, even in this place where we come to be real. Underneath that conditioned-to-please niceness ("Oh, thank you for the compliment, but let's focus on YOU"), there is actually a good woman. If you take the mask off, you may at first find a frightening array of selves—layers of hurt and anger which have yet to find expression. But under everything else, there is an essence that is good. Genuine and delightful niceness. So, no more pretense.

One way of making sure your group gets past pretense and is real with each other is to use an exercise early in the life of the group called "Class and Ethnic Backgrounds." It provides a structure for women to tell their stories, and encourages healthy development of several processes: bonding, honest information exchange, and self-reflection.

Ask each woman in turn to spend about ten minutes responding aloud to a short set of questions:

What is your class and ethnic background? This question provides an opportunity to tell about parents, grandparents, where you grew up, and what it was like there: a

. . . rebellious women have always been central to any kind of major transformation of culture.

—bell hooks, writer

63

Black women have to look out and through all those people who have traditionally been on top of them: the black man, the white woman, the white man. This creates a different way of looking at reality.

—Alice Walker, Pulitzer Prize- winning author

tiny hard-scrabble farm in rural Alabama, an upper class suburb on Long Island, or Mexico City. Talking to these three women today, you might not guess that where they came from was so different. But, inside, those are the landscapes they still sometimes inhabit. When you can see those scenes along with them, you'll be more able to join them on their journeys to power, helping them take the actions they envision.

What was difficult for you as you grew up? The focus here is on the challenges. "I was always hungry." "My parents were always working so hard, I never saw them." "I felt different from other kids because . . ." Our challenges were as various as our numbers.

What has been a source of strength? This question gives women a chance to connect and ground themselves in their deep, historic strengths. "I was always so loved." "I came from a big family. Everybody knew me, knew my relatives, so I felt wherever I went I had friends." "My grandmother was an amazing woman. She rented out rooms to make ends meet, and eventually she bought another house, just for boarders." "I got a great sense of playfulness (or a work ethic) from my family . . ."

Where do you want to grow, and what might be in your way? "I am working on taking leadership in my job, taking myself seriously. I want people to respect me and not give me any grief. I see they tremble when Helen comes in the room. I want that same kind of respect." This question helps women identify and focus on an area of growth, and also think about obstacles. "I have so much trouble taking myself seriously—realizing what an accomplished sociologist I am—that I think other people pick up on that, and they feel they can get away with acting out all their stuff on me. So, I guess I need to loop back and pick up the stitch of that inner work." "I want to make more money." "I want to help other women who are (whatever I am: recovering from something, or poor, or Chinese . . .) to get a foot in the door. I want to start an agency.'

What kind of assistance will be helpful for you?

Encourage women to think about and ask for help. It is so much easier for most of us to offer assistance than to ask for and receive it, that this can be a real challenge. "OK, I'd like someone to talk to for five minutes when I'm feeling that familiar powerless feeling. I'd like a buddy system."

Or, "Let me know how much you respect me." Or, "Give me ideas about how to start an agency. How do I set up a business? Where can I get this information?"

These questions provide a skeleton around which women can hang their stories, which will probably take off free form—and that's fine. These are just starters.

Adapt the questions to the purpose and composition of your group. For example, in a group of coworkers, give women a chance to tell how they got to that particular job, something about their satisfactions and challenges in the position, and what support they want. In a group of women with disabilities, ask women to talk about how disability is viewed in their community or their family. Specifically, then, how is their disability regarded?

Try to add some humor wherever you can. Without being superficial, you don't want women to sink each other either. Remember, the purpose of the group is to strengthen each other. You could add a time for funny stories, or simply insert your own levity as possible. But whatever you add, keep some questions about background and current areas of growth. They provide an essential base for communication—and action.

Teach or remind the group about listening skills: Pay rapt attention while each speaker is sharing what may be difficult information and feelings. If your group is over ten women, you probably would have only half the group tell about their backgrounds at one session, with the other half sharing their stories at the next session, unless you are meeting for more than a few hours.

At later sessions, pose other questions for disclosure and discussion. These are tools to help you get closer and understand each other's needs and strengths. They also provide a snapshot of women's lives.

The center of the universe is everywhere.

—Hehaka Sapa (Black Elk), Oglala leader

Other questions could be:

What are early messages you got about: being nice, being female, being ladylike, being good?

What was your family's definition of a woman?

Where is your power as a woman?

What is the most powerful and "unladylike" thing you've ever done? Done this year?

After individuals respond, have a group discussion. What were themes the group noticed? Differences, and conjectures about the reason for the differences (age, class, regional, or ethnic backgrounds)?

You may also role play new responses to situations where you typically fall into your "nice" patterns. If you observe that you always fawn with car mechanics or at the doctor's office, with supervisors or parents, try playing out fresh behaviors, with the support of the group. You'll be surprised at the creative, comfortable repartee and retorts you develop.

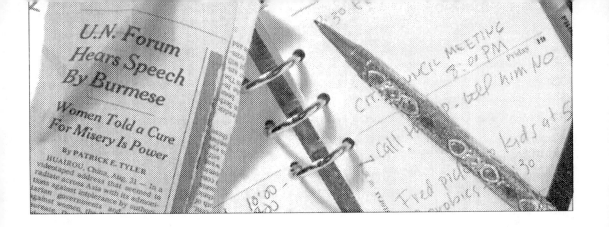

Highway Two:
Taking Action

●

Mile Marker Four:
Set Goals

This chapter introduces a powerful
tool for action: Setting goals is the next
key to having our lives be the
way we want them.

Mile Marker Four:
Set Goals

Goals are dreams taken seriously. They are the large things in life we aim for, the basis of the maps we have in hand when we come to the next forks in the road. When we exercise choice, part of what makes things turn out well is our prior goal setting.

Goal setting is like writing orders to the universe. The miracle is that they are often delivered. Once we set our sights toward a certain end, the universe seems to rearrange itself in accordance with our desires. We make many little decisions to support movement in the new direction, without even being conscious of all the small choice points. One day, years later, we look up and say, "How did I ever get here? Oh, that's right. Ten years ago this was just what I said I wanted to do. I longed to own a business and be my own boss. I forgot that was my dream. And now here it is. I'm living it."

Many women haven't spent much time consciously constructing goals, other than those concerning partner relationships. Even these may be no more tailored to specific needs than the generic, "I want one." Most of us fall, topsy turvy, into and out of jobs, careers, occupations, and commitments, only later to discern a pattern, understanding that choices were made—by us!—but we were often unaware of them at the time. Many men's lives, of course, don't always appear as straight lines, progressing logically from A to B and on to C. But more do. They are more encouraged from birth to think this way about their lives, setting goals that will shape the future. And men have so many taillights to follow when the road gets dim or foggy—men who have gone their way before, sometimes just a little ahead of them—that they are more typically able to keep going in one clear direction.

As Mary Catherine Bateson writes in her aptly entitled book, *Composing a Life,* women's lives today are complicated partly because it is no longer possible to follow the paths of previous generations. "Our lives," she writes, "not only take new directions; they are subject to repeated redirection." Thus, she describes women's lives as having "multiple commitments and multiple beginnings." Women, therefore, have not been permitted to focus on single goals, but have "tended to live with ambiguity and multiplicity."

Tania, a computer programmer, is typical. She is dreaming of some day becoming a professional musician. She'd love to teach music in schools and be a free-lance performer. Tania drifted into work with computers because her parents both worked with them. She still doesn't quite believe that she has the right or the ability to set her own goals. She's a gifted singer, drummer, and composer, just starting to imagine that she could actually create the life she wants. Used to "settling," she's finding that a women's support group for artists in eclipse is giving her the courage to believe she could actually turn her dream into goals.

At Equity Institute programs, when men and women do lifelines that map their pasts, there is a startling gender difference. Women's life markers are almost always relationship- and family-based while men's are about careers. And women's lives tend to show less a pattern of linear development towards some clear goal than a cumulative, cyclical structure. Like housework or child care and domestic life in general, women's lives are defined by concrete, repetitive tasks. Daily life—always a process, never a conclusion. As Bateson reminds us, women's lives are more often like music or patchwork quilts, created as we go. Successful women are able to improvise, combining both familiar and unfamiliar components in response to new situations, and in the process exploring the creative potential of such flexibility.

Of course, women's lives are not without commitment. We do know how to set goals—just not for ourselves. Women know how to accomplish huge tasks, like squeezing a six hundred dollar welfare budget to feed and clothe a family, or saving change for eighteen years so a child can go to college.

Whatever you want to do, you're the only person who can make it happen. Believe in yourself. Follow your heart. And set five-year goals.

—Shirley Nelson, CEO of Summit Bank, Oakland, California

As long as you don't know where you're going, any road will get you there.

— Anon.
(Often a woman)

Women can figure out how to make twenty impossible pieces of a puzzle fit into one picture: shop for groceries, pick up medicine for a sick parent on the way home from work, prepare dinner, iron, help with homework, return phone calls about important community business, write late at night in a journal, and actually get some sleep before rising at six to go back to work the next morning. And do it all with love.

Goals? We know how to set them and how to meet them. We simply haven't had as much practice applying the skill to our own dreams.

One of the few women I know who lived with a map for herself since childhood is a politician. When I was eighteen and first met Eleanor Holmes she amazed me. She was going to be a judge, a politician, a national leader who worked for equal rights. Everything she did was put against this map: would this new road move her forward or not? If so, she usually took it. If not, she consciously measured its value. I'd read of men who set early goals—in politics, science, or literature—and went on to achieve them. But never a woman.

Eleanor planned each step, professional and personal, with her goals in mind. She went to Yale Law School, married another lawyer, and then did something that made my jaw drop and my eyes pop. As soon as Eleanor married, she arranged for child care for children who weren't even conceived, much less born. Her mother-in-law would babysit when the children were to arrive, years later. I was astonished that someone—a woman—could plan her life so far in advance. It wasn't how I had ever seen it done. I was simply trying to do something "interesting." And hopefully, "useful."

Eleanor became, in short order, New York City Commissioner of Human Rights, Chair of the Equal Employment Opportunity Commission under President Carter, and is now Washington D.C.'s delegate to Congress, where she is having the time of her life.

Ten years ago I was appalled when Eleanor told me she was planning to fly from Washington to San Francisco to give a speech, and then return immediately on a red-eye.

"Why don't you stay a few days and enjoy yourself?" I asked her. To which she answered, "I don't have time. Every hour counts." I couldn't imagine a life which didn't have a few extra days to fritter away in a pleasant place. Today I recall this conversation wryly as I do just the same thing myself. In and out of cities. Now I get it.

We all have different bases for setting goals. Eleanor made hers clear in a 1994 interview on the District's budget crisis and the new Republican majority. "I love Congress," she said. "Look, I tell you, people come to me and say, 'Oh Eleanor, are you all right?' But it serves me well. I grew up in the nation's capital that had segregation everywhere...When I was a child I thought segregation would last forever. And I was prepared to fight forever. So I don't regard this as daunting."

Eleanor set her career in motion and focused on it for forty years. Since active parts of our brains constantly get fresh oxygenated blood, and inactive areas don't, her sit-in-the-ashes Cinderella brain cells have no doubt withered by now while the road-to-power cells have surely multiplied. Conscious evolution.

Another woman set a different kind of goal. Tirsa, a social worker, had a tumultuous relationship with Ed, her long-time partner. She was tired of their fights. In their last battle, which pushed her over the edge, Ed yelled that she embarrassed him whenever they were out in public together. She talked too much and too loudly, and he was sick of her "low class" behavior. This wasn't the first time he'd made the accusation, describing her family of origin—and herself—as socially uninformed.

Tirsa made her own action plan: she decided to tell Ed she wasn't going to listen to his attacks any more. She set about accomplishing her goal methodically, thinking about what she planned to do, even rehearsing what she'd like to say. She role played it until she felt sure of her ground.

"With all my years working with families and knowing about women's roles, you'd think I wouldn't have the same

I am stunned that at only twenty-one years old I knew enough to know that if I wanted to pursue a dream, now's the time to do it.

—**Lisa Kudrow, actor, Emmy Award nominee**

damn fear every woman seems to have—of abandonment. And to feel this way about my own husband of twenty years. It's ridiculous. But I'm terrified of losing him and the relationship. Even for a woman like me, it's just as hard to stand up to him as it is for any wife. It's taken me two years to decide that I'm willing to put the relationship on the line, and say, 'No more. You can't talk to me or about me that way. It's unacceptable.'"

The next time Ed began to criticize the way Tirsa was talking, she got furious. Ed mumbled, "Here we go again." Tirsa told him they each had work to do. She didn't know what he had to do, but she had to stop taking all this crap from him. She demanded full respect from him, she said, and she wasn't going to put up with anything else.

When she stopped talking, there was silence.

"I went outside and started to cry, just as I always do after our fights, but then I began to laugh. I did it! For once in my life, I stood up for myself, and to a man. I've done it for my clients for years, I've urged them not to listen to destructive comments, I've counseled them through it, and now, I finally claimed my own right to be treated well. So many times in my head I have imagined saying, 'I won't let you treat me like this!' but I'd never done it before in real life."

A few days later, Ed started again making sarcastic comments about how ignorant she was. This time, Tirsa simply reminded Ed that she wasn't going to accept anything other than complete respect. This meant no more criticism of her language, her background, her body, or blame for her personal habits. They could fight, but not with these slurs thrown in.

"I was actually shaking when I said it," she related. "It must have taken me at least five minutes to get it out. I was waiting for the blow-up, when he said, 'That sounds reasonable.' I was shocked. It couldn't be that easy. It still amazes me."

Later, Ed told Tirsa he realized that his attacking her only kept him from getting in touch with how rotten he was feeling, and, understanding this, he felt like a "new man." Tirsa's refusal to put up with unfair treatment forced him to confront what was really bothering him: his fears that he was going to lose his middle management job in the next wave of "downsizing." He hadn't talked much about it because it was simply too frightening; goading Tirsa into fights had let him vent a little anxiety and allowed him to blame her if he did lose the job (her background wasn't "high society" enough to pull him through). But he was starting to understand that wasn't getting him anywhere. After the dust settled after each fight, the reality remained. So, in the end, he was relieved to be pushed to end the cycle.

Tirsa's insistence on respect also forced Ed to think about what he needed for respect. Soon after he figured out what was really bothering him, they begin to problem-solve together about their careers and family finances. In the process of meeting her goal—being treated with respect—Tirsa created a much closer relationship with her husband, and a chance to do some joint planning on a realistic basis.

Goal setting is helpful in many circumstances. Kendra told an Equity Institute seminar that she is at a place where she has met her current goals and needs to set some new ones.

"What's next for me?" she asked. "I have a good job. I have it now. So how do I enjoy it or live it? I have a family. I'll have my first child in six months. I've got it all balanced. So what comes next for me? Because I feel like I'm stagnating, I need something to strive for, a new goal.

"I've accomplished what I set out to do: marriage, child, a good job. Maybe I need to go back to school, or get more involved in community organizations as a board member. I'm wondering, 'What is my next move?'"

Other women offered their experiences. Selena went back to school for a graduate degree in her late thirties; Gloria started a catering business in her early forties; and Jaqueline wrote a book, each when they got to one of those "Been There, Done That" stages.

We must concentrate on what we can do and erase "can't," "won't" and "don't think so" from our vocabulary.

—Cardiss Collins, first woman to chair the Congressional Black Caucus

My grandfather once told me that there were two kinds of people: those who do the work and those who take the credit. He told me to try to be in the first group; there was much less competition.

—Indira Gandhi (1917–1984), Prime Minister of India

With the group's help, Kendra strategized her next step. She realized she hadn't gone back to school for the graduate degree that would give her a better chance at career advancement because she didn't want a long commute into the city at night. Someone told her about a program for non-profit management—just what she was looking for—at a university near her job.

So Kendra's current goal is finding what she calls that "extra activity" to stimulate her creativity. She thinks the graduate program will do it, but she realizes that isn't the main goal. It's simply a means to an end. The main goal is to keep herself growing.

When I asked Kendra how she had gotten so powerful, she replied, "My mother and my environment. I saw my mother get divorced, and how she managed to operate the home and the job. I saw my mother go out and get what she needed. She did it all. My mom worked seven to three, so when I got home, my mom was home." She paused. "I hold my mother in high esteem."

Another woman her age, Tamyra, a sales manager, chimed in, "The fact that my mother had two infant babies and held three jobs at one point so we could stay in a basement apartment showed me it could be done. My mom was pregnant with my older brother when she was in high school. She was forced by her family to marry our biological father, but he was abusive and she didn't stay in the relationship. I admired her for that.

"My mom has always worked, even when she married later. I was two.

"My step-father (actually he's the only father I've ever known, so he is my father) encouraged my education, even after I left home, leaving a note, at eighteen, after I moved in with my boyfriend of three weeks," she laughs. "Now my husband of ten years, Mike, has always encouraged my education and work. Because he grew up with a single mother, he's more supportive. He shares the household tasks, and it's no big deal.

"The challenge for me," she went on, "now that I have a new baby, is the guilt. I wonder if I should be at home. People tell me I'm going to miss this time. Also, the fact that I waited until I was twenty-eight to have the baby."

We all expressed surprise at "waiting until twenty-eight."

"Oh yes," she said, "back home people thought there was something wrong with me because I didn't have a child yet, and then I was 'living in sin' out here in California with Mike. They wondered.

"But how to balance home and work, with your child, your husband or partner, your job. I'd never want to not work. That superwoman expectation isn't what it used to be, but it's still there, we carry the baggage.

"We're caught between the old and the new. We're not in the traditional roles that our mothers were (or were supposed to be—my mom worked three jobs). But I found when I was pregnant that people either put me into the old picture, where I was just a body carrying the big event—the BABY. (That was all some people could talk to me about, and I was supposed to be in constant bliss.) Or else I was supposed to be the new woman: at my office, just the same as always, without noticing that something amazing was happening in my body. It felt like there was no right way to do it. It's hard trying to live up to some image. The feminist who hardly notices the pregnancy— except when I'm shopping for baby clothes on Saturday. Or the pregnant woman who's in bliss and thinks of nothing else.

"I remember the first time I realized I was getting lost in the 'Baby Event' was at a wedding when a friend congratulated me on my pregnancy but then wanted to know how I was doing with work, my home, and other interests. He really made me notice that the entire day no one had even asked me about any of that.

"Now that I have the baby, people still make you feel bad: 'Oh, you had to go back to work after only two and a half months. I hope there's no problem later with your son as he grows up.'

Success is important only to the extent that it puts one in a position to do more things one likes to do.

—Sarah Caldwell, symphony conductor

It doesn't happen all at once. You become. It takes a long time.

—Margery Williams Bianco (1881–1944), novelist

"I explain to people that work is fine, my son is fine, my husband is fine."

"What about you?" I asked Tamyra. "You mentioned everybody else."

She laughed. "Yeah, I'm okay. But I do feel guilty sometimes. And I see my friends, like my sister, with an older child, dealing with the difficulty of going to see her daughter in her school play. It's not like where I work, where I take the baby to work two days a week. Her company isn't flexible. They wouldn't let her leave two hours early to see her daughter perform. She's changing jobs, partly because of that."

"Don't expect the employer to sympathize," pitched in Kendra. "Use personal or vacation time. Didn't she have any? Don't say why. It just adds to the stigma of women always having to take off because of 'my child.' It's none of their business anyway. Just tell your sister to use her own time and tell them she has to leave at a certain time. They don't need to know why."

"You're right," Tamyra said. "It reinforces the stereotype of women not being committed to work.

"For me," she went on, "getting over the guilt is the main thing. That's my goal, being able to brush off the comments of people who say, 'It's too bad you have to work, and you can't stay home with your son.' I'd always want to work, though it would be nice to have the choice not to have to, financially."

Other women in the group helped her strategize how to meet her goal: not feeling guilty. She planned to observe her own mother more often. Her mother always worked, with much less support than Tamyra has. She's going to remember how close she is to her mom today, and how she, Tamyra, did get what she needed—in spite of, or perhaps because of, her mother's demanding work schedule. And that in fact she did grow up to become a clear-headed and strong twenty nine year old.

Tamyra also decided to form an informal support group with two friends who also like their jobs and have young children. She planned to get them together once a month: A young working mothers' Action Team.

Her doctor had actually suggested a group like this, but Tamyra hadn't given it much thought.

Two weeks after the seminar, Tamyra did start a Working Mothers Group with three other women (one of her friends brought a friend). At their first meeting, the four women came up with enough topics for a year:

- Finding Day Care
- Balancing Family and Work
- Parenting: Sharing Responsibility with Partners
- Fitness
- Trouble Shooting
- Support
- Returning to Work after Family Leave
- Finances
- Raising Sons/Raising Daughters (The group had both)
- Part Time/Full Time Work
- Is There a "Mommy Track"?
- My Life Goals
- Is Motherhood, Work, and Romance Too Much to Expect?
- Is Guilt Required?

The group decided to tackle one topic each meeting, sharing solutions, resources, fears, and successes. They have now held three monthly meetings, are wildly enthusiastic and report less stress already. Knowing that others are there with support, ideas, and a waiting ear is making a difference.

Maddy, a professionally trained actor, discovered the power of group goal setting at a period when she was floundering. Several years after her training, Maddy found herself surviving on a series of part-time jobs, getting few acting parts. She became discouraged about theater and began to doubt herself. Did she have the creative core to thrive as an actor?

Then she joined an artists' support group, made up of five women committed to developing their creativity. Together they

Challenges are as necessary to our existence as air . . . Without the physical challenges of managing our environment, our muscles would atrophy, our bones grow brittle. Without life's inevitable challenges . . . we might never discover our resourcefulness.

—Susan L. Taylor, editor-in-chief, Essence

Keep in mind always the present you are constructing. It should be the future you want.

—Ola, fictional character of Alice Walker, Pulitzer Prizewinning author

came to an Equity Institute program. They each set goals about their acting careers, strategized, commiserated, committed to meet monthly, and within a year, four of them—including Maddy—began working steadily. (The fifth decided to leave acting.) Today Maddy is a rising star in regional theater, working in play after play, getting good parts. She credits her renewal to the support group she was lucky enough to find, already formed, and to the group goal setting.

Today Maddy's struggle is maintaining her energy. She is tired and wants a break. So perhaps she'll find another support group, tailored to her current needs—a women's Resting Group, as my friend Akaya describes a gathering she facilitates for women on the edge of burn-out.

Sometimes people set goals individually. Suzanne, a nurse's aid in an Equity Institute seminar, told us that ten years ago she set four major goals, with the help of the workbook, *What Color Is Your Parachute?* Her goals were:

- Raise happy, healthy children
- Shift to a career that pays more money
- Impact social policy about race and gender discrimination
- Have a stable life-partner

These objectives set Suzanne's life course, giving her markers when she wondered which fork in life's road to take.

As a single mother with a flexible schedule, she tailored her job to her children's school hours so she could give them the attention she wanted to provide. She became active in a community group working on inclusion in schools. And she developed a committed life-relationship with another woman. Six years ago, she wrote me recently, they bought a house together.

She was on the way to meeting her first and last goals—stabilizing her family. Then, last year, inspired by the outcome of several high-profile harassment suits, Suzanne began to focus on making an action plan to fulfill goals two and three—the new career. She decided to take on racism and sexism through the courts, setting herself the goal of becoming a lawyer. While continuing to work at her day job, she plans to attend law school at night.

Now she has to get very specific, breaking her long-term action plan into attainable steps. She needs to research local law schools, find out what preparation is necessary to apply, figure out financing, and perhaps seek out support networks of women in law.

At the seminar, Suzanne reduced her plans to a series of steps, each with a timeline:

- Find out what local law schools exist—this week;
- Send for catalogues from all of them—this week;
- Get the names of five lawyers specializing in civil rights law, including public interest advocacy firms—next week;
- Make appointments with three lawyers—two weeks;
- Get information about local LSAT courses and send for information—this month;
- Find out about "Women in the Law" networks—next month.

With her overall goal in clear focus (her intention), and setting timelines for the steps necessary to reach it (focusing her attention), Suzanne has the basis to accomplish her plan.

If your bigger aim is to be more empowered, try breaking that down into concrete and detailed bits as the basis of an action plan. What would being empowered look like for you?

For Inez, a physicist, the answer is: doubling her research space at work. So she creates short-term goals: "I plan to negotiate for a better work space. I have plenty of logic to back me up. There is room available and I'm not going to take No for an answer. By the end of the month, I will have a commitment for more lab space."

This kind of goal setting means refining choices, which are already identified, and designing an action plan. Include a timeline for benchmark data to check progress.

Look forward. Turn what has been done into a better path. If you're a leader, think about the impact of your decisions on seven generations into the future.

—Chief Wilma Mankiller, Cherokee Nation, citing traditional precept

There are multiple paths Inez can take to meet her overall objective of more lab space. We each get to continually choose, revise and tailor plans to fit constantly changing environments. Her scenario could go: "Uh oh, it's already the end of week one and I haven't even made an appointment with my division head."

"Week two. I have the appointment and I've met with two supporters. They're coaching me."

"Week three. My case was unassailable! I had the specifics, I knew what I wanted and that it was reasonable, I had a solution to the problem—and I even showed him how giving me the space was going to make him look good. He said yes!"

Or her story could unfold differently: "Week three. No way am I going to get it, now that the vice president just turned down a similar request yesterday. I have to go back to the drawing board and design another solution. I'll invite Harry and Veronique to a Think Tank on Friday to help me devise a new strategy. I'm going to cancel my meeting until I get a new plan."

"Week four. Great Think Tank. New plan: all the women in the division—all three of us—are going in together, to demonstrate how unequal the space distribution is by gender. That's the tack I need to take."

As women increasingly take on issues of economic empowerment, many are setting financial goals. One friend, Elizabeth, who has the goal of getting enough money for a down payment on a house, joined a women's investment group, in which women pool their resources—as immigrant groups often have—to invest. The fee is $150 to join the group. It is each woman's contribution to an initial investment. The women meet monthly to learn more about investing together.

Elizabeth has also made her own first stock investment, and is searching about for other ways to generate that down payment. With her goal clearly in front of her, she is becoming more aware of options: getting more income through investing, or obtaining a low-cost first-time homeowners loan, which requires little down payment. She has just started to research opportunities, and has the goal of buying her house within two years. With the clarity and focus she is bringing to the goal, she will probably meet it.

The Tool Kit: Strategies for Setting Goals

Success is a failure turned inside out.

—Anon.
(Often a woman)

Now that you have remembered who you are, made yourself central and gotten over boiler-plate "nice"—it's time to set goals. They are the basis of the map—your action plan—to get you where you want to go.

Think about your life goal or goals. What are they, at this moment? Have they changed over the last decade? Which ones have you met? This question sets a life direction and involves your broadest purpose. It could be spiritual, social, or material. Whatever it is, it's what you really are "about."

Write down three current long-term goals, as a record of your intentions and a reference for later check-ins.

Write down your one- and two-year goals. Think about your long-term goals as you make these shorter ones. Do the intermediate goals support the longer ones? It's helpful if there is a relationship between the two. For example, if you want to become a manager in two years, how does this relate to your life goal of becoming a congresswoman? (It might. Figure out what skills, credentials, and, contacts you will accumulate as a manager that will boost you into elected office).

Write down your goals for this week and this month (short-term goals). Be specific. Break your long-and mid-range goals into attainable steps. Decide what you have to do to reach your goal. Think, for example, about

Suzanne, the nurse's aid who wants to become a lawyer, and the way she planned out each segment she needed to accomplish in order to get into law school, putting a time line to each task.

 Ask yourself, honestly, what assumptions or beliefs you would have to give up in order to meet your goals. Your first step in challenging the old notions that keep you from fully achieving your goals is to identify them in yourself and in those who surround you.

Does your partner think you could never be an entrepreneur? Are your parents waiting—with some urgency—to be grandparents? Does your best friend believe that women "your age" (forty) are days from being hopelessly over the hill? You may not be able to re-adjust the attitudes of the people around you the way you can fine-tune your own opinions, but you can listen with a more critical ear. And you can choose to spend more time with people who don't share those limiting opinions.

 If you work outside your home and have a young child, find out what your company would be willing to offer to meet your needs. Could you bring your infant to work several days a week? (A congressman does it. Equity Institute does it. Major corporations are doing it. Most are finding this innovation provides an unexpected benefit: a source of pleasure and morale-building for everyone in the office.) What about on-site day care for children and elders? Generate some noise about this. More and more firms are recognizing and accommodating care-taking relationships. You don't stop being a mother—or a daughter—once you punch a time clock or come in the office door.

Setting Goals in Your Action Team

Use the group as a supportive place to set individual goals. Your goal could concern work, self, spirituality, family, wealth, creativity, self-esteem, community, or any aspect of life you choose.

Announce your plans: then check in at subsequent meetings. How are you each progressing toward your goal? What's working, what's not? Because we're unused to setting goals for ourselves, women often forget between meetings what objectives they had set. In this case, a group memory is helpful. You may want to keep a written record of goals—each woman writing her own, or a group note-book—so women at least have a chance to say, "Oh, yes, that's right. In fact I have been working on that, and this is what's happened...." or "Hmm, I think I'm on a different track now. I'm going to set some new goals."

Celebrate achievements. Provide assistance for each other in devising new methods to accomplish your objectives. Identify barriers and get group thinking and encouragement as you move around road-blocks.

One effective format is to provide a period of time (anywhere from five minutes to an hour, depending on the time you spend together and how many are in your group) for "group think." One woman describes her goals, her progress, if any, and what gets in the way or may prevent her from meeting her goals. The other women act as consultants, listening to her (which itself has an astonishingly forceful impact, as she gets a chance to hear herself think out loud with all this good attention.) After she's had a chance to talk about her own feelings and observations of her journey toward her goals, other women comment, offering their thoughts and suggestions.

Goal setting in groups is so powerful that it is an essential component of all Equity Institute programs. Making commitments publicly is inspirational as we observe each other make and meet goals, while remaining flexible to

You need to claim the events of your life to make yourself yours. When you truly possess all you have been and done, which may take some time, you are fierce with reality.

—Florida Scott Maxwell, author

new and unexpected options that open before us. Hearing each others' goals also gives us the opportunity to thoughtfully support each other, with information about the directions others are taking. And getting a group snapshot of aims helps us understand more broadly the context for some of our own struggles.

Mile Marker Five:
Make Choices

A key issue in every women's life is
how to retain the choices we have while
expanding choice arenas, so we can make
decisions in every aspect of our lives,
rather than accept limited options.

Mile Marker Five: Make Choices

Following the road to power means claiming our ability to choose the direction of our lives. From the right to select a mate, to get the job, or attend the school we want, we've had to battle for every choice. And we've won, in arena after arena. For example, who among us, until recently, consciously selected the mother role as one among several reasonable options?

Thirty years ago my friend Ann Mari, ten years older than I, decided not to have children. I was bewildered by her choice, without even the language or concepts to think about it rationally. I accepted motherhood as a given, and was startled by her putting this "inevitability" into the realm of choice.

Choice has many faces:

"Yes, I am going to fly that airplane."

"No, I will not accept the life I watched my mother squeeze into."

"Yes, I will become an astronaut."

"I will become President."

And on and on, in a never ending cascade:

"Yes, I will go."

"Yes, I can do."

"Yes, I am."

Young and old women all have options that didn't exist even a generation ago. We've created a social space within which women can live on their own, if they choose to, or live with other women and men in any combination. We've crashed open doors to jobs that weren't possible for us to even consider until the last two decades; we've insisted that we all have options. In order to freely choose our life paths from among them, we need, as the writer Elizabeth Mitchell says, to "to put the training we received when we cared for dolls into perspective. Or we will be compelled to experience only shadow lives… Through dolls, the heart muscles of females are strengthened, ensuring that they will be ruled by compassion and, through that compassion, by others, for the rest of their lives." Putting behind the internalized commands to follow the wishes of others—parents, friends, partners or an imaginary ideal feminist superego—leaves us free to really choose our lives. What shape do we want them to take, what do we want to explore, who do we want to be?

We all make choices constantly; but now, as our options are opening, we need to become ever more conscious of them. Understanding that we are choosing, we can't really blame the outcomes on other people. We can notice that our selections are sometimes limited. We may not have access to the easiest or most direct routes, and part of what we need to do is demand access, alone and in concert with other women.

But meanwhile, there are always choices. As the sister of a man who was imprisoned in the old South Africa said recently in court, her brother had been so lonesome in solitary confinement that he retained his sanity by making friends with a fly, the only living creature allowed in his cell. This man made a conscious decision to remain sane, and to begin a unique relationship. With a fly.

We all get to make choices about our responses in any situation. We get to decide when to say "Yes" and when to say "No," when it's time to shift to drive, and when to go on to high gear, when to accelerate and when to brake. We get to decide where we're going and which route to take.

Women have been so circumscribed that when we do make choices outside of the narrow prescription for female lives, we sometimes stir up fearful reactions. A friend told me of her first solo camping trip. Robin had never done this before and planned it, with great enthusiasm, for months. When her vacation finally came, she traveled up and down the California coast for two weeks, enjoying the freedom in packing up camp when she wanted to, going at her own pace, reveling in the unaccustomed solitude. She found, however, that when she met fellow campers they often asked, "Aren't you afraid of traveling—or camping—alone?" (Women in pairs or groups even

I get optimism from the Earth itself. I feel that as long as the Earth can make a spring every year, I can!

—Alice Walker, Pulitzer Prize-winning author

*They never imag-
ined we'd stick
with the officers'
training program.
They figured we'd
stay on the job until
we got married and
had babies and
then go back home.*

**—Beatrice
Vormawah,
Ghanaian ship
captain, the only
female ship captain
in Africa and one of
twelve in the world.**

get this question when traveling or dining "alone"—that is, without men. The singer Holly Near wrote a delightful musical spoof on this experience: A gentleman asks two women in a restaurant, "Are you alone?" To which they respond, "No, we're together.")

Robin wasn't afraid of camping alone—truly alone—before she got these comments, recycled fears that have often kept women at home, longing for adventures we are too afraid to seek outside "romance novels." Fortunately, Robin kept going, brushed off the remarks, and had a marvelous trip.

When we make unconventional choices, it is particularly helpful to have our Action Team or other support group cheer us on and provide guidance. Sophia, a chemist in the South, described in a seminar how much she relied on the few other women in her specialty, nationally, to give her job and friendship contacts when she moved from one city to another. Rosie, the midwestern bus driver, described how vital other women's support—both drivers and riders—was to her ability to stay on the job.

Socorro Valdez, interviewed by Yolanda J. Broyles for research on the theater ensemble El Teatro Campesino, described how the women in the company during the 1970s struggled to be viewed and treated as equals. Only fifteen when she joined El Teatro, Valdez chose to confront the limited roles offered to women. "You were either the novia, la mamá, la abuela, or la hermana. And most of the time these characters were passive." At one time, she said, there were only three women in the company. "That was a real interesting time. We were either going to remain members of the company, or just be 'the women of the company.' That made a real difference, you know, because I hated to be put into a mold like 'These are the ladies of the Teatro.'... We ended up in the role of fighters, because that's what was needed to get the men's heads to a place where they would be able to discuss something with you."

When they protested the limited roles, the women were told they could write their own plays if they didn't like what was offered. They tried a number of strategies, including getting several women in administrative positions. And Valdez chose to play some male roles—old men, whom none of the male actors wanted to play—which allowed her to stretch as a performer. Over the years, she and another core group member, Olivia Chumacero, developed additional ways to utilize their acting expertise, eventually directing and teaching as well as acting. "From the backstage perspective," Broyles wrote, "I witnessed dramatic and inspirational breakthroughs...Many of the women managed to transform old frustrations into new options, creating new spaces and models in which they and other women—and men—can move."

Today many women are choosing to operate in new spaces and activities: riding motorcycles, taking jobs no woman has held before, openly choosing other women as lovers or life partners, or straightforwardly having children outside of marriage. Women continue to expand the possibilities of what seems "normal," in spite of fears and attacks. In order to move outside expected behavior, it is necessary to make deliberate choices. Women are no longer falling into lives. We are selecting them.

This doesn't mean it's easy. Women in non-traditional work, like men of color or other men not "in the loop," are often scapegoats. For example, the first person dismissed from the police force for misconduct in 1995 after a group of New York City officers rioted in Washington D.C. was a woman. As author Connie Fletcher told a *New York Times* reporter, "There's a blue curtain. The men close ranks and the women are left to hang. They're the ones who get fired or suspended or hung out to dry." She cited a female officer who posed for Playboy and was dismissed, while a male vice detective caught on film having sex in a massage parlor was only suspended.

But, ironically, Fletcher sees hope in a woman's implication in a recent New York corruption scandal. "It might be a good sign that women are being accepted if they're allowed to be part of the corruption."

I never had a man ask me for advice on how to combine marriage and career.

—Gloria Steinem, author, co-founder, Ms.

I always believed that if you set out to be successful, then you already were.

—Katherine Dunham, scholar, dancer

In spite of the difficulties, women continue to choose previously closed fields like police work. In San Francisco, female cops have made major headway in the last decade, with 13% of the force now made up of women. After years of resistance, male colleagues and superiors are finally recognizing that not only can women perform physically, they bring additional skills. Deborah Erdy, a triathlete who's been on the force for two years, said in a *San Francisco Chronicle* interview that the public can still give women cops a hard time. "Some people think women shouldn't be cops and they won't listen to you. They laugh, think it's a joke. They say, 'Why don't you send some real cops?' You get it a lot."

On the other hand, she reports, a woman's presence can take down the heat a few notches. Many times, especially in cases of domestic violence and child abuse, families are happy when female officers show up.

"That's not to say men aren't as caring—but we as women are socialized to deal with things differently," Erdy says. "We have the ability of talking to people. It's a real advantage. But if we need to do business, we can do business. I like working with a man, for the balance. We can offer more."

Police Chief Fred Lau, who joined the San Francisco force in 1971, admitted he was "skeptical" at first about women coming in. But Lau—who himself had to fight to get in because he didn't meet the height requirement at the time—changed his mind. Now he says women have improved some parts of police work. "I think some of our training methods have changed," he told reporters Carol Ness and Rachel Gordon. "Where we used to rely on a lot of physical skills, we rely a lot more on stronger communication methods. Women helped pave the road for that."

An example of a woman who consciously and ultimately successfully made new choices is the character played by Kathy Bates in the movie *Fried Green Tomatoes*. Stuck in a boring life and stagnating marriage, she made a decision to expand her horizons. In a series of humorous but deadly serious moves, she goes to a relationship group seeking remedies to put zip back in her marriage ("dress in saran wrap") and befriends a fascinating older woman who helps her begin making other choices in her life. She experiments with new recipes, gets a job, begins to work out, and finally creates another identity: Towanda, an alter-ego who is a take-no-prisoners Amazon.

In one transformative moment, Bates refuses to take the insults of younger women who yell at her in a mall parking lot, and repeatedly rams their parked car while they watch in disbelief. She further experiments with her new power by knocking out a wall in her home and, for the first time, makes direct demands on her husband, rather than trying to wheedle, plead, and cajole her way to goals. Having made this series of choices, Bates ends the movie a more centered and powerful woman. She has a career, is in charge of her physical health, and is developing a more equal relationship with her husband—a man emerging from his bewilderment at the unexpected new woman who appeared in his living room one day, riding her exercise bike, shouting, "Towanda!"

As *Fried Green Tomatoes* depicts, the shape of each of our lives is determined by the choices we make. Whether we choose to linger in depression and resentment, as the Kathy Bates character initially did, or experiment with new avenues of self-expression and empowerment, as she later found the courage to do, is up to us.

Sometimes our thinking is so limited that it's hard to figure out what options we potentially have, and what choices we therefore could select. A useful technique to open ourselves to possible new choices is to imagine another identity. What if you were a man? What do you imagine would be possible? How do you think people would treat you, and what would you demand? What would you expect of yourself? Let yourself hypothesize that you had been born male. Who would you be today? Here are some women's answers:

"If I had felt so entitled since childhood, today I'd be a full professor, maybe chair of my department, instead of hanging

They've always said, poor Indians, they can't speak, so, many speak for them. That's why I decided to learn Spanish.

—Rigoberta Menchu, Nobel laureate

One day I found myself saying to myself, "I can't live where I want to. I can't even say what I want to!" I decided I was a very stupid fool not to at least paint as I wanted to.

—Georgia O'Keefe (1887–1986) painter

forever in the junior ranks, going from one university to another. I would have pushed my promotion more, and fought for the validity of my research on quilting as art rather than craft. Or even refused to buy into those distinctions, which usually get applied in a sexist way."

"I'd be a musician. I never even saw a female drummer perform until recently. That is definitely what I would be today."

"I'd be CEO of the company."

"Maybe I would have chosen a job in maintenance—which makes almost twice as much as my job as secretary, for the same hours."

These are aspects of yourself that you can still consciously choose to develop, once you realize what options you cut yourself out of because you didn't realize they were available to you.

Or what if you weren't Mexican-American, for example, or Jewish, or a member of any other stigmatized group? What if you had never experienced backlash? What would you have seen your mother and your grandmother do? What might you be able to do?

Of course, that's what you can actually do.

Or what if you were suddenly twenty years older—or younger? Who would you be?

In a seminar a thirty-year-old South African woman living in the United States imagines that she is sixty-five and the president of South Africa. It's exciting to hear of her high political ambitions, but why can't she picture being that powerful for thirty-five more years? While it's refreshing that she correlates age with power, now that she has envisioned that future, perhaps she could jump even further, and imagine navigating her way to President in ten or fifteen years, instead of waiting so long.

Whatever you conjecture for that "other" self—the one without the limitations you think you carry—you can choose for the real you. Maybe you won't make it happen today, maybe some of your fantasies are old daydreams that you don't even want any more, but, just like Kathy Bates, if you really wanted to live out any of those dreams, you could.

Letting yourself open up to a big-picture view—no limitations—gives you some clues about choices you thought you didn't have and the boundaries you unwittingly accepted. So for a moment, try on a different identity. For this instant, be someone you imagine as unfettered by your particular shackles. What does it feel like to be you, with that one part of your social profile—your gender or race, your sexual orientation or religion, your age or your size—altered?

"I could speak in public."

"I'd be less afraid."

"I could live anywhere."

"I could take leadership."

Your choices must begin with imagination. Too often we make major life decisions from inside the trappings of identity boxes that come with restrictions: my mother didn't do it, my father didn't do it, no one in my family has ever done it. So I don't do it.

When we make deliberate and conscious choices, with no boundaries to our imaginations, we can redefine those identities we thought were so restrictive. We get to claim what strengthens and builds us, while rejecting the socially imposed limitations. Women often haven't been there as role models to show us that, yes, we can implement a corporate-wide information system, produce an MTV video, be the national vice president or the school superintendent. We can be architects and stock brokers and secretaries of state. We can impact our towns, and our states. We have to exercise our imaginations to give ourselves a full set of choices. Saying, "Yes, I want to do that" is the first step to learning how to do it.

Making conscious choices is a subset of making any decisions. Since historically, many decisions were taken out of our hands, we've lacked practice, at least in making them confidently and openly. But we can learn how to make decisions from a large universe of possibilities—including choices about our lives. There are numerous processes, each of which is

How we spend our days is how we spend our lives.

—**Annie Dillard,** author

effective for different women, or for the same woman in various contexts.

Let's say you're a credit analyst at a bank. You recently realized that men tune you out during team meetings. Whenever you bring up a new topic, there is absolutely no reply. But when Fred or Sam rephrases your thought, he gets the response: "Great idea!"

You consider a number of possible interventions:

- Put this inequity on the agenda as an item at the next team meeting;
- Talk to your division manager privately, telling him dispassionately about your observation. Ask him what he thinks it's about;
- Blow up the next time it happens. Try to scare them;
- Repeat each of your comments twice in future meetings;
- Lobby a male ally prior to meetings, who will second your ideas and deliberately return the spotlight to you;
- Give up wanting to claim credit for your ideas;
- Advance your suggestions to power brokers before the meeting, knowing that usually the real meeting happens before the meeting;
- Glare through the next meeting until someone asks you what is wrong, and then explain your perception of the situation;
- Leave the bank;
- Write a memo to each member of the team detailing your observation of past conversations.

How to select the best tactic, or group of tactics, for you?

Some women make a list of pros and cons. You could select your favorite one or two possible tactics and subject each to the Pro/Con treatment. It's like a cost-benefit analysis in that you get to project what you might win and what you might lose, for each intervention. This helps get all of the thoughts that are running around your brain sorted into logical sets. Sometimes

Whenever I have to choose between two evils, I always like to try the one I haven't tried before.

—Mae West
(1892–1981), actor

it is startling to see what some of the "pros" or "cons" are when you actually list them. The answer may be immediately apparent. Other times, this technique simply serves to clear your mind and objectify the factors going into your choice.

If you were the bank credit analyst faced with the choice of what to do to get listened to, you might choose the first two possible interventions listed above as ones you wanted to subject to a pro/con treatment. Your first choice is "Putting the behavior I've observed on the agenda" and you put on your "Pro" list these probable positive outcomes: making all your coworkers who are in on these meetings aware of the subtle tune-outs; demonstrating that this is "business," not something personal, which is why it appears on a business agenda; and, making it public like this, you might get allies who would call attention to the mistreatment if they see it again. "Cons" might be: you could subject yourself to humiliation and become the butt of jokes if coworkers don't get it, once you've gone public; you risk stimulating others' resentment if they perceive valuable time they need for other urgent business being taken up by your "over-sensitive, self-centered" complaint.

After looking at the pros and cons, you might decide that putting it on the agenda is for you, and now that you've identified a few cons, you may be able to ameliorate them by lobbying an ally or two before the meeting, so you won't become isolated. And knowing the possible pitfalls will inform the way you present your case: maybe you'll name the "over-sensitive" issue yourself, and use that to launch the presentation, or as part of a joke you create.

A second method is to imagine yourself into the scenario and try out different strategies to see how they feel. You can do this alone or with a friend or colleague, who role plays with you. What solutions do you conjecture might emerge, say, from bringing the topic of your invisibility up at the next team meeting? And how would you do it? With humor, with anger, with professional detachment, with righteous indignation, with bemusement, with statistics about how common

Every time you don't follow your inner guidance, you feel a loss of energy, loss of power, a sense of spiritual deadness.

—Shakti Gawain, author

If you refuse to accept anything but the best, you very often get it.

—Anon.
(Often a woman)

this is, with anecdotes about similar situations? There are endless possibilities here for action within just this one strategy. You could try on different demeanors and see which, if any, seem suitable and effective for you, and how you feel after you've tried them out.

A third method of decision-making is trial and error. You try out, in a low-risk situation, several of the interventions that appeal to you the most. Perhaps you find a comparable situation to the bank meetings with a community group where you are active, with your Action Team, or in your family. In this somewhat safer place, you act out your strategies and assess the outcome. Following the credit analyst example through this method, you might have noticed the same behavior (or something similar) in another group you're a member of, but one which doesn't have the economic power of a job. You bring up your observation and objections there, as a dry run, getting the practice and assessing results. If speaking up firmly got results in this setting, for instance, you can assume that it will probably be successful at work, and you've had a tryout.

A fourth way of selecting among choices is to solicit other input. Gather information from books for women at work or from people you suspect have had similar experiences—in this case, those frustrating tune-outs. As the credit analyst, you ask for advice from networks or from professional industry-specific associations. You talk to your Action Team and other friends. Certainly other women in mostly-male meetings have experienced the same response you've been getting; what have they tried? What worked for them? Out of the data you get this way, you select that which best seems to fit your situation, and your style, and has a track record of success.

A fifth method is to put yourself together with others in an information-rich environment and let solutions unfold. In this model, solutions are always unique and unexpected, arising as they do out of particular contexts. So, utilizing this technique for the bank credit analyst, she might either put herself with the team members in a novel context (say, a restaurant at lunch time), or situate herself with other women in banking at a conference. In either of these contexts, answers and resolution might emerge without conscious structuring. The assumption underlying this method is that the universe is self-organizing. We don't have to struggle; answers emerge when we relax, letting go of the illusion that we have to make everything happen. We are still in charge of our choices and our lives, but solutions may emerge unexpectedly. We practice awareness, looking for answers without anxiety; in fact, we have confidence that they will emanate from our environment.

Each of these methods has something to recommend it. You may join elements of one with parts of another.

Practice making conscious decisions. And remember, when making choices, few are final. You usually get to choose again if you don't like the outcomes of your first venture. You can try one strategy, and if it doesn't work, try another. It's also all right if you get part way into something and decide it's not right for you after all. You are developing valuable experience in making good choices. As you choose, remember the words of Hillary Rodham Clinton at the Fourth U.N. World Conference on Women: "We need to understand that there is no formula for how women should lead their lives. That is why we must respect the choices that each woman makes for herself and her family. Each woman deserves the chance to realize her God-given potential."

In order to actualize that potential, you're entitled to all the information you need. In order to get it, you're going to have to ask questions. In an Equity Institute seminar, Maria told us that the most disempowering message she got as a working-class girl was: Don't ask questions! If she transgressed, her family was afraid she would appear embarrassingly uninformed or stupid. She didn't want to look like Archie or Edith Bunker—or a "foolish immigrant"—so she grew to be a woman who tried to glide through life without ever asking questions, thereby missing critical information. She never asked for details about tasks required of her at her job or about new

The choices we make determine who we become, offering us the possibility of leading an authentic life.

—Jean Shinoda Bolen, psychiatrist and writer

assigned projects, thinking that to do so would reveal her ignorance. Thus, she sometimes went off on the wrong track and had difficulty collaborating with colleagues.

Once Maria realized how this childhood prohibition was cutting her off from data she needed to perform well—and that it was permissible to seek it—she inquired more often about project directions, even though it felt uncomfortable to do so. She had to remind herself that the most intelligent people often ask a lot of questions. And that no one knows everything.

Maria was astonished at the difference asking questions made in her ability to excel at her marketing job. Freed from the fear of appearing ignorant, her talents became more apparent, she was able to coordinate her work with others, and her questions (often going right to a potential weakness in presentation) moved projects forward more effectively.

The Tool Kit: Strategies for Making Choices

 Ask questions. In order to make informed choices, inquire about options and their repercussions. Ask questions at work, and request information from those serving you: doctors, lawyers, clerks, repair people. Employers or service providers may not encourage questions, but you are entitled to all the data you need to make good choices and to effectively implement your decisions.

 Take the time to know what it is you want. In order to choose well, we have to know our true desires. Many of us have been so busy attending to others that we haven't allowed ourselves the quiet to attend to our own inner stirrings.

Sam, the woman who drove west from Oklahoma to escape a battering husband, finally had a Saturday "off"

from her daughters when her new partner said he would take care of them for the day. He encouraged her to have an adventure alone, do something frivolous or exciting: A museum, a hike, a movie, anything she wanted to do. He wanted to give her this gift of time.

The distressing outcome was that she had no idea what she wanted to do. She had been denied choice for so long that her attunement to her own desires had deadened. She ended up going to a beauty salon and getting a permanent—to look more beautiful for him.

To stay attuned to your own desires, deliberately schedule in regular time when you take an hour, a day or an afternoon away from family, work, or friends. In those times alone, attend to the inner voice that has been trying to be heard: "I want to paint," "I want to go bowling," or "Take me to the new coffee house in town"—which actually opened five or six years ago, but still seems new, since you've yet to get there.

If you don't know what you want to do, simply take a walk or do something else that quiets you. You will soon know what your soul has been yearning for.

Practice consciously exercising choice at least once a day. At your job or in your community, select one important task where you can employ some choice. At home, decide to pick the foods you want, the clothes you enjoy, the recreation you desire. Practice choosing the timing that suits you—even for simple events like dinner. You don't always need to dance around others' schedules.

Expand your choice categories. Historically, women have been restricted to making decisions about a small range of items: food, clothing, domestic technology. Women who worked outside the home for pay generations ago (and they were more than many of us imagine today) mostly lacked choice in their occupations. They took

Mistakes are part of the dues one pays for a full life.

—Sophia Loren, actor

The strongest principle of growth lies in human choice.

—George Eliot
(Mary Ann Evans,
1819–1880), novelist

what was available to them, in their locale, for women of their legal or social status. Until World War II, for example, virtually all employed African American women saw before them only two choices: domestic or agricultural labor. (Even then, a few women, like Madame C.J. Walker, burst out of those limited confines to become entrepreneurs. She became a millionaire selling cosmetics to African American women.) But we are truly in a different era, to which we have to catch up mentally and emotionally.

Make a list of categories, like Work, Entertainment, Cars, Education, Health, Body, Spirituality, Sexuality, Reproduction, Exercise, Sleep, Food. Write down your choices in each category. For example, under Sleep, write the time you like to go to bed and the time you like to wake up. Under Work, record what jobs you choose to do, what work you enjoy. For a week, observe how many of your choices you exercise. Keep a log tracking what choices you make, noting how frequently you drift into others' programs.

 Make sexual choices. The relatively new legal concept of marital rape (i.e., women are not automatically sexually available simply because they become wives) is vital to all women, and has been hotly contested, because it establishes the concept that women have sexual choice everywhere. Even within marriage, where we have so often been legally subsumed, women have choice. A woman has, at any time, the right to decide whether to be—or not to be—sexually active with a consensual partner.

 Choose humor whenever possible. Humor provides the seasoning that makes our efforts palatable. The impossible becomes possible with humor. It lightens up 'life and death' situations, so that they are more easily handled.

To laugh with good humor in the face of fear is to fully reclaim our power.

Erma Bombeck is a good example of a woman who transcended the potentially mind-chilling effects of sub-urban housewifery by casting her witty eye upon the inequities to which she was subject, thereby gaining some control. She, like Moms Mably and a long tradition of comics before her, developed an effective platform for highlighting bias through humor.

Read humorous books and columns to keep your funny bone exercised. Go to comedy clubs and shows. Choose friends who make you laugh, find movies that tickle you, and consciously expand your HQ: humor-quotient. It, like other abilities, can be stretched and maintained with deliberate use.

Try on different identities. You're not limited to the stereotypes of who you've been perceived to be. Give yourself the opportunity to thoughtfully choose what you really want by trying on various identities. Could an "X" like you (a woman or a Lebanese refugee, a lesbian, or a woman born poor) become a "Y" (scientist or legislator, mother, or patron of the arts)? You bet.

Practice a new decision-making method. At your next choice-point, notice your decision process. How well does it work for you? Try one or two new ones, selecting from the five methods outlined in the chapter:

- A Pro/Con list;
- Putting yourself in an imaginary scenario;
- A low-risk trial and error simulation;
- Soliciting other input;
- Placing yourself in a context in which unique solutions can unfold.

Giving people choices enhances our capacity to attain dignity and reach our capacity.

—Faye Wattleton, former president, Planned Parenthood

Maybe some combination of these will work best for you, or perhaps you will utilize another effective method. Whatever process you select, be aware when you are choosing, how and why.

Make it a rule of life never to regret and never look back. We all live in suspense, from day to day, from hour to hour; in other words, we are the hero of our own story.

—Mary McCarthy (1912–1989), novelist, critic

Action Team Choices

Make choices about your group. If you find it isn't meeting your goals, remember that you have the power to stay, working to change the team so that it becomes the appropriate one for you. Or to leave and join another group. Or start one of your own. There are many possibilities.

The power of choice means that you get to have your life—every aspect of it—work for you. Your life, including your Action Team, can be just the way you want it, once you know what you want and decide to construct the life that will bring it to you.

Your team is a microcosm of your life. You contribute to choosing its direction, structure, and composition. As you assert your needs, you inspire other women to be honest about what they want, and the team becomes stronger.

Select women to be in your Action Team who stretch and genuinely support you. You truly will be creating powerful visions together.

You also want to choose styles of meetings, and content, that suit you. At this point in your life, what atmosphere is going to be most conducive for the success of a group for you? Do you want weekly dinner meetings, monthly retreats, one evening a week or a quarter? What level of support are you seeking?

And what topics do you want to address? Your choices here, like everywhere else, will help determine the kind of group you are in, and how effectively it meshes with your current needs.

Mile Marker Six:
Take Charge Everywhere

This chapter emboldens us to be
alert and powerful in even the smallest of our
daily interactions, which we sometimes
experience as burying us in
a ton of feathers.

Mile Marker Six:
Take Charge Everywhere

With our multiple commitments, women's lives are complex. Many of us have gotten our lives "together" in one sphere or another—yet few dare imagine lives with no limits.

Several client stories illustrate the common situation of women who are succeeding, perhaps extremely well, in some portion of their lives, yet still having a rough time until they decide they have to—somehow—take charge everywhere.

Elana is an engineer, a woman in a profession that's 92% male. After ten years in research and development for a Fortune 500 company, she loves her job and still can't quite believe she has it. She pinches herself sometimes, and has to remind herself that she's a real scientist. (Her mother was a maid, her father a porter.) From the time she was a child, this was what she wanted to be. She never had any doubts. Before her time at her company, she's heard, women were completely frozen out of the information loop, openly laughed at when they offered suggestions. The few who endured were isolated, hard-working loners. But for Elana, that's ancient history. She gets along with her male coworkers and is well-respected. In fact, she kind of likes being an "only" and the special status it confers. Her problem, the one that drifts into her mind in down-times all during the day, is childcare.

Elana practically runs over pedestrians screeching to get to the day-care center before the 6 P.M. pick-up deadline, when the late charge kicks in. And she feels guilty that she doesn't have more time—or home-cooked dinners—for her young child. But with little leisure in which to contemplate either her regret, or her competitive urges toward the few other female engineers, she simply keeps on going, racing from home to work and back again, trying to extract as much pleasure as she can from both places. Her husband "helps" at home, but it's not enough.

This was Elana's story when she came to an Equity Institute

seminar. What finally brought her there, she said, was that she'd begun to cry in the car as she rushed back and forth. She realized she had to do something different—quickly—because she was on a fast road to meltdown.

In the seminar, after she described how frantic she felt, Elana role-played possible discussions with her boss and coworkers ("I have to leave now to go home"), her husband ("We have to talk. I can't go on this way; we have to replan our lives, with you pulling your weight at home"), and the director of her child's day-care center ("We need a little slack in the to-the-minute 6 P.M. cut-off before overtime charges"). She was surprised to notice how terrified she was in each script. Elana realized she had felt so lucky to have a job, and one that she loved, as well as a child and a loyal husband, that she was frightened of rocking the boat. Demanding change would do just that, so she'd been trying to cover all the bases herself. Since that clearly couldn't go on much longer, she decided to take one step at a time. She opted to begin at work. Elana was going to stop putting pressure on herself to be a perfect star (to "make up" for being female and African American) and simply be a competent worker, like most of her colleagues. She had established herself well; but overwork became such a habit that now she has to deliberately ease off.

She also recognized that her antagonism toward the other women in her field came from her assumption that there was only room for "one." And she was determined to be it. She had seen the tokenism scenario played out several times during her career, but as she talked to other women in the seminar—and came to value their insights and support—she understood that she didn't have to play into that story line. The plot could unfold differently if she chose to play a different role. She realized her power in the situation. Elana promised to investigate a women's forum, part of an annual conference she attended. She'd seen the notices, but always avoided checking it out.

As for sharing the load at home, Elana knows that "taking charge everywhere" means just that. She's not yet ready to

What I wanted to be when I grew up was—in charge.

—**Brigadier General Wilma Vaught, U.S. Air Force**

Women need to see ourselves as individuals capable of creating change. That is what political and economic power is all about: having a voice, being able to shape the future. Women's absence from decision-making positions has deprived the country of a necessary perspective.

—Madelaine Kunin, Governor of Vermont

attempt to change the house and child-care work distribution, which implies a significant shift in her relationship, but has it on the back burner. With fully equal sharing at home a long-term goal, she's convinced she'll move in that direction over the next two years. Meanwhile, she plans to ask Wendell, her husband, to speak to the day-care center about relaxing the pick-up deadline. And, once he's initiated the relationship there, maybe that will be a logical place for him to start taking more childcare responsibility.

She left the seminar with plans on all fronts, and with hope.

Another woman, Arlene, part of the explosion of female small business owners, opened her own gardening company four years ago. She had worked in sales at several other firms, getting experience to fulfill a long-standing dream of opening a business. While she enjoys gardening, she finds supervising four employees difficult ("I hate to tell people what to do"). Arlene is wondering how to take charge of the business more comfortably. She is not part of any network of other female business owners, and feels isolated with her problems. Some days, she is so discouraged about management and personnel that she is filled with remorse about giving up her former job, remembering how easy it was getting a paycheck from someone else (and forgetting what it was that made her want to open her own firm). She was on the verge of burnout when she turned to Equity for assistance. In weekly executive coaching sessions, she practiced taking charge with her employees. As she began the work, she realized that, like many women in management, she'd been treating the firm like a family. And to her, that meant, as "mom," she was responsible for everybody (else)'s well-being. She spent so much time "taking care of" her employees, and was so personally hurt when they didn't perform well, that she was chronically exhausted and disappointed.

Simply recognizing the pattern was illuminating for her. Arlene wanted to run a humane business, not treating her employees as harshly as felt she'd felt she'd been treated. But she was caught. Once her workers realized what a safe space this was for them—with "mom" always ready to pick up the slack—they responded much as many of them had in their own families, to their real moms. Sometimes this was with careful and patient work; at other times, it meant anger and avoidance.

Once Arlene understood that it was all right to assert herself as a business owner—that didn't make her bad—she was able to examine job functions, and employees, more dispassionately. Yes, she could treat people well by paying them competitively high wages, recognizing good work, being kind and equitable, and having rational policies. It didn't mean, however, that she was responsible for her employees. She had a right to take care of herself, and run her business like . . . a business.

Diane has a different problem. She's the director of a non-profit cultural center for women. She represented her agency at the historic 1995 Beijing Women's Conference—"See the World Through Women's Eyes"— and believes women are preparing to lead the world. "Women," she says, "do the world's work. We carry water, cook the food, hold men together, care for children, work the night shift. And then we feel bad about ourselves! How strange. I think we're about to get over it." Internationally recognized as a women's cultural leader, her problem is money. Diane makes 20% less than an average man who directs a non-profit agency the size of hers, in the same region—and 40% less than comparable men in the private sector. (The non-profit ghetto, like any field dominated by women, pays less.) So, while Diane also loves her work and feels fortunate to be in such a creative field and able to contribute to women's lives, she can't imagine how to empower herself financially. She feels she's offering her talents at her own expense, and she's tired of it.

In their careers, all three women wildly outstripped their grandmothers and mothers. They dared to take charge in some parts of their lives, yet were stuck in extending this attitude to

Audre Lorde clarified for me that a woman's place is anyplace she damn well pleases.

—Korva Coleman,
journalist for
National Public Radio

Everything's a circle. We're each responsible for our own actions. It will come back.

—Betty Laverdure, Ojibway leader

life at home, fears of competition, comfortable supervision, or feeling entitled to make enough money to buy a house. Women's expectations have historically been so low—we were "lucky" if we hooked a decent husband or got anywhere at all in a career—that it's new terrain to imagine the opposite extreme, "having it all," which has itself become a derisive phrase. And why not? Why shouldn't we have it all, the components of enjoyable lives?

We are still learning the guideline that one corporate vice president says is her watchword: Never take "No" for an answer. Whenever someone tells her it can't be done, she goes back to the drawing board and takes another tack. Once she decides she's going to do or have something —a job, a raise, or equality at home—she figures out how to make it happen. At work, she's learned to make friends with her boss' boss, so she can go around (usually him) if necessary. This woman simply anticipates success, and counts on her ability to make it happen.

If for women there are few expectations about what we can achieve and do, for men there are many. There is an unwritten rule we've all absorbed, men and women, that men will always take responsibility, take charge, take initiative—and drive the car, no matter what.

This rigidity can have tragic consequences. Several years ago a family drove two days to their daughter's college graduation at an elite women's college in New England. Marilyn was the first person from this working-class home to go to college. Finally, graduation day: Her parents, brothers, and sisters all piled into the car and set off on the celebratory trip. They drove day and night. And day again. Although the mother had a driver's license, only the father drove. He (and maybe she) must have felt it was his responsibility to take the family to the big event. He became so exhausted that he fell asleep at the wheel, crashed the car, and most of the family was killed.

It's sometimes hard for us to remember that when women say, "Move over, I'm going to drive for awhile," we are not only salvaging our lives, we may be saving others as well. So we're probably not as selfish as we feel. No matter what we're told.

Taking charge everywhere means looking thoughtfully at all areas of our lives, seeing where we've gotten used to giving up power—in fact, gotten so used to it that our lack of authority looks normal. One such area where many of us have lost charge of our well being is in the development of physical strength and ability. We're told we're weak, in need of masculine protection (from other men) and that to appear truly feminine we must be delicate. Many of us are proud of our "petite" bone structure or our small feet—and correspondingly ashamed of big ones.

Most of us don't learn, as girls, how to get hurt, fall down, and pick ourselves up to play again. Avoiding the label "tomboy" (with all its promised adventures but terrors of being shunned), we tend to think of injuries as events to be avoided at all cost. And, as caretakers, we hold the preservation of our lives as the highest value. (Those rare women in movies who care more about themselves and the quality of their lives than simple physical survival display an unusual attitude. Choosing death rather than a return to unsatisfactory conditions is usually a male prerogative.)

Were we to make the decision to take charge of our physical abilities, many of the limitations placed on us would crumble "like cookies in a blender," according to one female athlete. A willingness to take risks—and take charge—politically, personally, or financially, often follows.

I sometimes have the opportunity to watch girls play soccer and lacrosse when I run at my local school track. Recently I watched a sixth grade boys' soccer team play a girls' team. When they ran for the ball, the boys repeatedly rushed forward at the crucial last moment to close in on the ball; the girls, at the same moment, when they got a foot or two from the ball, usually took a step backward, or hesitated a moment, thus protecting themselves—and ensuring that they rarely got the ball. (This was overwhelmingly true of all the girls, although I noticed that those who appeared to be European or

> *We are disabled more by barriers of access than from the specific conditions of our bodies. . . . To consider it a special privilege to use a telephone, ride a bus or use a public bathroom is absurd. . . . By accessibility we mean access to the same choices accorded able-bodied people.*
>
> —**Susan E. Browne, Debra Connors, and Nanci Stern, authors**

Yize uvalo, inqobo yisibindi. Fear is nothing, the real thing is courage.

—Ndebele proverb

Asian American did this even more often than visibly African American girls, possibly reflecting their greater conditioning to retreat in the face of conflict.)

I have watched girls play lacrosse on gender-mixed teams and observed the same phenomenon. Almost all the girls hung back, repeatedly, setting themselves up for failure over and over again, in games they certainly had the strength and size to play well.

But fortunately that is not the whole story. Today almost two hundred colleges field female rugby teams, a rough contact sport. The physical nature of the game, players say, has made them more assertive and heightened their sense of teamwork.

As one senior at Penn State, Wendy Heslin, who weighs one hundred and fifteen pounds, told a *New York Times* reporter, "I'm much stronger and more confident. To knock a big girl down is a feeling I can't explain. Your head is spinning; you feel like you're floating on air. You can't hear anything but the cheering…" While we might not all want to "knock a big girl down" or even cheer those who do, the impact on the women's self-confidence was extraordinary.

Princeton's senior captain, Julia Worcester, from Andover, Mass., said she felt a sense of power "knocking someone else down and coming out on top." And, best of all, "after a few tackles, you realize that you are going to get up."

Players report that the assurance they gained in the games extends to daily life on campus. A Princeton player, Taur Null, was feeling so tough after one game that she joked to a reporter, "Maybe we should send out a warning to the rest of campus— rugby women on the loose, stay in your rooms."

Angela Bassett had a similar response when interviewed about her role in the movie *Strange Days,* an apocalyptic thriller directed by Kathryn Bigelow. She was asked by her interviewer, on television, what drew her to the part. "Was it the romance?"

"No," Bassett laughed. "It was the action. To slug it out, run, fall down. It was fabulous." Bassett was absolutely radiant as she described her joy in the physically demanding role.

Most of us are not going to go out and start playing rugby or become major "action" heroes, duking it out with killers. But women have destroyed lifetime habits of timidity by making the decision to develop physical strength in just one area. While it was liberating for the rugby players and for Angela Bassett to find that scratches, scrapes, and bruises come with the territory—they heal—and a relief to discover they're not made of glass, the rest of us can get the same information by trying wrestling or a tackle. Yes, a tackle! A fortyish friend of mine, Alicia, participated in a women's physical power workshop and described to me afterward how astounding it was to tackle and be tackled. "We found out we can fall down a lot without being hurt," she told me. "It felt so joyous to do that, we were all screaming with delight. Everyone was. It was so much fun. I'd never been very athletic. I never even thought of tackling someone. It seemed like such a male thing to do. It never occurred to me that it was something I would, or could, or even wanted to do."

"It was amazing," she said, her voice reflecting the surprise she was still experiencing. "Out of thirty women, no one got hurt. Some of the women had physical disabilities, some were young, some were old. And we were all laughing and giggling. It was one of the most liberating things I've ever done. You should try it sometime!" (I haven't, but hearing her enthusiasm helped me decide to take up a strenuous form of yoga. I had been wondering if it would be "too much." It isn't, and I feel the same delight she describes. Getting out of bed early to be at the 7 A.M. class twice a week is turning out to be less traumatic than I'd expected, because I easily recall, even in the morning dark, how alive my body feels after class. And I'm already developing strength in my upper body—an area I'd given up on for years.)

A client, Nanette, reported she felt the same way when she took up weight lifting at fifty. During the four years she stuck with it, she felt more powerful all the time—not just when she was working out. She developed a slight swagger and a

When I dare to be powerful—to use my strength in the service of my vision, then it becomes less and less important whether I am afraid.

—Audre Lorde, New York State laureate

more "can do" attitude in all parts of her life.

Writer Julia D. Russell recalls her childhood in similar terms. "Smoking was out because I wouldn't do anything to jeopardize what I loved most—getting a ball in the goal, running fast and hard, breathing so deep my lungs burned. From junior high on, teams and practice and games became a refuge for me, a place to be wholly and unselfconsciously myself—strong, aggressive, competent, and sure."

Indeed, a good antidote for any of us who are giving up somewhere in our lives is watching a game of women's basketball. They elbow each other, bump and push, without ever saying "sorry." Whatever our own physical abilities, seeing female athletes jump, run, and shove expands our image of what women can do. Just as another powerful woman, Sojourner Truth, did, when she spoke in 1852 at the second annual convention of the women's rights movement, thundering to the narrow range of female images that excluded her: "That man says that women need to be helped into carriages, and lifted over ditches, and to have the best place everywhere. Nobody ever helps me into carriages, or over mud puddles, or gives me any best places, and ain't I a woman? . . . I have plowed, and planted, and gathered into barns, and no man could head me—and ain't I a woman? I could work as much and eat as much as a man (when I could get it) and bear the lash as well—and ain't I a woman?" Yes, and she describes a female image we hardly recognize.

Boys grow up playing competitive games. They learn that "the rough and tumble of competition doesn't harm relationships, and that conflict is not always bad," as business consultants Pat Heim and Susan Golant write. "They learn a kind of aggression which later becomes the basis of workplace interactions."

Women in settings with men who have been thus socialized often face unexpected dilemmas. Brenda, for example, an architect for a large hotel chain, came to an Equity Institute program, where she described an interaction that stunned her.

I had the best serve in women's tennis. I had the best overhead in women's tennis. And I had the most killing volley in women's tennis . . . I was ruthless on the court.

—Althea Gibson, tennis champion

She had been on her way to a meeting of managers from a variety of divisions from across the country—people with whom she had met many times before—when she ran into one of the men in the hall. They stopped to chat.

Hal opened up. "So, how's it going?"

"Great."

"What's new?" he inquired, "What are you thinking about these days?"

"Oh," Brenda beamed at him, "I'm excited about the idea of consumer surveys, and thinking about how we can utilize them in our new campaign."

She went on to fill him in on her new ideas.

Ten minutes later, in the meeting, the boss turned to Hal. "What's the latest from those brain cells you've got trapped in your head?"

"Consumer surveys," Hal began. "They're cutting edge, and I've devised some strategies for using them in our new campaign."

He ran down every detail of Brenda's ideas, never giving her credit, while she sat there, first in shock, then in fury.

She thought about her Action Team, where another woman had reported an almost identical scenario and had made a bold play. Within a few minutes Brenda recovered herself enough to begin laughing. And she took charge of the moment.

Light-heartedly looking over at Hal, Brenda said, "Oh, Hal, when are you going to get to the part where you tell them that I told you all this?"

It was Hal's turn to be startled. He evidently never expected a woman to call him on his power grab, and he didn't have a plan. He just looked at her in confusion for a moment.

She covered for him, smiling. "I know you were getting there. Let me pick up the end of the idea." And she went with it.

Later, as they were all leaving the meeting, Brenda cornered Hal privately and said, "Don't ever do that to me again," and walked away.

He didn't.

There is no limit to the ideas the open heart can create, once powerlessness is challenged.

—Fran Peavey, author

This "guy culture" dominates many fields. A male physicist in an Equity seminar, Tómas, described it as "fast, competitive, and critical, with scientists beating on each other (mostly verbally) to get to the truth. We put ideas—and that means each other—to the rack," he explained. His female colleague, Arvonne, summarized the difficulties of that culture for women, most of whom haven't grown up battling in the same adversarial mode. She told a story demonstrating the misunderstanding and missed cues that fly past each other when these two cultures intersect.

Arvonne described a conference at which a female presenter left in tears, after a man in her field rose to tell her that her work was "bullshit." He was stunned at her response; he had simply expected her to come back with a strong defense of her ideas. When she failed to do so, and left, he assumed her research was flimsy—not that she was hurt by his condemnation. And it never occurred to the presenter, with whom Arvonne spoke later, to defend her ideas, as he had expected she would. She took his denunciation at face value, and moreover, she took it personally. And blamed herself for her response.

Finding the resources to take charge wherever we are—as we work or conduct other daily business—is possible, though certainly challenging. It may mean jumping into "male mode," practicing how to come back with the kind of responses male colleagues expect (or don't, as Brenda's coworker illustrated). It may mean developing our own manifestation of a "don't mess with me" attitude. It often means being persistent. And it always means deciding that our integrity comes first. In her book, *The Alchemy of Race and Rights,* law professor Patricia J. Williams describes an incident in which a white clerk refused to buzz her into a Soho boutique, "when I pressed my round brown face to the window and my finger to the buzzer, seeking admittance." The teen-aged clerk mouthed through the window, "We're closed," although it was two Saturdays before Christmas, at one o'clock in the afternoon, and there were several white shoppers in the store. After going home and writing in her journal, Williams discovered the next day she was still brooding, so, she writes, "I turned to a form of catharsis I have always found healing. I typed up as much of the story as I have just told, made a big poster of it, put a nice colorful border around it, and after Benetton's was truly closed, stuck it to their big sweater-filled window. I exercised my first-amendment right to place my business with them right out in the street."

Later, Williams persisted in describing the incident in speeches and published articles, although law school journal editors tried to silence or censor her account, complaining, in one instance, that her story was "unverifiable;" in another, that she was not giving "equal time" to the "other side." That moment at the store was a humiliating and enraging one, in which Williams' power of choice, to be admitted to a store to buy, for her mother, a sweater she'd seen in the window, was taken from her. Yet by publicly posting her account of the event, then writing and speaking about it, Williams took charge in every way she could.

Whatever the external limitations we face, taking charge means we have to do the internal work to overcome our fears, however they surface: anxiety about disapproval, conflict, or isolation; annoyance or fury at having to take on yet one more energy- and time-consuming battle. It isn't easy. This is the moment when having done the work of getting centered, and having the support of others in place, is crucial in our ability to act powerfully. Having a shoulder to cry on eases our pain and clears confusion before planning next steps. And having others remind us that no matter how poorly we've been treated, we don't deserve it, can make the difference between folding and going forward. When we get good support from others as well as from within, we can use all our experiences as grist for growth.

Once we establish internal dignity and the absolute conviction that we deserve to be respected—in our work and in our selves—we can choose any method (or try several in turn, as

Many women have more power than they recognize, and they're very hesitant to use it, for fear they won't be loved.

—Patricia Schroeder, Colorado Congress-woman

We do not want another Algeria, in respect to women's issues. We do not want another America during the second World War. We're not ready to go back home after the independence.

—Suha Hindiyeh, Director, Palestinian Women's Resource Center

Williams did) to redress mistreatment. Having that rock bottom certitude in our own worth is basic to overcoming it.

Taking charge everywhere is especially important right now as we watch the United States polarize. To provide leadership to these fractures, we need to take a major leap in our picture of ourselves as women. Only when we understand who we are will we understand that we have the power to take charge in every aspect of life: from controlling our poses when we are photographed to demanding credit for our ideas, to insisting that our exclusion from any arena is unacceptable. And to directing local, state, national, and international policies.

Margaret Wheatley, the organizational consultant, lives in Utah. At a public lecture, she described an astonishing example of an organizing effort, a taking charge, by a neighbor. This woman called together a group of friends and asked them, "What do you—what do we—want? Let's decide what our needs are, and then set about getting them met." The group selected as their first priority a traffic light, making a major street crossing safer. The women worked with the City Council and within six months had a street light installed.

Continuing as a group, they asked repeatedly, What is possible? With this process, they became a major force in the city, accomplishing greater and greater successes until, after six years, they brought in a forty-three-million-dollar urban neighborhood redevelopment grant. This group of women is now redesigning their city to meet their needs.

Another woman, Cynthia, told us in an Equity program of a smaller but nonetheless impressive example of taking charge. She felt that her town lacked a sense of community. So, with a friend, she decided to put a bench in front of her home to encourage informal gatherings. With no authority from the city, Cynthia and her friend paid to have a beautiful wooden bench installed, with the inscription, "Good neighbors, good friends." It has now been there three years, serving its purpose of bringing people together. Neighbors gather at the bench, spending mornings and long summer evenings sitting and talking. People of all ages use the bench. One simple object—a bench; one simple idea—providing a place to sit; and one woman's decision. She is making a difference in the quality of life on her block.

In many communities, groups of women have taken charge by driving drug dealers out of their neighborhoods. Carol, working at a Southern community center, organized her neighbors to pressure the owner of a building where drugs were being sold to evict the tenants. (She doesn't want her city named, for fear of retaliation. Taking charge is not always an easy process. Nonetheless, it's often better than the alternative.) In Berkeley, California, neighbors of one such building sued, alleging hazardous conditions—and won. The owner was ultimately forced to forfeit the building after several years of unwillingness to take responsibility for her tenants.

And yet another woman, Ellen Malcolm, frustrated by the barriers women candidates for public office faced, decided, in 1985, with a group of friends, to found EMILY's List (Early Money is Like Yeast). The idea was to provide early money to the campaigns of pro-choice Democratic women, giving them credibility by showing the political establishment they could raise serious money. Since 1985, when there were only twelve Democratic women in the House of Representatives and none in the Senate, EMILY's List has helped elect 33 women to the House, five to the Senate, and two as governors.

Today, EMILY's List is the nation's biggest resource for federal candidates. It has expanded to become a full-service political organization that raises money, helps women build effective campaigns, and mobilizes voters to elect pro-choice Democratic women. It also networks candidates so they can access resources. Eva Clayton from North Carolina describes herself: "As a woman running in a rural minority district, I knew few of the experts and donors across the country whose support I needed to win. EMILY's List put me in touch with them, and I was off and running." (She won, and is now a U.S. Representative.)

Even the most hard-nosed physicist is beginning to admit that the flap of a butterfly's wings in one place can change the weather thousands of miles away. Everything we do matters.

—Gloria Steinem, co-founder, Ms.

We have to do whatever we have to do in order for there to be a new day. That means dealing with practical reality in a way that keeps you very close to the ground, always knowing what you have to deal with in the everyday sense . . . You understand that what you have to do is make up the difference, whatever that is.

—Bernice Johnson Reagon, curator, founder of *Sweet Honey in The Rock* vocal ensemble

Founder Ellen Malcolm continues to have large goals. In 1995 she said, "We will use our considerable resources—financial and intellectual—to take back the Congress with pro-choice Democratic women. The more than $8.2 million our members contributed to women candidates during 1994 makes EMILY's List the biggest funder of House and Senate candidates in the country, bar none."

In addition to raising money for the campaigns of candidates who meet their criteria, EMILY's list helps them "spend it right" by making their campaigns more professional, cost-effective, and efficient. The organization trains campaign managers and press secretaries, and helps them get out the female vote, through their WOMEN VOTE! program. The group anticipates that the new women voters they target will not only help women win, they will build a political foundation to break the hold of the radical right.

"The Christian Coalition grew powerful by delivering radical right voters in Republican primaries," Malcolm says. "They told candidates, 'No more moderate Republican nonsense. You must be anti-choice. If you don't support our social agenda, you will lose the Republican primary.' EMILY's List will mobilize progressive women voters on the Democratic side. By making a long-term investment, we will turn out an increasingly higher proportion of women to vote in Democratic primaries. Then, if you are running for office, you had better be pro-choice—and you had better pay attention to the issues that affect working women and their families.

"I can't promise that we can turn around enough seats to win in 1996. But there is one prediction I am confident making: whether Democrats win or lose, EMILY's List will emerge as a leading political force in Democratic politics. Because while other partners of the party stand shell-shocked and paralyzed, EMILY's List stands out as an organization with direction, energy, resources, drive, and political savvy.

"Women," she says, "can transform the political landscape. We've shown it can be done."

This is thinking big.

One challenge as we make the leap to deciding we have the power to shape the world that works for us—in our families, in our communities, at our jobs, in our states, country, or planet—is to believe that we, as women, are actually capable of such influence. The sense of inadequacy, feeling we don't have anything important to contribute—at least not on that scale— has been with us so long that it takes a real push, from ourselves and from others, to move into leadership. We are so used to devaluing ourselves as we've been devalued, even to the point of letting ourselves get repeatedly interrupted by others, meeting their needs, that it's a real stretch to realize that we could take charge of world affairs.

And, of course, we also face external barriers, such as the conviction by many male political leaders that a woman is not "electable" as President. These limitations, repeated during the entire course of our lives, seep into us, and we need to jump out front to get rid of them, even when we think we don't know how or have a clue about what to do. (Neither do men, much of the time. They've just been taught to tough it out and never let on. We have the luxury, sometimes, of being able to acknowledge our terror as we plunge ahead.)

"Feel the fear and do it anyway," as the writer Susan Jeffers entitled her book, should be our rallying cry as we learn to take charge everywhere. As we do, we make it easier for the next woman who comes along. The poet Audre Lorde said once in a speech I attended at Smith College that she too was often afraid, with no models of how to be, but she kept breaking ground anyway. I was surprised at how deep her terror was, and inspired by her determination to keep opening new territory with her imagination and her sense of what she was entitled to.

Women have been taught—perhaps because of our history as caretakers of children, who needed us so much—to avoid taking risks, at least until we aren't afraid. An example is my friend Marita, who wanted to leave classroom teaching to run seminars for other teachers. She was excited about the idea and

The least I can say for myself is that I forcefully created for myself, under extremely hostile conditions, my ideal life. I took an obscure and almost unknown village in the Southern African bush and made it my own hallowed ground. Here, in the steadiness and peace of my own world, I could dream dreams a little ahead of the somewhat vicious clamor of revolution and the horrible stench of evil social systems.

—Bessie Head, South African novelist, died in exile in Botswana in 1986

got an excellent response from a few programs she piloted. Yet, year after year, she hesitated to leave her guaranteed paycheck. She kept waiting to feel completely unafraid before she made the jump—but it never happened, so she never made the leap to her "dream career." Then she died in an automobile accident. Marita's unfulfilled dream always reminds me that sometimes we just have to make the decision to act, without waiting until we feel completely comfortable; and then deal with the fear once we've made the leap.

Courage is the price that life exacts for granting peace.

—Amelia Earhart (1898–1937), pioneer aviator

We're often going to wonder, before a major choice, whether it's the right thing to do. (That's what makes it a choice.) We rarely imagine our heroines as fearful. Especially when we see them moving forward. Was Shirley Chisholm terrified when she became the first woman to run for President? (And where did she get the moxie to imagine herself as President?) She was rarely considered a "serious contender," yet she took herself seriously enough to run a campaign.

Was Ellen Malcolm afraid at the beginning of EMILY's List? I recall talking to her the year she started it, and along with her contagious enthusiasm for what was then a completely new idea, was some anxiety that the whole thing might be a bubble. But she nonetheless moved along her road, creating an organization that will make an impact for generations.

Was Senator Carol Moseley-Braun afraid when she and her ally, Senator Paul Wellstone, led a spontaneous filibuster to block a major budget cut—a done deal—they considered reckless? Perhaps. But she did it anyway. As Moseley-Braun said, "Senator Wellstone and I aren't exactly the senators who get to go into the room and carve up deals on how things run around here. But we are senators." So she used her power, against the wishes of Democratic leaders, to derail the deal.

Taking charge everywhere can mean using humor to assert power. In 1977, at the National Women's Conference in Houston, 14,000 women—a record-breaking number—gathered to observe International Women's Year. They came to create a National Plan of Action and make policy recommendations to the President. Women from across the political spectrum showed up, as did a few men. Some men came as long-time allies. Others, including several well-known KKK members, arrived as part of an attempt to disrupt the conference. Their presence was locally billed as 'Klan versus Feminists.'

During the opening forum in the Sam Houston Coliseum, the proceedings were interrupted by the loud-speaker:

"Emergency telephone call for Mr. X (the leader of the KKK). Please come to the podium."

There was a hush as his name was recognized. In that moment of absolute quiet, a friend of mine, Nancy, yelled out from the upper bleachers, with all the power she could muster,

"Your sheets are back from the laundry."

Silence. Then amusement rippled in one section of the stadium, building in rolling waves until the whole coliseum was a sea of delighted laughter. The red-faced KKK leader—who appeared smaller and smaller as the clamor rose—made his way out of the stadium, not to be heard from again.

There are all kinds of ways to assert political power. Remember the Boston Tea Party? "No taxation without representation" was the rallying cry I learned in elementary school. It's a cherished part of our folk history—that canon of stories we tell and retell—establishing who we are and what we believe. "No taxation without representation" was the clarion call to dump British tea in Boston Harbor, initiating the revolution that culminated in the representational democracy we have today.

Yet if we consider gender, most of the United States population still doesn't have political representation. Women, fifty-two per cent of the population, have never had one of our own group as a president, vice president, or Speaker of the House. Half a decade after the much-ballyhooed Year of the Woman, we still make up only 10% of elected governing bodies. Our particular visions, styles, and agendas are barely present in these powerful groups of people whose actions are so critical to our lives.

But we are taxed.

Until we have numerical equity in county, town, state and national houses, we could take charge in any number of ways. Once we decide that a situation is unacceptable and we are going to change it, a variety of creative strategies emerge. We could, for instance, like Ellen Malcolm of EMILY's List, focus our energies so that more women who reflect our visions get elected. Or we might organize to propose that we, like our fore-bearers, pay taxes in proportion to our representation, until we reach parity.

Or perhaps we'll decide it's just about time for an end-of-millennium women's tea party, a re-enactment, updated with a late twentieth century sensibility. Maybe it's tea-dumping time again.

The Tool Kit: Strategies for Taking Charge Everywhere

 Commit to never again "settling" for less than absolutely everything you need to live the life you choose. "For me," you say or write, "this means_____."
Once you complete the sentence you know where you have been compromising. For instance, you might say, "For me, this means not being afraid of my team leader at work. I'm going to talk to her (or him) about the way (s)he speaks to me. It's so rude. I won't put up with it any more."

For you, "settling" may mean you are working for wages below fair market value, so your commitment would be to negotiate a raise, or enter another line of work. No longer settling for a half-life may mean redesigning your job description or leaving your job altogether.

You can do this exercise repeatedly, and come up with different answers each time, for every one of us gives up in so many ways we hardly notice unless we take the

It would probably be easier for me not to speak out, not to ever say anything about the issues of sexual harassment or the role of women in the work-place and politics, not talk about those things ever again in life. But I think it would be irrespon-sible. . . . I will not be satisfied any-more with living my life simply for myself. Other issues are much broader than my own little world.

—Anita Hill, law professor

time to scrutinize our lives with this lens. Even a shrunken world looks normal when one is used to it.

For one week, repeat to yourself, "I'm in charge of my life." Notice where you didn't feel in charge until you remembered to say this. And notice where you thought, "I knew that." That's where you haven't given up.

List the ways you haven't given up your power. All of us have held on to wonderful capabilities of many kinds. Our mental power, for example, is continually expressed in the strategies we've figured out to navigate our way this far. We have physical power of varying degrees. We have exercised our ability to determine many of the conditions of our lives, making decisions and choices.

Claim the power you do have—that which has been given you and that which you've demanded.

It's exciting to realize what we have under our belts and at our fingertips. We're starting with a complex system of power as a basis for further growth.

Describe (in writing or to a friend) how you've exercised your talents and skills throughout your life, in little ways as well as big ones. How have you actually used all the kinds of power you've had, as a girl and a woman? When you chart your life, examining the past for power, what do you notice? Many females, for instance, begin to subtly give up power as young teens, reclaiming it later as mature women. What is your power lifeline?

Reclaim one area of physical power. It might be a sport, a form of body building, or other exercise. It could be walking, lifting weights, playing basketball, running, dancing, or heavy gardening. If you haven't been doing this, you will be astonished at the difference in every aspect of your life. Your walk will change, your whole sense of physical—and mental—capability will increase.

> *If there are difficulties along the way that would hinder them from fulfilling their potential, they will not stand by idly and let those barriers stop them, and in that sense I think Chinese American women have found their places.*
>
> **—Judy Yung, Director, The Chinese Women of America 1848–1982 pictorial exhibit**

If you have already reclaimed, or kept, many areas of physical strength, expand and develop expertise in yet another arena—the one you've been putting off for years. Take the wet suit or the bowling ball out of the closet, research the aerobics class that's tailored to you—the one for people in wheelchairs or with chronic low-back pain—and jump to another level.

 Decide you won't take "No" for an answer in any area of your life, for one week. You'll be open to hearing why No makes sense. But if, after listening, you still want to go ahead—with a new venture, a raise, or getting the support you need—make a decision that you're the one who gets to decide. If your answer is Yes, stick to it as you figure out a way to make it a reality.

Action Team Tips For Taking Charge Everywhere

Your team is your home base. Nurture it, take charge of it, give it your wholehearted support, and be committed to the other members.

Do everything you can to deepen trust between you. Women together can do anything; alone, the prices we pay for success are often so costly they negate our victories. Like Shannon Faulkner, the lone female cadet who pioneered women's attendance at The Citadel military academy, we may even find ourselves unable to go on in isolation.

Bonding successfully with your team requires ridding yourself of any remnants of negativity you hold about women. Whatever criticisms or fears you continue to hold about women as a group—or some subset to which you belong—will surface, and you'll be running from others like you.

For example, if you're turning thirty with terror about going "over the hill," and you look at women over thirty as ancient, you probably won't be able to assist your age mates (or older women) very well. Nor, if you're busy distancing, will you be able to take in the support they have for you.

If you're a lesbian and want to run the other way when a stereotypical "dyke" sits next to you in the lunchroom cafeteria, that's a clue: work to do.

If you're Japanese American and still carrying your parents' or grandparents' humiliation (along with the anger) for the Relocation—the World War II internment— you may have difficulty getting close to other women with a similar heritage, due to the strange habit we humans have of projecting our own discomforts onto others, thinking *they* are weird, or unpleasant.

If you're Jewish and embarrassed to acknowledge it, subtly accepting slurs you've heard about Jews—you're not going to be able to fully sustain other Jewish women. Or be sustained by these powerful sisters.

If you notice that you still want to cancel a meeting with a woman in order to have one with a man; if you walk into a room and automatically believe that the men in it are more important than the women; or if you find yourself suddenly simpering attentively in the presence of a man, in a way you never would conceive of doing with a woman— the first step is simply to acknowledge it.

Relax. We've all been there. We are all still there, on many issues. Take time to identify your discomforts. "Oh, that again. I thought I'd dealt with it. I guess the lies coming in are more pervasive than I realized; they're continually nourishing that old gunk. All right, let me notice this one fully and watch how it's operating in my life."

Talk about your self-observations in your Action Team. It will be a relief to each of your listeners to hear she's not the only one. You won't be shunned, but, paradoxically, cherished more as you shine the spotlight on issues every woman needs to excavate. The power released in such unearthing is marvelous.

When my friend Mei-Ying, for example, was bold enough to reclaim her birth-name after a more Anglicized name—Janie—had been forced upon her by an employer years before, she restored her entire heritage. This liberated her power on her new job, in her community, and at home with her husband; she was also set free to associate more comfortably with other Chinese American women. No more ambivalence, no more chagrin, confusion, or remorse about her adoption of "Janie." Fully grounded in herself, she was more able to encourage and cherish women both similar and different from herself. But before she could take the step to change her name, she had to go through some previous steps, acknowledging the embarrassment she felt about ever accepting "Janie" in the first place.

In order to view the women in your Action Team as valuable and central to your life, you need to feel that way about the woman you look at in the mirror every day. Go back to the "Remembering Self" strategies at the end of Milemarker One for a tune-up whenever you need one—every three thousand miles, or every three months, whichever is sooner. Taking these bodies and minds on the road, where we absorb all the dust and dirt of misinformation, requires regular cleansing.

I have to make things happen through the force of my personality. Most power is illusionary and perceptual. You have to create an environment in which people perceive you as having some power.

—Carrie Saxon Perry, first Black female mayor of a major U.S. city

Highway Three:
Building Alliances

●

Mile Marker Seven:
Build Women's Alliances

This chapter details how women have
been pitted against each other. It provides
rationale and strategy to overcome the
difficulties of this inheritance.

Mile Marker Seven:
Build Women's Alliances

When we do manage to act authoritatively, women sometimes, unexpectedly, find hostility from other women. They may fear there's only room in God's heaven for one: If we're in, they're out. Born of our conditioning to compete, this theme is a distressingly common one.

Some years ago I noticed with shock how I automatically scan other women's bodies to see how they stack up to my own. It's a constant hum in the back of my brain. Are their tummies more prominent or—a more recent addition to the scan—their necks more wrinkled? Yes. Oh good. "Mirror, mirror on the wall, who is the fairest one of all?" It's me! I am (still) the fairest one of all! Relief. One more time.

Then I began to realize how I also slid into comparing lives. My children are more accomplished and all around "better" than yours. (Which, not incidentally, means I must be a better mother.) My life-mate relationship is healthier: we are autonomous and committed. And between the two of us, who contributes more to social change? Or makes more money? Oh no, you do! You travel more or command a greater fee for speeches. The chatter is as endless as the yardsticks, and is always a variant, however updated, of the old mirror chant.

The reality is: We are all driving down this road together, and the journey is easier if we help one another along the way. Twenty-five years ago, when I first met my neighbor Maxine, she seemed to me from another species. A professor, she had a housekeeper, traveled internationally to conferences, and— most impressive to me—carried an appointment book.

As we became friends, I discovered Maxine wasn't really so different. She just had some goals at a young age different than my own, and, growing up in New York City, more options. Knowing her helped me decide I wanted to pursue similar goals. If she could do it, so could I. Six years after I met Max, she helped me apply to a doctoral program, where I was accepted with a fellowship. I went on to get an Ed.D.

Later, after my friend Barbara began writing her first book, I started on mine. The book process became normal—and thinkable—when I saw a woman up close do it. I know I've had a similar impact on other women. So now, when tempted to jealousy, I reframe the thought by reminding myself that every time a woman breaks a boundary, that limit is broken for all of us. Which includes me. Every time you succeed in a project, another woman is encouraged to try. Every time you take charge in some area of your life—when you organize your neighbors to make a safer community, or demand that a mechanic explain your car's malfunction clearly—you inspire another woman to take charge similarly.

Yet, we are so used to comparing bodies, children, possessions, and lives, in endless dress rehearsals for lifetimes of insecurity, that it becomes second nature. It's hard to rejoice in another's success as it highlights our own sense of inadequacy. And when we don't even notice our own achievements, we can easily resent someone else's getting whatever it is we crave: attention, money, love.

Such comparisons—or the urge to pull each other down—don't come only when we see those like us succeeding. When other women are in trouble, distancing ourselves can also be enticing. Suzanne, we think, is getting sexually harassed (or raped, or having trouble with her silicone implants, or getting breast cancer, or losing her custody battle, or having a rocky time at work) because of something she's doing wrong. So long as we hold that thought, we can imagine that if we don't make that same mistake, we'll be safe. We don't want to think that her condition is generic to women.

But in reality, it usually is. Women's troubles—and gains—are widely shared. We are linked, and our transition to various kinds of power over the last two decades is coming, in large part, because we are pushing together. That's why taking the road to power means leaving comparisons, criticism, and competition behind. And why it begins with our own solid centering.

It was maybe four years ago that I sat with Ntosake Shange and raised this question in relation to black women: "Where is the healing place?" That evening we had no answer. Now, I am more confident that community is a healing place.

—bell hooks, professor, author

The women's movement has been about not "settling" for the lives of limitation passed down to us. We're expanding our image—bit by bit—of what life could look like if we truly took charge. And our vision grows fuller each time one of us goes where no woman has ever gone before. Our possibilities grow as we watch each other bloom.

From the consciousness-raising groups of the '70s to today's Action Teams, we're bringing each other along. We started out naming and sharing miseries, convincing ourselves, when we heard it from one after another woman, that having to do all the housework, for instance, was neither trivial nor idiosyncratic. Over the years, "girl talk" has shifted from naming problems—that essential early stage—to solving them. Not that the naming is ever done. It continues, and is one way we sustain each other. But to that sacred telling and listening, a staple of women's lives, we are increasingly adding action.

One stunning example of women who took off together in high gear occurred in Boston, where twelve women in health care began to meet in 1977. "We had no agenda," one of the group's founders, Elaine Ullian, told Andrea Gabor in a *New York Times* interview, "except to create a safe place to discuss our professional concerns. We wanted a place where we didn't have to worry that someone would say, 'She isn't very good, is she?'"

After seven years of monthly meetings, in 1984 the group made an historic decision. "We realized that we had started low, and were now among the senior management of our organizations." Ullian continued, "We were all working for new CEOs. We could be CEOs. But none of us was. There were three or four search firms that recruited for these jobs. And they didn't even know we existed."

The women realized the reason was twofold: They themselves had limited their aspirations, and they weren't hooked into the networks of power. They hadn't regarded themselves as CEO material, and nobody else did either. One woman said she was in her twenties before she fully recognized that a woman could be a doctor, much less the chief executive of a hospital.

Without models, she never envisioned herself in such a role until she began to consult to other CEOs, and the job was demystified.

Despite fears of appearing too assertive—one woman said she'd been warned by male coworkers about aggressive women—the group decided to set a goal: to establish three of their members as CEOs within the next few years. Having made this decision, the A Team, as they called themselves, was systematic. They made a plan to get known and crack the health care power structure.

A Team members networked with female executives in other industries and senior men in their own field. They met headhunters, politicians, and hospital trustees. Every time a top job came up, they contacted their new network to recommend each other.

"We knew if we didn't initiate an organized approach, it would never happen," Linda Shyavitz, one of the women, commented in the *New York Times* interview. In less than a year, the group had invited several leading headhunters to its meetings, met the president of the Massachussetts Hospital Association, and taught themselves to read hospital financial statements.

They took an all-for-one approach, in which they all pulled for one woman at a time, as jobs became available. Their success was dramatic. Several A Team members recommended Linda Shyavitz for a CEO job—and she became the first A Team member to head a hospital. A few months later, a headhunter who had attended an A Team meeting approached Elaine Ullian for the top job at another hospital. The women hooked into their network, worked the phones, and Ullian became the A Team's second chief executive.

The group continued to expand connections and advocate for each other, simultaneously educating themselves on issues like executive pay packages and how to navigate the state legislature. They became ready to handle power.

The results of this focused work were extraordinary. Within five years the A Team doubled its original target. One woman

The Glass Ceiling hinders not only individuals but society as a whole. It effectively cuts our pool of potential corporate leaders by half. It deprives our economy of new leaders, new sources of creativity—the "would be" pioneers of the business world.

—Lynn Martin, former Secretary of Labor

Hit one ring and the whole chain will resound.

—Sotho proverb

went from being a manager to a chief financial officer; another, who was a director, became a vice president; two more, formerly vice presidents, became the group's third and fourth chief executives. And they continue to provide each other with a base of support in coping with new dilemmas.

Imagine thousands of A Teams. We all need this kind of thoughtful, strategic sustenance. My friend, Harleen, recently applied to be line-supervisor in the lipstick factory where she's worked for fourteen years. She didn't get it. What if Harleen had been part of an Action Team—her own A team—with women from her company helping her as she built confidence, perhaps pulling strings and putting in good words for her? It might have made all the difference.

Sometimes even two other women can be a powerful support group. My friend Kerry in Massachusetts is part of a three-woman support team ("The Girls Group," they've dubbed themselves) formed by a management consultant each had been seeing individually. After a year, when the consultant left to pursue another career, the three women—all owners of small, service-providing businesses—continued to meet monthly for several hours at the end of their business day. Five years later, the outcome is astonishing. As a result of observing each other underpay themselves, for instance, they've pushed, challenged and supported each other to take huge pay increases. One woman more than doubled her salary; all have gotten large increases—and, contrary to their fears, the companies are flourishing.

Kerry described to me how she came to raise her own salary. After several group discussions about issues of self-worth and money, she found herself meeting with her attorney and accountant to set up an employee stock bonuses plan. The accountant, a man, told her matter-of-factly that she would need to almost double her own salary. The attorney, a woman, understood how flabbergasted Kerry was, and commented, "If you have a problem with that, I know a good therapist." Kerry did it—the money part—and looking back now, can't believe she was taking such low wages from the business, which she founded eleven long years ago.

The Girls Group follows a regular structure set up by their original facilitator: they each check in for ten or fifteen minutes about their companies and their own issues, and split the remaining time for group consultation about topics each has raised. Most of their time is spent on personnel and money ("How do I create a humane, and efficient, workplace?" "Am I terrible if I fire someone?" "How do I get more business?"). Additionally, they network, using each other's services directly, and recommending each other for work they hear about.

Many of us have been trained to do our work well. Often very well. We've thought that was all that was necessary to succeed. We were also raised with an ethic that says we have to "make it on our own," although the power of the old boys' network, which we continue to understand better and better, belies that credo. In fact, there are rules of the road that aren't in any handbook, tickets we need to have stamped in order to pass through the next toll booth. And there are those who can give us the information we need to prosper. There are formal and informal networks; mentors who would love to watch us flourish. As we discover the power of these connections, we are figuring out how to make them work for us.

Sarah, a lesbian who produces business videos, told an Equity Institute group how she realized, on a business trip to Los Angeles, that she hadn't kept up her connection with Yvonne, a friend from long-ago lesbian-activist days, now a corporate media executive. Sarah changed her travel plans, staying an extra day. She liked Yvonne. But she also had a nagging thought that it would be a good idea, professionally, to reconnect, although she didn't have any concrete assistance to ask for.

A year later Sarah got a call: Yvonne wanted her to collaborate on a proposal for a video series on women in corporate America. Sarah jumped on it.

I come from a family of very strong women. In Chile, and in most of Latin America, the women are strong. In order to survive in a patriarchal society, you have to be organized, you have to have good women friends.

—Isabel Allende, writer

Women have at least three kinds of power: Dollar Power, to boycott with; Vote Power, to take over structures with and maybe even get somebody elected; and Body Power, to get out and support our friends and make a damned nuisance of ourselves with everybody else.

—Flo Kennedy, activist attorney

That was the old girl network at work. (And, in this case, the old lesbian network. Such networks exist among Chicanas, Filipinas, and every other ethnic or cultural group. Use them. It's not crass. You get to contribute, and as you rise, you're in a good position to do more for other women.)

The three rules of networking are: Relationships, relationships, relationships. And women have it covered—this is one game mother not only taught us to play; she invented it. We've developed the skill for social reasons; now we need to put it to work for work. So polish those affiliating skills and keep your connections fresh.

This isn't a new "technique." Women have been acting collectively for a long time. Mary Kenney, a Chicago bookbinder in the 1890s, describes in her autobiography the process of her own empowerment, followed quickly by the desire to extend it to other women:

"The bindery was on the top floor, the seventh. One morning the elevator was stopped for about ten minutes and, for the first time, I was late. When my week's pay came, they had deducted ten cents. I went to the foreman and asked him if he would go to the man who had my ten cents and say that if I was worth ten cents for ten minutes when I was not at work, I was worth at least ten cents for ten minutes when I was. He agreed and brought back the money."

Once when the man in charge of her section went on sick leave and she was asked to fill in, she said she would only do the job if she got the pay he had been getting. But the foreman told her that she was already getting paid more than female workers who had been there ten years.

"I refuse to do a man's job without a man's pay," she replied. And won. She even took work breaks—unheard of at the time—stopping work for fifteen minutes at ten and three o'clock, insisting that if she didn't, she couldn't work well. She also refused to have her pay docked or be subjected to other routine harassments.

Mary quickly understood that most of the women couldn't

win breaks as individuals. So she left her job to organize, successfully creating a strong Chicago women's trade union movement. Later she co-founded, with several other women and a male ally, the National Women's Trade Union League, which lasted until 1950.

A modern-day "Mary" described her organizing work to a rapt audience at an Equity seminar. Rosie, a city bus driver in a large midwestern city, told us about her job. When she started driving fourteen years ago, only ten percent of the drivers were women; now it's up to fifteen. That doesn't sound like a lot, but she notices the difference the 50% increase makes. Back when she started, Rosie said, she wasn't thought of as a "real driver." This was conveyed to her by numerous passenger comments. One of the kinder was, "Oh, a girl driver. I bet you can do just as good as a man." This remark doubly infuriated Rosie when she found out that female bus drivers have better accident records than the men.

During the early years it was critical for her to create friendships with other female drivers. They made clear to each other that they were "real drivers and good ones at that." Looking back, Rosie realizes the female drivers' support of each other was essential to her being able to stay on the job, which she is passionate about. She loves getting to know her "regulars" on the line, the physical act of navigating the bus, her flexible schedule, the sense of camaraderie with other drivers (especially the women), the pay, and the job security.

Understanding how crucial the solidarity with other women drivers was to her success, Rosie recently formed a women's caucus of drivers and other employees. The caucus "helps us recognize we're special," she explained. "It's under the union, and deals with attacks by other employees or safety on the line, safety issues that particularly apply to women, like being assaulted on the line while driving. Women have to work nights more since there are no women with much seniority. So we get the worst picks—the weekend nights—and being women anyway makes us more vulnerable.

Power over must be replaced by shared power, by the power to do things, by the discovery of our own strength as opposed to a passive receiving of power exercised by others, often in our name.

—Petra K. Kelly, German Green Party leader, murdered in the 1980s

We must remember that one determined person can make a significant difference, and that a small group of determined people can change the course of history.

—Sonia Johnson, author

"We deal with our general treatment and things that apply just to us, like maternity leave. The caucus sponsors events and shows films, and sends women to regional and national events about women workers. Plus we lobby for the things we need." Through its unifying efforts, the women's caucus is making the daily lives of female drivers and employees significantly different than they were in the days when Rosie joined the company.

Passengers are making their lives better too. Rosie reported that female riders increasingly say, "Right on!" when they see her, or smile, or comment that they prefer riding with women drivers. This nurturance from other women feeds her for days, she says.

Women's support, as Rosie found, was critical to her survival. Another young woman got an extraordinary public display of sustenance. When Qubilah Shabazz, Malcolm X's daughter, was accused of plotting to assassinate Nation of Islam leader Louis Farrakhan, several female support systems went into motion. One was a recent group: the daughters of celebrated civil rights leaders, who gathered to give public support. The young women—from the families of Martin Luther King Jr., Medgar Evers, Jesse Jackson, Andrew Young, and Alice Walker—came together to "extend support to a troubled sister," in *San Francisco Chronicle* writer Evelyn White's words.

"Regardless of what happened," White quotes Rebecca Walker, the twenty-five-year-old daughter of Alice Walker and co-founder of Third Wave, "I felt a real obligation to come forward and support Qubilah. I know how vulnerable we can be as young black women out in the world."

An older support group, The National Coalition of 100 Black Women, helped organize the event. The Coalition, an influential advocacy group, was founded in 1970 by a small group of women in New York City to address problems and opportunities facing black women. Advocating women's leadership development, the Coalition has been so successful that by 1996, with Jewell Jackson McCabe as president, they have a membership of over 7,000 women.

African American women have a long tradition of organizing for mutual aid. In the 1890s they created a massive club movement involving hundreds of thousands of women who gathered for social, religious, and political purposes, in the process defending their communities. One twentieth century version is the National Council of Negro Women (NCNW). Organized in 1935 by Mary McLeod Bethune, the NCNW, with a million members, is one of the oldest and largest women's organizations in the United States, providing advocacy and direct service. Typical of its projects was the 1964 "Wednesdays in Mississippi," a creative interracial civil-rights program to establish lines of communication between Northern and Southern women. Today, NCNW sponsors programs for four million women in the U.S., with offices in Senegal and Zimbabwe.

African American women continued a tradition of sustenance when, in 1991, University of Oklahoma law professor Anita Hill was widely denounced and disbelieved for accusing Clarence Thomas of sexual harassment. That November, sixteen hundred African American women signed their names to a full-page ad in *The New York Times* supporting Hill.

Due to our combined efforts, we've traveled a way since 1991, when seven female congressional representatives stormed the Senate to protest Anita Hill's treatment by the Senate. By 1995, under Senator Barbara Boxer's leadership, Senator Bob Packwood wasn't able to wiggle through the old boy network, as Thomas did. Sexual harassment is now a recognized issue of major concern. Even Republican Senator Mitch McConnell, chair of Packwood's Senate ethics committee hearing, said, "No workplace in America ought to tolerate this kind of offensive, degrading sexual misconduct." This shift in national consciousness has come from the persistence of millions of women, many working in groups to come forward together about harassment.

The impact in workplaces is enormous, reaching to the highest levels. In 1995, J.P. Bolduc, the CEO of a giant chemical

The process of empowerment cannot be simplistically defined in accordance with our own particular class interests. We must learn to lift as we climb.

—Angela Y. Davis, scholar and activist

*If the first woman
God ever made
was strong enough
to turn the world
upside down all
alone, then women
together ought to
be able to turn it
back, and get it
right side up again!*

**—Sojourner Truth,
abolitionist**

and health-services company, W.R. Grace & Company, resigned upon request, after his board investigated complaints that he sexually harassed employees. This was a first. "We have done a thorough search, and can't find any similar situation where a chief executive was asked to leave for this reason," according to Marcia Bremit-Kropf of Catalyst, a women's advocacy group. Given the stigma women face when they bring complaints, it is women working in groups who often successfully force such resignations or terminations at any level.

Women supporting each other have the power to effect amazing change. Twenty years ago a young woman named Tracy Gary inherited a large amount of money. Feeling isolated and alone in the investment and social justice worlds, she founded Resourceful Women as a resource and network for wealthy women who want to contribute to other women's empowerment.

"In the last ten years," Gary says now, "the United States has witnessed a revolution in how women think about themselves and how they think about money. Learning about money—managing it, talking about it with our loved ones, using it to bring about social change—is as important for women today as it was for our mothers to learn to drive and our grandmothers to secure the right to vote.

"At Resourceful Women I've been in a position to see not only how much women with wealth need information about finances and a chance to break out of their isolation, but also how badly the nonprofit community needs them. I've been most fulfilled when I've been able to act as a broker between the two and have seen them both gain from healthy partnerships.

"I soon saw the level of pain and isolation in some women inheritors, their sense of being used, and their mistrust. I realized how deeply disenfranchised they felt and that they didn't have the level of resources and support they needed to be full societal participants. As a woman of wealth myself, I fully understood the irony and contradictions in this. I saw how talented these women could be and how much their leader-ship was needed.

"My work continues to be exciting because members of Resourceful Women have so much potential to effect change. In one meeting of the Women Donors Network the combined net worth of the women present was $1 billion. Imagine what a group of such dedicated women can do if they are fully able to use all the resources available to them.

"Today we continue to believe in the financial empower-ment of women with wealth. We found that when women first contact us they often feel isolated and lonely, overwhelmed by unfamiliar paperwork and financial terminology. Our new-comer meetings and mentoring programs let them know that they are not alone, and that others have made the passage before them." To date, Resourceful Women has helped over two thousand women with inherited wealth utilize their power so that they and other women benefit.

Today there are literally thousands of organizations devot-ed to women supporting each other: professional and political advocacy groups, caucuses at work, neighborhood alliances. As the millennium approaches, we're continuing to learn how to share skills, how to find and give mentoring, and how to strengthen and inspire each other. Women who are harassed at work, women who suspect they are being paid less than male coworkers—all are turning to other women for advice and mutual action.

A group of faculty women at a small college recently ques-tioned whether their pay was equal to that of their male peers. Believing it wasn't, they hired a statistician to analyze the col-lege's salary data, but were refused access to the data they needed for a comparative analysis. Forced to research their rights, they eventually sued, through the Equal Employment Opportunity Commission, for the information and obtained it. Using that data, the group was able to issue a study demon-strating that, campus-wide, they were indeed receiving unequal pay, although the average was not as drastically low,

Masterpieces are not single and soli-tary births; they are the outcome of many years of thinking in com-mon, of thinking by the body of the peo-ple, so that the experience of the mass is behind the single voice.

—Virginia Woolf (1882–1941), novelist, critic

I discovered that, invariably, one of the reasons Asian and Asian American women had decided to depart from the norm and enter seminary was because of an example set for them by another woman.

—Greer Anne WenhIn
Ng, professor of
theology

comparatively, as they had suspected. Using their report, the group pressed for "equal pay for equal work" and, after several years, received it. The college now makes an annual report, itself, about comparable pay by gender.

The origin of this triumphant action was a small gathering of four women, who decided, after one too many gripe sessions, not to sit around feeling angry and powerless anymore. They determined to work together to make change, which was much less frightening than attempting to "take on the administration" alone. They lobbied a few senior female and male allies, getting them to sign on to the project, requested the information they needed, and when it was denied, learned about external resources like the EEOC which could help them in their quest for data and, ultimately, parity in pay.

We aren't driving on the road to power alone. From A Teams to labor caucuses and political groups, from impromptu news conferences to workplace support teams, from small local organizations to large national ones, women are learning how to successfully sustain and expand each other. We get to share the driving, switching off as we tire. We get to have cartographers for guidance, we can share directions and read maps for each other. We are, truly, on this journey together.

The Tool Kit: Strategies for Building Alliances

Notice when you feel competitive toward other women. This is good evidence they are doing something you'd like to do. Utilize this information for your planning process as you make choices and set goals.

Notice the women you want to get as far away from as you can. Be honest. What is it about them that makes you so uncomfortable or disdainful? Do they represent qualities you're uneasy with: your class, body, age, or sexual orientation? Again, the discomfort is a clue. It's astonishing to discover that as we actually move closer to women whom we initially dislike, we are often able to accept the aspects they mirror in ourselves more easily.

Notice how you already support sisters. Think of specific situations. Each of us has something to build on. We have stories of solidarity, along with those moments we'd rather forget. Focus on all you've done to nourish and advocate for other women.

Choose one woman or girl to mentor. Think about someone you know who could use your assistance, subtly or explicitly. Offer your knowledge base, your contacts, your perspective, your emotional support, or your material resources.

Create a Network. Decide that relationships with other women are vital to your growth and spend "prime time" developing or expanding friendships. Remember, you get to make these choices.

Join a network that already exists for women who share some important aspect of your life: your occupation, interests, or ethnicity.

Provide support for women in general. Make a decision to call put-downs of females as they pass you—whether the source is male or female. Those pervasive, subtle comments eat at our self-confidence and at that of other women who often, without thinking, recycle belittling remarks.

Write down what support would look like for you. What is it that you need? In what circumstances do you feel most alone, and what is it you would like from other women to help you end that isolation?

The way I see it, if you want the rainbow, you gotta put up with the rain.

—**Dolly Parton, country singer, song-writer**

145

Once you know what it is that you want, think about how you can get it. From a group, or individuals? What do you need to tell them about you that will help them give you that support? What gets in the way of your asking? Go through these questions with a friend, or write down your thoughts about them.

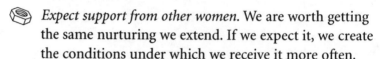 *Expect support from other women.* We are worth getting the same nurturing we extend. If we expect it, we create the conditions under which we receive it more often.

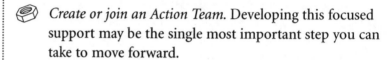 *Create or join an Action Team.* Developing this focused support may be the single most important step you can take to move forward.

Your Action Team: Supporting Each Other

Tell your team about the one-for-all and all-for-one approach that was so successful with the Boston A Team and the National Council of Negro Women. What replication would work for you? You may want to set group goals, as the A Team did.

Be committed to each others' successes and strategize about what steps will get you there. Give concrete support by getting information for each other. Make calls, check up on progress, and give encouragement when teammates hit bumps in the road.

The connectedness we experience in our Action Teams is one strand we'll use to weave a vision of the world as our perfect home, a world into which we fit exactly.

One way to express support for each other and provide feedback for growth is to regularly give appreciations. At the end of meetings, allow a few minutes for each group member to express what she values about other members. Be sincere; look for and think about what it is that your sister has done that you appreciate. For example, you might mention her openness in talking about her challenges, or her courage in seizing opportunities and plowing forward, regardless of fears. You might tell her how much you value her participation in the group, or describe some quality you admire: her humor, her compassion, her toughness. Whatever it is that you appreciate, let her know directly.

If you have team leaders, allot extra time for them. These women have taken the time to plan and think about the group's needs. They also put themselves on the line, risking disagreement with their ideas or leadership styles. Give them a double dose of appreciation—even if you disagreed with something they did. Focus on what did work.

The desire to criticize usually comes from disappointment. How can our leaders not be perfect, when we need them so much? Often when we (finally) find a group that seems to work well, with effective leadership, we pin all of our hopes on this new star in our lives. "At last, people who understand and support me . . ." we feel, adding whatever past disappointments we are carrying to the mix that we imagine this new group won't have. It's kind of like falling in love. When the inevitable occurs, and other people in the group—or the leaders—show their human frailties, we can be bitterly disappointed. "Oh no, not again!" When we get this feeling, it's a good time to: a) check out what we may be bringing to the situation; and b) think as clearly as we can about how to support the leadership, or other members. What do they need to get past some confusion? A listening ear, or new information? If we can see that they get it, everyone in the group will benefit, both from the process and the outcome.

The rush to attack flows easily from the sexism we've internalized, as the self-criticism we heap on ourselves overflows to others like us. We need to learn to monitor those attack juices. What seems to turn them on?

Leadership is often isolating. Supporting the leaders in your Action Team is crucial to group success. When you disagree with your leaders, talk over concerns and doubts

> *One of the important functions of leadership is to ask questions of group members that allow them to tell enough of their own truth to get their feet moving.*
>
> **—Fran Peavey, author**

147

One loses many laughs by not laughing at oneself.

—Sara Jeannette Duncan (1861–1922), writer

privately and directly with the leader, in as supportive a way as you can, remembering that she is just a person like yourself, who has volunteered to take a necessary and important role. As you think together about your questions, you will strengthen the whole team. Explore every possible method of resolution before bringing in other people, which can begin a drama.

One interesting way of resolving conflict and disagreement is to take turns arguing in favor of each other's positions. It is surprising what can happen when you use this technique. At first, it may feel artificial. Soon, you can find yourself actively agreeing with what you are saying, as you marshal thoughts in support of "your" opinion! In fact, when I have used this method, I have several times ended up switching positions with the person I had the original disagreement with. It is fascinating to experience this shift, and makes me wonder how much of the original tightly held assertion was based on a habit of opposition, or having to be "right."

One way to support other women's growth outside the Action Team is help each other within it. We can expect each other to take leadership roles in every area. Every woman is a potential leader; many need encouragement to step out of feelings of powerlessness or past experiences of leading in ways that separated us from others. The Action Team is a perfect place to talk about our development as leaders, as we figure out what—for some of us—is a new role. Those women who have a history of leadership often find we've led in ways that were detrimental and costly, sacrificing ourselves along the way and probably feeling isolated. The group is a safe place to retool our leadership styles and get support for acting powerfully and deliberately. With a little help from our friends, we can learn to take initiative, think carefully about the circumstances and people around us, and ourselves. We don't have to end up being separate from others.

Take turns reporting and listening to each other's challenges and accomplishments in leadership. You might pose a few questions:

- My accomplishments in leadership since last we met are_____.

- My analysis of my group—at work or in my community, the group where I have decided to provide leadership, whether or not I am formally "the leader"—is that they need_____

  _____.

- My goals as a leader in that group are to_____

  _____.

- Difficulties and fears I have as I set out to accomplish meeting my own leadership goals and group needs are_____

  _____.

To feel valued, to know, even if only once in a while, that you can do a job well is an absolutely marvelous feeling.

—Barbara Walters, journalist

After hearing from each woman, provide help with her challenges. Simply listening carefully and non-judgmentally as she thinks aloud is one valuable form of assistance; she gets to reflect as she hears herself talking amidst the caring attention of the group. You can also provide concrete suggestions, based on your experiences in similar situations and on your knowledge of her. For example, you may remember that Marissa has difficulty speaking confidently to groups in English, so that is an area where she needs validation of her considerable dexterity with the language. She's carrying so much old baggage about English, left over from school days as a new immigrant, that she doesn't realize how articulate she is. Your ability to help her frankly confront and let go of her discomfort will be essential in overcoming her timidity. You could also encourage her to, additionally, lead a group while she speaks in Spanish, her first, and still most comfortable, language. And you might provide Marissa with material support: information, contacts, and other resources helpful to accomplishing her goals.

Or you may realize, when you ask these questions, that Michelle constantly feels she has to manage everything

Our struggle today is not to have a female Einstein get appointed as an assistant professor. It is for a woman schlemiel to get as quickly promoted as a male schlemiel.

—Bella Abzug, feminist, former New York congresswoman

and everyone. That is her definition of a leader. And she's burning out. No wonder. Helping her to see that she doesn't have to take care of everything, that others are there to do their part, will assist her immeasurably in asserting a more relaxed—and therefore sustainable—leadership style.

You may remember that when this woman, Rita, described her childhood, she said she grew up in a working class family often on the edge of terror about survival. She had three younger siblings and felt she had to pitch in to take care of everyone. Today that isn't the reality of her life, but that's her baggage.

Without being a therapy group, your awareness of each other's vulnerabilities and strengths will be useful as you give each other a hand. You can talk to Rita about how to get enough fun and rest, the challenge she identified as the biggest barrier to her effective leadership. You might remind her that the nature of life is to be both playful and self-organizing; even if she doesn't do everything, the planet will probably survive. She can midwife change, but doesn't need to direct it all. At the same time, you can appreciate her for caring so much.

As you grow to know each other well, and the months wear into years, your Action Team could become the most important group in your life.

Mile Marker Eight:
Support Across History's Divide

There are so many ways we are
sliced one from another. A powerful part
of creating strong teams is building
alliances with women who seem
significantly "different."

Mile Marker Eight:
Support Across History's Divide

I'm not certain how many friends one needs, but definitely one or two who think your gift, whatever it may be, is pan de cielo, the bread of heaven. Every woman is entitled to an Allelujia Chorus.

—Clarissa Pinkola Estés, Jungian analyst, story teller, author

We need each other's support. So how do we build alliances across the divisions that our histories have ripped between us? Our ethnic pasts, our class backgrounds, all have taught us that safety lies "with our own kind." Yet as long as we stay apart from each other, we're losing vast sources of potential, women to point out vistas we're completely missing as we speed through life on our familiar route.

What would being allies to each other even look like?

If you are an African American woman who helps a Cherokee woman you work with to succeed, through mentoring, friendship, or simply taking the time to notice her skills, you are an ally making a difference in her life—and in your own. As a result of your positive attention, your colleague contributes more to the team, helping you both become more successful. And she expands your horizons at unexpected moments as you benefit from a new perspective.

If you are heterosexual and assist a lesbian colleague (or family member) to talk easily about her weekend—just as you describe yours, with little thought about what to include, and no thought at all about your pronouns—you're bridging a chasm that has deeply divided women. You can assist her to do this by speaking comfortably yourself about gay and lesbian topics, yet without always bringing them up when you see her. (Before I came out, in my attempt to be an ally, I over-lesbianed conversations and holiday gifts with a lesbian friend, until my daughter wisely pointed out, "Ma, she's not only a lesbian, you know.") When you've made clear your own willingness to stretch, your friend no longer has to use part of her creative energy for censorship, worrying about revealing herself through the careless use of a "she" instead of a "he;" you are generating an environment in which she can be fully present. As the two of you model this comfortable relationship, you provide safety for others to be themselves and to form friendships across history's partitions.

If you are Gentile and cancel meetings on Jewish high hol-idays (or better yet, keep the holidays in your calendar so you schedule around those days in the first place), or if you are able-bodied and figure out what a person with a disability might need to flourish, you're being a champion for those whom history has relegated to the sidelines. The talent you unlock through your inclusive behavior may bloom to change the course of your group, your branch, or your firm.

Becoming an ally is the outcome of creating relationships in which you value your friend or colleague. Fortunately, nurtur-ing relationships is one of the traditionally female abilities women have retained. Most of us have some idea how to make friends and be friends.

As women, we also have good preparation for being allies. Some of us have had mentors ourselves. And most of us know what it feels like to be excluded, to be kept out of the informa-tion loop and miss opportunities. We know what it's like to be ostracized, to not get invited out for a drink after work with the guys. Or to the gym with the boss. Having felt the sting, we are extra motivated not to exclude in turn, especially as we become aware that the exclusions weren't personal. (Sometimes, if we've been hurt too badly, we may take guilty pleasure in watching others suffer as we have. In this case, back to the self-nurturing strategies at the beginning of the book. And remem-ber, it's not your fault you're mentally passing on the hurt. You're only trying to get rid of it. There are more effective ways, however.)

Even with all the preparation most women have for being allies, we face barriers. When it comes to working or socializing with women who are "different," we realize our comfort zone is rather small. We often find we're happiest with women just like ourselves.

When given the opportunity to hire, most of us tend to select a woman much like ourselves. She is easily recognizable as meritorious. We understand her references and how she

Shared joy is double joy, and shared sorrow is half-sorrow.

—Swedish proverb

thinks. Maybe we have friends in common or went to similar schools. We know how to "read" her. It's a stretch to see women who are significantly different as qualified.

"Stay" is a charming word in a friend's vocabulary.

—**Louisa May Alcott (1832–1888), author**

We acknowledge this comfort zone when we think of a prospective group member—at work or socially—as "a good fit." And we all know it in our guts, when we enter a new place and look for the cues that tell us we belong.

Rather than succumb to the ease of hiring or supporting only women with social profiles like our own, it's worth the extra effort to seek out inclusive pools and push through the discomfort zone. That's the territory with the annoyingly familiar buzz. When we hear it, we start to think, "Uh oh, I don't know what to do, what to say. I don't have a clue. Do I bring up her disability, or pretend I don't notice? My God, I'm staring. But if I don't look at her, I don't want her to think I'm avoiding looking at her!"

"Should I ever mention her race? Should I tell her she's the 'first'? And ask her how she'd feel about that, or what support she'd want? She might think I'm patronizing her."

Or, "I think she might be a lesbian. What shall I talk about with her? Will she think I'm totally retro if I mention my husband and kids?"

Or, "She was so fat." "So tall." "Too beautiful." "Too unattractive." "Too old." "Too young."

In these or other scenarios where we're considering bringing in a woman who is different, we may be shrieking inside, "I'm lost. How do I act 'casual' when I'm feeling confused? It's easier if I simply avoid her altogether."

To the world, we simply say, "I don't know if she's going to be a good match," and we're relieved as she drifts out of our lives.

When that dis-ease buzzer goes off, we need to ask what it's really about. Is it the lack of a shared language, literal or metaphoric, that makes us uncomfortable? Is it some other difference of social identity—class background or religion? Or is it that the woman truly is not right for the job, the committee, or the Action Team?

Being an ally means asking ourselves some searching questions, entertaining a willingness to enter that discomfort zone and keep on moving until we come out the other end.

Being an ally across history's great divides means figuring out how to develop new networks, putting ourselves into situations where we are likely to encounter women not found in our regular daily loop, and then sticking with it when we feel the inevitable uneasiness of strange territory.

We also need to examine the screens used to filter out who fits—and who doesn't. If someone in your workplace speaks of a rush of ideas as being like a wave of hot flashes, what reaction would she get? When an Equity Institute client, Mary, used that metaphor recently, a younger woman glared at her and asked, "Did I really need to hear this?" "Yes," Mary responded, "You did. If we're going to talk every day at the office about pregnancy, we can speak of hot flashes."

Women in their twenties and thirties often report their discomfort around middle-aged feminists, because of the unreasonably high expectations they believe are held out, as well as the lack of media attention they feel they get, compared to older feminists. "You young women have everything going for you," they hear subliminally. "We were back there in the Stone Age, making a movement, creating an open world—for YOU. So get to work. Get a great job, don't have kids until you're thirty, and on your lunch hour, work for choice—or peace, or something. We busted our guts for you, so don't blow it. We expect great things from you. No pressure. We just want you to be happy."

When those of us who are different across any of these boundaries try to work or socialize together, there are challenges. We may come into the relationship with resentments, such as the ones described above. We usually don't get each other's jokes. We don't understand cultural references, we don't know the same people, or have the same concerns. We definitely don't watch the same TV shows. It's easy to feel uncomfortable with each other, bad about ourselves or furious at one another.

Fear and guilt are the only enemies.

—Elisabeth Kübler-Ross, psychiatrist

The more I traveled, the more I realized that fear makes strangers of people who should be friends.

—Shirley MacLaine, actor, author

Yet making allies is about creating relationships. They become links over the fissures that have kept women apart: singles from married women, lesbians from heterosexuals, white women from women of color. Women without disabilities are often separate—socially, culturally and in workplaces—from those with disabilities. Older women feel distant from younger women. We live in parallel universes.

We have grown up so segregated that most of us who are white don't fully understand a T-shirt that a friend of mine loves to wear: I'M TIRED. I'VE BEEN BLACK ALL DAY. We don't know about the cumulative slights that led her to make this statement.

Yet if we become friends—even through our discomfort—we start to hear the first-hand stories that explain the slogan. About being stopped on the highway in a late-model car, detained for three awful hours on suspicion of having stolen it—even though it is clearly registered in her name. Or having her husband pulled over in the evening driving a U-haul truck (while already under the stress of moving), handcuffed and forced to lie on the pavement, with a gun to his head. Again, "suspicion." Of being a thief.

We hear about our friends or close colleagues shopping and being watched constantly, or being overlooked in a store when a white woman came in. When it's a close friend calling up, hysterical, to say she was stopped on the highway because she was driving a BMW (and that's why she missed the business presentation she was on her way to), we suddenly realize that when we drove down the highway yesterday and didn't get stopped, or when we shopped and received immediate service—or, at the least, didn't get followed or searched—when we go about our daily lives relatively unimpeded by "officials," we're being treated differently.

And we begin understand that this differential treatment has an impact—on blood pressure, on frame of mind, on outlook. And on success.

We also learn about the support systems women under such

duress have historically kept in place; we learn about strategies for coping we never thought of.

When we have friendships across the great divides, we newly hear—if we're not Chinese American—from the Chinese woman afraid to go back for her next appointment in the citizenship process, because the officials grilled her so badly and roughly fingerprinted her at the first visit—even though she's here legally. And when we hear that story we know something strange is going on, because our friend from Ireland who just went through the immigration process had a much more benign experience.

The broader our network, the more complete is our picture and our understanding of what happens to women: what is distinct treatment by race or age, and what is simply bad treatment for all women—or all people.

And we not only hear about the different responses, but directly observe it when we travel with a woman who is in a wheelchair or from a targeted ethnic group, if we aren't. We notice when the waiter or hotel clerk speaks only to us, even asks us about her: Does she want this, or can she do that?

The first guideline for broadening our ability to support each other across history's divisions is to find out, through conversations and media, about the issues other groups of women confront. Many of us are well-intentioned, but we lack the information we need to be good allies.

If we are not immigrants ourselves, for instance, and English is our first language, we need to know about the sense many first generation women have of stumbling over their own voices, until they forget they have one. And then we understand why the woman we're attempting to have a conversation with seems "shy" or "modest." She may be trying to survive by being invisible. Knowing that, we won't give up so easily. Maybe we make the effort to learn Spanish, or some phrases of Japanese or Tagalog, indicating our awareness that there is a universe this woman inhabits, a cosmos in which there is much history, events to celebrate, a universe we respect enough to learn

When alone, I am not aware of my race or my sex, both in need of social contexts for definition.

—Maxine Hong Kingston, author

something about. And, when we are successful in establishing a relationship, we remember that national borders are not the most prominent feature of our planet. Certainly they are not obstacles to the movement of global capital—why should they be to us?

The second guideline to becoming effective allies is that, once again, even if we think we've already done it, we need to continue rooting out our own unconscious biases. None of us is immune, and new forms keep coming at us.

For instance, I recently read a newspaper review of a female band. The reviewer commented that, while the band played, its lone African American member "swung her dreadlocks menacingly at the crowd."

Menacingly? How do you do that with hair?

No one else in the band was described as hostile. Images like these are presented so frequently and so routinely they just slide in and most of us don't even notice it happen. We may perceive women with dreadlocks as faintly menacing, and we're not sure why.

At Equity Institute introductory programs, we often ask people to draw the first image that comes to mind when we ask, "Draw a white woman doing something." And then, "Draw an Asian American woman doing something." "And a Black woman doing something."

We give this instruction for each ethnic and gender group. The images people draw are stunningly similar across regions, age groups, genders and ethnicities. We all got the same messages, even about ourselves. This is some of what we've found:

White women are everywhere still viewed primarily as mothers or performing household chores. In the few images where they work outside the home for pay, they are often teachers.

Black and Latina women are also with children (not always their own), are often cleaning (not always their own homes) and frequently are entertainers. A small minority are educators. Asian American women are usually seated at computers—

It's so clear that you have to cherish everyone. I think that's what I get from these older black women, that sense that every soul is to be cherished, that every flower is to bloom.

—Alice Walker, author

when they're not farming in rice paddies with big grass hats.

White men everywhere have briefcases, sit at big desks or are otherwise depicted as professionals. They are virtually never with children, never doing indoor household tasks, never shopping, never dancing, never hanging aimlessly about or engaged in criminal behavior—all activities ascribed to other groups.

Hopefully this rigid cast of characters will soon change. We're just starting to get a critical mass of news photos of fathers with children at work, and see real-life men wheel babies in carts down grocery aisles or push strollers on city streets.

The old representations of "male" and "female," or of various ethnic (or age) groups have an amazing reach. We don't drop them at the door when we get to work. They are in our minds and become the basis of how we relate to each other. The 1995 Federal Glass Ceiling Commission reports cite this as one reason 95% of corporate officers are still white males. The rest of us are regularly viewed as uncommitted to work, likely to have high rates of absenteeism, or incompetent in some way that matters. All of which has been documented repeatedly as untrue. But who said reality had anything to do with this?

I can testify to the reach of the old images. I've had lots of practice with diversity, with inclusion. That's my business and my life experience. Yet I once wondered how a woman who got a major appointment would know how to manage 4,000 people. And I've never wondered this about a man!

We all carry the same mental garbage. Even if it's only in one little brain cell, it's still there. Having the courage to notice it helps keep us from acting on it. So a commitment to being an ally across any kind of historical divide—race or ethnicity, religion or sexual preference, age or ability—means we enter a lifelong program of unlearning the old images.

The more we are able to catch ourselves when we rely on them, the better our chances of seeing people for who they really are—which gives relationships a whole lot better chance

It's impossible to say what we've lost when we cut off one group. We are all diminished when one group is diminished.

—Maya Angelou, writer

of success. As we continue to build connections and coalitions, we need to be especially mindful of those little slips and slurs—the "menacing" dreadlocks of our imaginations.

"So what if all the other physicians got door-plates with 'Dr.' in front of their names and you got 'Ms.'?" an Equity Institute client, an oncologist, was asked, when she protested this special treatment. As the only female physician, she, along with the secretaries, got 'Ms.' "It doesn't really matter. It's just a word," she was told. But she knew it did matter. Words usually do exactly what they're supposed to: give information, with subtle differences in status transmitted by our choice of words. Probably the person who ordered the name-plates made an "honest mistake," i.e., an unconscious one. Whoever the orderer was, man or woman, when that person saw a female name, it was not supposed to have "Dr." preceding it.

Language, conveying our understanding of who people are, is powerful. When we ask, for instance, for "African American" images instead of "black," women usually get upgraded in their jobs. Remember this the next time someone asks why it matters if you're called a "woman" instead of a "girl." Or what difference a title makes. Monitoring our own language—and thoughts—as we interact with women different from ourselves, is a necessary condition of undertaking a multicultural life—in other words, a twenty-first century life.

The last guideline for being an ally is to deal with guilt. This involves noticing that strange and uncomfortable feeling that tends to creep into our relationships with people different from ourselves, especially those targeted for a discrimination we don't face.

If there's one thing deadly to relationships, it is guilt. When we are full of contrition about the plight other women are in—especially, what "my people" have done to "your people"—we can't treat each other as full human beings. We aren't going to have the same high expectations, and eventually, we're going to be resentful:

> *The world has improved mostly through people who are unorthodox, who do unorthodox things. They're always shaking up the establishment.*
>
> —Ruby Dee, actor

"Here I've been good enough to go around feeling wretched about the situation "your people" are in, and you still don't thank me! Well, I've had enough of being your friend." Or, "I let you slide by on your schoolwork (or your job), because I know how rough life is for you. Is this how you repay my generosity?!"

Letting another woman "slide by," because she is disabled or old, or poor, or in any other disenfranchised category—and touches your heart—is a set-up for failure all the way around. Instead of encouraging her to remain stagnant, fulfilling less than her potential, we might choose to mentor her, or see to it that she gets the environment she needs to perform well. We could do this by working to change the climate of the organization, or its more formal rules and policies that may be unintentionally exclusionary. (I deal more fully with how to do this in a previous book, *The Future of White Men and Other Diversity Dilemmas*.)

The impulse to let someone "slide" may spring from a sense of compassion, but the outcome will be awkward at best, and, more often, a disaster that leaves you all embittered. So scratch the guilt. It takes some discipline, but it's worth it. Tell yourself that you are not liable for the past. But you—and we—are responsible for the present.

Once you follow the three alliance-building guidelines—you get more information about women different than yourself, you become conscious of your own biases, and you shed guilt—what do you do? How do you go about becoming an ally in the world?

There are lots of opportunities every day. You might, for instance, name harassment when you see it. "Yes," you affirm, "that really did happen. Bizarre as it seems, that action did take place. He did just touch your bottom as you walked past him. I saw it happen. You're not imagining it."

Or, "Yes, your manager did treat you incredibly rudely. I'll strategize with you about how to intervene. We won't let this happen again."

The spiritual ways have maintained us over time, especially through five hundred years of oppression. The sun will come up. We have had five hundred years of building our strength as a people, and now we come into the spring.

—Henrietta Mann, Ph.D., a Southern Cheyenne Elder

A woman's organization was the catalyst to trigger a flip-flop in my mind that I wasn't a follower, I was a leader. And in spite of my first reaction, that of fear, and a feeling that I couldn't do it, I took the risk. Learn to trust your own feelings.

—Ginger Purdy, feminist leader

Or, sometimes: "I'm not sure you were passed over because you're female. You haven't been here as long as Len has. I know it's happened to you in the past, but I honestly don't think that's it this time. He probably was the best person for the job—obnoxious as he is, and sorry as I am to admit it. But let's make sure you get the next slot. I'll help you plan. Let's see, what do you need to know—and whom do you need to know?—before the next opening comes up?"

Supporters provide a reality check to perceptions ("Am I imagining that I'm always ignored at staff meetings?") and, if necessary, help strategize a response, or offer to become part of a response-team. As an ally, you may become a mentor, offer to intercede in a difficult interaction, or see to it that a woman excluded from the information loop gets cut in. You use whatever access you have to "the club" to change its culture.

A man came up to me after a speech I delivered at a conference on this topic and shared a wonderful story about his granddaughter's use of her access to power. He told me, with enormous pride, about the difference she made in her workplace. The granddaughter, Greta, was a white lawyer in a Southwestern city. She was new to her job, but had made friends, among them an African American colleague.

Not long after being hired, Greta was invited to interview with another firm, one of the most prestigious in the city. Flattered to be recruited like this, she met with one of the partners. As Greta spent time at the firm during the interview process, however, she became increasingly uncomfortable. And she couldn't figure out why.

Suddenly, she realized what it was. There were no people of color anywhere. When she mentioned her discomfort, and her curiosity about the absence, to a senior member of the firm, Greta was shocked at his blatant response: "We've found they usually don't work out, so it's a waste of our investment. Anyway, they prefer to stick to their own kind. It works out better for everyone this way. No disappointments, no hard feelings later on." After a shocked pause, Greta replied, "I couldn't work here. When you change your policies, I'd love to talk to you again." And she left.

Back at her own company she told her colleagues what had happened. Word got around and, according to her proud grandfather, Greta was "a hero" among the local African American legal community. She broke ranks. Using her entrée into a setting of power, where the white partner of the law firm recruiting her assumed she would share his prejudice, she made an impact on segregation in her field and in her city.

Sometimes women don't act, even when they want to, because they don't know what to do or say. They wonder, "What's an irrefutable statement?" Lacking it, they don't do anything. But you don't have to have the most answer-proof rebuttal to a slur or a slight in order to be effective. You don't have to know all the "facts" or statistics.

Simply breaking silence can be immensely powerful. (As is silence itself, in certain situations. If you're uncomfortable with a stereotypical joke, for instance, and can't think of anything to say, you can simply not laugh. That's rather strong.) Most people appreciate even an awkward ally. And, like every skill, this one improves with practice.

Once we make the decision to enter the discomfort zone and believe that it's worth it, that there is something good enough waiting on the other side, all kinds of things start to happen.

We learn how to make visible to ourselves events occurring all around us. (Their former invisibility was part of our social-ization to segregation.) We begin to see more. It's like brushing water over a page encoded with a picture, awaiting our brush stroke to bring it to life. We begin to notice. And to talk.

The only time most white women talk about race, for instance, is when there is an incident, a daily occurrence that for once got headlines. The only time many heterosexuals talk about lesbian issues is when a custody case makes headlines. Part of the alliance building process is that we begin to take in the bigger reality that exists around us, all the time. One of the things we may start to notice is how strangely segregated our own friendship circles are.

In recent years it has become good form to lament the small numbers of some targeted group at our gatherings: Young or old women, lesbians, women of color. And then, typically, after the lamentation, we move on, because we haven't known what to do. After all, we invited "them" to "our" party, and is it our fault that not many of "them" came?

It's like the complaint we hear from businesses and universities: "Well, we advertised the position, and no women applied."

We need to desegregate our lives—from all the forms of segregation to which we've grown accustomed—because otherwise it's too easy for others to fracture us. It's like not having strong bones. Without a broad range of experience and thinking amongst our numbers, we can't be as strong as we need to be to move forward. It becomes easier for others to break us apart.

How do we make these strong bones? By plowing through that discomfort zone, gaining understanding about each other's struggles, values, and triumphs. When we take the risk to break ranks, we see what miracles lie on the other side.

One white woman, Ellen, told an Equity Dismantling Racism seminar about her experience crashing through the barriers. Even though she was married to a Latino, raising their children to be proud of their dual heritage, she had never noticed that all her close friends were white. One day a Chicana coworker ripped her up and down for all the ways she was racist, in every detail of her being—her speech, the clothes she wore, her attitudes, where she lived, the job she had—and her all-white friendship circle.

Ellen listened, went home, sobbed, and made a commitment to never again participate in white-only settings. She found a fully integrated day-care center for her youngest daughter, which coincidentally was closer to her job than the center she'd been using. She started to make friends with some of the other parents, she went to meetings and subscribed to periodicals intended primarily, but not exclusively, for segmented audiences of color. She joined in activities and groups that she thought would be inclusive.

Ellen began an odyssey of making new friendships, and of being scared: "What if 'they' don't like me?" she sometimes wondered. "Why would she want to be my friend?"

She told us how she had been plagued by embarrassment. She remembered thinking, repeatedly, "Oh, I just said something so racist: I asked my new friend if I could touch her braids. What was I thinking?"

Or, "Ten years ago, when the language was still more in flux, I called the new secretary Afro-American and she told me, with a definite look, 'There's no country I've ever heard of called Afro.'"

Ellen had puzzled over names: "I never remember her Swahili name," she told us. "And then I think, 'It was Swahili, wasn't it?' I can't remember."

She had agonized over mistakes. "I called Allan by the name of the other Asian man in the office, who isn't even Filipino like he is. Oh, I said 'Asian' when I should have said 'Asian American.' Or maybe he's a Pacific Islander. What does that mean and who can I ask? I don't want anyone to know that I don't know what that means.

She told us that she had often thought, "This is so hard; it was much easier before." One day she found herself realizing that she couldn't say her new teammate's name—Maria—in any way that sounded at all like Maria herself said it, without feeling like a foolish Anglo making an idiot of herself, so she just never said Maria's name. It was too embarrassing.

Nonetheless, Ellen persevered. She formed a white allies group with a few friends. They were white women committed to eliminating racism in any way they could, including breaking down personal boundaries. Similar to another ally network, Parents and Friends of Lesbians and Gays (PFLAG), this support group got together to share fears and successes.

Adventure, risk, transformation: the frontier is pushing indoors through uncaulked windows. Watch me reposition the stars, I whisper to the astrologer who floats cross-legged above my kitchen stove.

—Jane Ripplemeyer, fictional character of Bharati Mukherjee, author

The only safe ship in a storm is leadership.

—Faye Wattleton, former President of Planned Parenthood

Gradually, Ellen noticed that her friendship circle was changing. A decade later, she realized that her in-close friendships were amazingly diverse.

She had created a network.

When it came time to call together people—for ideas about how to handle the sexual harassment she was experiencing on her job, to carpool to children's events, to go to concerts, or when her mother died and she wanted close friends around her—this was the group she called on, and these were the people who called on her. It wasn't "us" inviting "them" to "our" party anymore. It was us and us.

As the years rolled on, when Ellen wanted to create an inclusive team at work, she had scores of references to call on for help. Since she worked with a wide variety of people, most newcomers to her network were comfortable with her, knowing they weren't her only Cambodian, Nigerian, Jewish, or Cuban American acquaintance. She had contacts with amazing reach, and was widely trusted by people from many communities.

All of us who undertake this journey find that, like any trip, it has its shares of tears and terrors—and its rewards. This process of crossing history's divides to support each other is very much like "coming out" in that it never ends. Because we are bucking the whole way society is constructed—to keep us apart—we have to figure it out over and over again. New situations keep arising.

Even after all the years of work, and successes, Ellen reminded us of that. She loves to sing, and finally she made the time to join a large gospel group where one of her friends had sung for years. One night Ellen said to one of her fellow sopranos, Adelia, who is African American: "Oh, you cut your hair."

"No," Adelia said.

"Oh, you didn't?" Ellen went on, "But it looks so different."

"No," she smiled.

"Really," Ellen pressed her, "It looks like you did."

"No." Adelia smiled again, perhaps a little frozenly.

Finally, Ellen realized that Adelia's hair was completely different each week. She had been wearing extensions and wigs to church, something that Ellen, with all her knowledge about African American culture—and its history of hair as an issue—just didn't think about as a possibility. But once again, she didn't let her humiliation at her own oblivion stop her. After a week or so of embarrassment, she reported, she continued to enjoy her choir and to grow as an ally.

We could substitute sexual orientation for ethnicity in this story. A heterosexual might go on and on to a lesbian about an upcoming wedding, never realizing what a sensitive topic this is to many gay people—because marriage is like a "white only club." We can't join it.

There are major consequences to the exclusion. I know several long-term lesbian couples who are cross-national: one partner is a U.S. citizen, one isn't. They have terrible problems with immigration. Since their union can't be legalized by marriage, the non-U.S. partner can never be recognized as a valid family member. The Canadian partner in one couple lived underground in the U.S. for years, sparking bouts of anxiety for both partners. Another couple chose to leave the U.S., after a decade of indecision, so the French woman could teach (her U.S. lover awaits legal resident status in France); and a third couple is in the process of selecting another unhappy option: living apart, in different countries, so they can keep the rest of their worlds—jobs, friendships, other family—intact.

I contrast these difficult stories with two other couples I know, both heterosexual. They both married recently—something they each said they wouldn't have done so soon—to provide legal status for the partners: one Nigerian, one from the former Yugoslavia. If I hadn't made friends with both sets of couples, I wouldn't know about the life-changing impact of this particular differential treatment: the right to marriage. Understanding some of the consequences fuels my work to extend this right to same-sex partners.

Into these stories of unawareness and awareness we could

I wanted a perfect ending . . . Now I've learned, the hard way, that some poems don't rhyme, and some stories don't have a clear beginning, middle and end. Life is about not knowing, having to change, taking the moment, making the best of it, without knowing what's going to happen next. Delicious ambiguity.

—Gilda Radner
(1946–1989), comedian

add other aspects of culture. Every group has trigger words. What hair is for African Americans and marriage is to lesbians, for many Jews it's Merry Christmas! (Accompanied by the annual office Christmas party, Christmas gifts, trees, and Christian songs blazing everywhere.)

Or we could substitute class for ethnicity. It's frightening to have cross-class relationships. How many of us have friendships with people at a distant end of the economic spectrum from our own current place? When we do, the relationship raises all sorts of issues about financial responsibility and equity, even if you merely go out to lunch together. Who pays? Avoiding this discomfort by remaining class-segregated is often easier—so women at each extremity (poor and wealthy) remain isolated.

We could substitute physical ability for ethnicity. How many of us have a teammate or friend in a wheelchair, if we're not? Someone we don't want to get too close to because they can't get into our homes. I was mortified a few years ago to realize, when I was having an office party at my home, that one Board member's partner couldn't come because he couldn't get up my three front steps.

We worked the details of that out. And then discovered that the bathroom was too small. So he could come but would have to refrain from drinking any liquids, which he chose not to do.

Now I know what to look for in my next home.

These are some of our challenges. Relationships aren't all we need to create the strong bones of coalition, but they are powerful glue. The Army understands this. That's what basic training is all about. People who are bonded will die for each other.

As we develop closeness across the road blocks that have been constructed to keep us apart, much of the rest of it—the work, the policies and agendas—will flow more easily. Then we can go down the highway together, truly powerful in a way that is impossible when we are splintered into fragments.

So many adults have told me in seminars that they never had friends from other ethnic groups until they left home as young adults. For many men it was the military that gave them a chance for closeness with people from backgrounds quite disparate from their own. For many women, it was college or a job far from home.

Fahimi, who is Saudi American, grew up in Detroit in a tight-knit community. Only when she left home in her late teens, going to New York and getting a sales job, did she begin to make friends with "Americans," as she calls everyone in the U.S. not originating from Saudi Arabia. She discovered, much to her surprise, how similar her interests were to those of other young women, and is now an active member of a women's group at her company, editing the in-house newsletter and organizing social events.

Sandra, a German American woman in her twenties, told an Equity program she was in college right after the Rodney King beating. The topic came up in a class. "I expressed my anger and surprise at this kind of mistreatment, but was put in my place by some other students who weren't so shocked. They had grown up with this in their neighborhoods. I was so glad to have gone to a totally diverse college. It was the first time in my life I really understood that not everyone lives in a little suburb with nice cars, homes and all the other things I had taken for granted. I was planning to go to a community college near my house—not so diverse—but in the end it didn't work out. And I'm so glad it didn't."

Because the social structure of the United States isn't constructed to facilitate cross-fertilization—of ideas and people—jumping across boundaries takes some work. But persistence in constructing these relationships will enhance your ability to function well. You'll be more widely connected, networked to many constituencies, and more savvy about the variety of possible perspectives on life's dilemmas.

I had assumed I was more or less free, not realizing that those who are free make and take choices; they do not choose from options proffered by "those out there."

—Mitsuye Yamada, English professor, writer

The Tool Kit: Strategies for Ally Building

 If you're looking for allies, try an exercise to identify the qualities you seek. You might do this if you're an "only" (the one woman of color or the only person with a disability, for example, in your workplace) or if you are in another vulnerable position where you seek the aid of an ally.

You might also elect to complete this exercise if you'd like to be a better ally yourself. You can do it alone, with a friend, or in a small group.

First, think of a time you were treated unfairly. Did anyone intervene as your supporter and, if so, what did they do? If not, what would you have wanted an ally to do? Create an imaginary ally. Take five or ten minutes to talk about this experience if you're with someone else, or to write about it if you're alone.

Second, remember an instance in which you or someone you know was a successful ally. What were the strategies used? And what was it about them that was effective? Again, tell or write about this experience.

Third, reflect on both situations. What are the qualities of a competent ally? What components make for success? Once you've analyzed ally behavior from both perspectives you'll know what to look for—or replicate.

 Recognize specific ways women's conditions are linked. Once women stop to think about it, they usually comprehend the bond immediately. Women understand at a visceral level that a chain is as strong as its weakest link, and thereby it serves us each to help other "links" grow.

As the implications of this become clearer, we appreciate the value of networking, role models, mentoring, or friendship, and the impact of the legal precedents we set for each other. How are your destinies tied to those of other women? Make a list of specific ways that the fates of other women (legally, socially, economically, politically, personally) impact you. And then, how you affect other women.

Pay attention to interactions around you. Wherever you go, notice what the social dynamics are and be prepared to act, as Greta, the lawyer-granddaughter did, even if it means going out on a limb.

Notice who is in your life and who is missing. Who is in your workplace or your neighborhood, and who is missing? What kind of person do you never meet?

Put yourself in situations where you will meet unfamiliar people. For starters, find periodicals at your local library or bookstore that serve targeted groups. Check out listings of activities, and attend one. Take a friend if you're more comfortable venturing into new territory with your own ally.

Follow up on media that looks interesting. Discover what topics are hot in various communities. Finding common interests is a good way to connect, so choose an issue that also interests you.

In your workplace, inquire about the existence of ethnic minority group (or gay, lesbian, and bisexual) associations sponsored by the company. Find out when the affinity groups serving memberships other than your own have open events. Stretch yourself to attend some, even if you're uncomfortable about going.

Mentally survey people you already know who are different from you in their social profile. Think about women at work you've met or heard about. Who interests you?

> *I leave you love. I leave you hope. I leave you the challenge of developing confidence in one another. I leave you respect for the use of power.*
>
> **—Mary McLeod Bethune (1875–1955), founder, National Council of Negro Women**

No person is your friend who demands your silence, or denies your right to grow.

—Alice Walker, Pulitzer Prize-winning author

Take initiative; make a call, introduce yourself, and invite her to join you for coffee or lunch. See if there's a potential friendship or collegial relationship there. Give it more than one try. If she's an "only" she may be isolated and be extra appreciative of your gesture. Or she may be triply busy, on everyone's committee and in every company photograph, and not have time at all. Nonetheless, she'll probably value the intention.

Identify your resources as an ally. Be specific. What do you have to offer? For example: information, access, skills, emotional support, encouragement, or cash.

Respond to slurs in a way that feels natural to you. Some women prefer to use humor. Others take a factual approach ("I disagree with what you are saying because …"). Still others find a simple, "I don't like that," or "Hey, cut it out," to be effective. Whatever your mode, develop a way of saying "No" that works for you.

At Equity Institute seminars, we often conduct role plays for participants to practice a variety of responses to hostile workplace environments. After only an hour, effective intervention skills can be developed. Role playing is a technique you may do with a few work mates, friends, or your Action Team.

Select, from several scenarios offered by the group, one or two. There are several ways to conduct the role play: individuals can play parts; small groups can play single parts (reducing isolation); people can relay in, tag-team style, to specific roles; or individuals can have coaches.

After you have selected the situation to role play, choose your mode. (With a non-facilitated group, the individuals playing single roles is simplest.) Open the scene, remembering that you don't have to have the "perfect response" in order to make an impact, and that you will get better with practice.

Once you've played out one tactic, debrief the players. How did each role feel? What did you think was effective? Then have any observers offer comments about particularly good strategies they witnessed, so you make them explicit and replicable.

Together (players and observers) brainstorm a list of all the strategies attempted, and discuss what might work best in this situation. Make sure people don't only talk about why every intervention won't work. There is always at least one, and usually many, elegant solutions for every challenge. Some women have been disappointed so often they forget this reality. If there is a lot of energy going into debunking any possibility of effective intervention, ask the group: Where is our (or my) power in this situation?

You can repeat this cycle of role play, debriefing and analysis as often as you wish, trying completely different tactics each time. It's an effective technique for generating interventions to any difficult workplace situation.

Talk with your friends about issues facing diverse groups of women. Make this part of your daily talk. Don't wait for that high-profile situation, an "incident," to occur. Inform and extend yourself to all constituencies.

Reach out, make friends, ask questions, read, and observe. Let yourself feel awkward, stumble, and just keep going. Allow yourself to not be a perfect ally. There is no such thing. You, like all of us, will say things that you know better than to ever utter. But you will be an ally-in-progress. Most people will understand and deeply appreciate that.

Participate in seminars on inclusion at work, in your community, or religious organizations. Good programs provide safe space for the exchange of experiences, foster

I believe that you have to force change . . . You rebel, you organize, you force issues, you threaten the status quo, you show numbers, you promise upheaval: there are numbers of things you have to do.

—Carrie Saxon Perry, elected mayor of Hartford, Connecticut in 1987

open dialogue and a chance to see the world through others' eyes in a way rarely offered out in the "real world." (Though as you change your real world you'll get that chance more often.) Good programs also assure positive outcomes, as participants emerge with concrete individual and group plans. Follow-up is built in. The learnings and action plans are applied to daily life in the organization.

 Make a commitment to expand your networks so they include all kinds of women. Give yourself time. It's a process. But do it. And have compassion for yourself.

> *The main thing in one's own private world is to try to laugh as much as you cry.*
>
> —Maya Angelou, writer

Building an Inclusive Action Team

Make sure that your group continues to be as inclusive as possible. Learn about the challenges facing each of you; utilize each other's networks to expand horizons.

A Speakout is one technique for exchanging information about the unique stresses and joys we encounter as members of particular groups (immigrants or Arab Americans, doctors or carpenters, single mothers or bisexuals). Even if the total Action Team has only three or four members—or as many as fifteen—you can conduct Speakouts. They are panels, structured to give several woman an airing about their lives. They are essentially testimonials: This is what it's like to be me!

Panels don't have to be on raised daises. The speakers may be seated next to each other on a couch, on chairs or on the floor, if they are comfortable there and your setting is informal. The guideline is: simply put panelists together.

Prepare several questions for panelists. They might include: *What are your joys, as a member of "X" group? Your challenges? What would you like from your allies? What do you want others never to say or do to you or your group?*

The panel is one-way communication. They provide opportunities for each member to share her story, without challenge. You can eventually have every member of the Action Team participate in a Speakout, focusing on some important aspect of their lives.

Speakouts promote greater group bonding and alliance building because, although they are designed around dimensions of difference, hearing about each other's vulnerabilities and sources of strength inevitably generates closeness.

They are empowering vehicles for speakers who have the opportunity to reflect on their lives as well as the chance to tell their stories to an attentive and caring audience. They are often cathartic and deeply moving events for the panelists.

Speakouts are also powerful experiences for listeners. How often are we offered an honest and thoughtful glimpse into women's life experiences that are quite different from our own—in an up-close setting? Such openings allow us the possibility of understanding both the connections and contrasts between women's lives.

Not only have we achieved victories, we have—despite the powers against us—become our own victories.

—Camille Cosby, philanthropist, educator

Mile Marker Nine: Develop Male Allies

No matter how much we remember who
we are, become central, get past nice, make
choices, set goals, take charge everywhere, and
support each other—sometimes we just can't do
everything ourselves. We need allies from
outside our group, who remind us that
we are not alone.

Mile Marker Nine:
Develop Male Allies

What we owe men is some freedom from their part in a murderous game in which they kick each other to death with one foot, bracing themselves on our various comfortable places with the other.

—Grace Paley, author and activist

When we wail, "I blew it. I'm such a loser. Who did I think I was, anyway?" we want advocates who understand this is sexism talking, recycling centuries of deprivation. We need champions who can see the big picture when we get lost in a maze of side streets. We want supporters with power, willing to use it for our empowerment.

Surprisingly, our best allies are sometimes men. They are in a good position to support us because they have access to resources—both mental and material—we've so often been denied. Men haven't been restricted in the same areas as women—told they can't think, problem-solve, or lead—so they can be excellent partners as we expand.

One anonymous woman in France described in an international report how she got encouragement from a male ally heard on the radio. "'One cannot hinder women from making philosophy in their kitchens!' a man said on the radio while I was doing my carrots. I have taken him literally. It is true; when I was doing my carrots, making 'my' beds, cleaning with 'my' vacuum cleaner, I was thinking and never stopped thinking. The only thing I had to fight for was a place to formulate my thinking, to express it. That means to find time for me, to write. That was to throw over my life and my oppression as a woman. That is what I have done. My philosophic essay is at an editor's!"

We can be good allies for one another because we each have what the other gender needs. Women want power—the ability to have our thinking taken seriously and the authority to choose our destinies. Men want connections with others. If women and men could share what sexism has allowed each gender to keep intact, we'd all have it all: the capability to be full persons. Members of each gender have been socialized to gain expertise in just one half of life. Once we divvy up skills, we'll all be able to be full associates, working together to take charge of making the world right.

When thinking about men as partners in growth, women often face a wall. That's because we've been told so often we can't trust men, that it's hard to get close without being drenched in sexual confusion (on our part or theirs).

Non-sexual intimacy between women and men is often challenging, especially for heterosexuals. Males have a long tradition of looking at women as collections of body parts. Most men have also been well trained to wear an "I don't care" look—Mr. Cool (belying the terror inside)—which triggers a corresponding urgency in women to get men to express their feelings. "It's all right," we say, "You can cry. Just tell me what you're feeling!" Which soon escalates to, "For God's sake, say something!"

And, with our own long history of measuring value by male approval, we still sometimes act differently around men. Our voices go up; one friend told me she notices women (including herself) crouching so as to be able to look up, when they're the same height as the man to whom they are speaking! We are stunned to hear ourselves acting as if we don't know what we do know. We radiate need. "Tell me everything about it." Or, "Do it for me, please."

Men in turn are triggered by women trying to get closer. "What is she going to want from me? Oh no, more responsibility." They hop right onto their own well-worn road, maturing the "relaxed cool look" into downright rejection.

It is possible to cut through this old dance by resolutely being ourselves—both women and men—regardless of the reactions we elicit (and when we do act as ourselves, responses are often surprisingly positive). Rosie, the midwestern bus driver, describes how she develops male allies. Over her fourteen years at the bus company, she's had quite a few.

"I'm clear about who I am. A strong woman and a lesbian, doing my job well. Men who respond in any positive way catch

Men weren't really the enemy—they were fellow victims suffering from an outmoded masculine mystique that made them feel unnecessarily inadequate when there were no bears to kill.

—Betty Friedan, author, feminist leader

my eye, and I think, 'Maybe this is a sensitive guy who could be a friend.' Then we would strike up a little kinship, a little 'hello' and 'how are you doing?'

"There's a fair amount of just milling around, playing cards, being on call. It's an odd environment that way, so there are many men I've spent hundreds of hours with, talking about everything. You get a sense of who you feel some alliance with. Actually, they become pretty important. We're out there alone on the line, so that's a source of support, just complaining about the finger I got, or telling what else happened today—the supervisor, or the traffic that sucked, or how the legislature is crazy to cut our funding.

"When Jane Roe (of Roe v. Wade) came out against abortion, I discovered I had an ally at work. There's a TV always on, and people often comment about it, responding a lot. Often that's really unpleasant, people make comments about women on the talk shows—and there's a million of them.

"But one day there was this news about Roe. I was just solemnly watching, maybe looking sad. A man I like a lot came up and said, 'That must be a bummer, huh?' There was a lot in that statement. Then we talked just for a minute or two. He doesn't even agree about abortion with me, but he knew I would be upset.

"He was somebody I'd just talked to a number of times before. Small talks, but we liked each other, and always gave a real friendly 'Hey there, how you doin'?' to each other. Having him acknowledge what I was feeling, without my having to say anything, helps the environment.

"Another time there was a supervisor on my bus and a male passenger was giving me a hard time. He used the word 'bitch' to me. Maybe I had started to close the door before he got on. I try hard to always wait if someone is running for the bus, but sometimes when there is lots of traffic and passengers, I can't tell who's waiting for the bus and who isn't. Anyway, he was cursing me.

"This male supervisor, who was riding up front as a

passenger, just turned quietly and said, 'This is one of the best drivers we have.' That completely shut that guy up.

"We had only had a slight relationship before, maybe talking briefly a few times. He was just a good guy. But we had made a good connection before, so he wasn't going to let me be abused like that. And he was being honest. I am one of the best drivers," Rosie smiled, as she told the story.

Male allies assist us by reminding us of our genuine strengths. Another example of this recognition was the man who, meeting his pregnant friend Tamyra at a wedding, asked briefly about the pregnancy, but then focused most of his conversation on her work and other interests. He was not regarding Tamyra as merely a storage vehicle for the baby, but as a complete person who included her unborn child among a range of current interests.

A third model is my son, with whom I tossed a ball for years, since it was something he liked to do. Malcolm was my main encourager in sports. "Ma," he used to say, "You're a good athlete. You should be on a softball team." He persisted in expanding my image of my athletic capabilities—which I thought were minimal—and finally I did join a team, enthusiastically enjoying several years of play. Malcolm walked his talk. My second season, when he was thirteen, he volunteered as an umpire for several of my games. While umping, he was respectful, thoughtful and always humorously interacting with members of both teams, who welcomed his support.

There are many ways to develop male allies. A story from an Equity seminar describes one. Joan met Guillermo in her early twenties, ten years ago, when she was a new manager-in-training at a software company. Guillermo was about to become a vice president. They became friends during her first weeks in the program; ever since, he has served as a significant mentor.

How has it worked? Sensing an affinity, Joan took initiative at the beginning, asking Guillermo for assistance in navigating unfamiliar terrain. She boldly set forth career goals, and, assuming she deserved it, asked for help.

If you talk to a young Sioux about why women do all the work, he might explain, "Our tradition comes from being warriors. We always had to have our bow arms free so that we could protect you . . . Every moment a Pawnee, or Crow, or white soldier could appear to attack you . . . We had to keep our hands free for that. That is our tradition." —"So, go already," I tell them. "Be traditional. Get me a buffalo!"

—Mary Crow Dog, activist, author

Seeing Joan's extraordinary potential in communications (and ultimately marketing), Guillermo made sure that she was in on key projects—first as a trainee, later as a player. He offered her material resources enabling her to do her job well, and continuously puts in a good word about her work with others.

Over the years he also became a friend. She explains, "Guillermo calls and says, 'How are you? I haven't seen you recently, and have been wondering how you're doing.' He does maintenance in the relationship. That's pretty unusual."

Shortly after her father's death, he invited Joan to his office. He listened as she attempted to sort out the tangle of emotions she was feeling: relief at the passing of an increasingly abusive and alcoholic man, sorrow at the loss of a friend, grief from her understanding of how shortened and distorted her father's life had been.

Guillermo listened, without judgment or advice, as she talked through her contradictory feelings about the man who had given her life. He offered supportive comments and commended her handling of the challenging final weeks, when Joan had taken charge in difficult circumstances, as hospital personnel fought the family's decision to finally cut off life support.

Finally, Guillermo asked Joan how she'd cope in the coming days and weeks. He pushed her to plan strategically: a day off a week for the next month; one visit with far-flung family; regular sessions with a company counselor.

And he talked about her work. How was she going to keep key projects going during the next month? Who would handle which pieces? What could she manage and what could she defer? Having an ally think with her this way at a critical moment—there were several important projects under way, and Joan was in no shape to prioritize—possibly saved her job.

Joan recognizes this is not a one-way relationship. While she has benefited from her powerful champion, he too gains from the connection. Joan produces brilliant work; her success reflects on him. In their discussions she often has excellent ideas which she passes on to him. And he uses her as a sounding board. Their association is mutually essential.

At the beginning of their relationship, Joan immediately became comfortable with Guillermo because his support of women includes life at home. Early in the friendship he mentioned how he was supporting his wife, Veronica, during her parents' visit. Joan, curious because of her own in-law issues, asked him what form his support took.

"I try to be emotionally available to listen to what is going on," he said, "and physically loving. And I put some effort into making practical things work, like sightseeing and dinner." He was giving up much of his own time that week, making Veronica's needs a priority so the family's visit would be a good one.

The story sounds remarkable. Yet if we reverse genders, and a female works to assure her male partner's smooth parental visit for a few days, we wouldn't give it a second thought. (Role reversals often highlight inequities, as they elicit exaggerated responses. Tamyra's husband, Mike, found that when he stayed home from work one day a week to take care of their infant son, he got reactions ranging from shock to wild applause. If a woman stayed home one day a week for child care, she might be regarded as uncommitted to her job. Surely not a hero.)

Guillermo's and Joan's relationship sprang up easily, and progressed over the years to an easy and deep regard for each other, personally as well as professionally. Sometimes ally relationships are more challenging. We may have to force discussion and demand support. Ellen told us about her repeated requests to her choir director to change the pronouns in songs they were singing to be either gender-neutral or at least to alternate "his" and "her." This was her choir's policy, and a reason she had joined, yet her director never made the changes until she insisted on it—with the support of several women and men—at rehearsals. The cycle of objection, heated discussion, and final change, recurred each week, song after song.

Finally Ellen took him aside. "Ben," she said, "I need you as

> *And if we think that our daughters ought to be in Congress next to our sons, we'd better let our sons know that now, so they get prepared to have women as colleagues.*
>
> **—Johnnetta Cole, President of Spelman College**

my ally on this. It really matters to me, and to lots of other people in the church. Please support me and make the changes before rehearsals. It's embarrassing to bring it up every week. I know you care about me and this is important to me."

"What's the big deal?" he asked. "It's just words. This is the way they were written. Plus it's unmusical to say 'people' or 'humanity' instead of 'mankind.'"

She continued to explain how she felt excluded, and asked him how he'd like it if everything was "womankind" and "her," which meant him too.

"Well, now that you put it that way," he laughed. "I'm with you."

"Thanks, I knew I could count on you. Please change the words before rehearsals, so we don't have to hash it out in front of everybody, and waste everybody's time. I'll help you rewrite any time you want."

After their private conversation, Ben came to rehearsals almost every week with rewritten songs. She was shocked a few weeks later when he directed a guest soloist to give "equal time" to both genders in a song the soloist had written himself. Ellen's persistence, and her private conversation, won her an ally.

Sandy, another client, found that in her job as a taxi dispatcher she also had to insist that the drivers (all male) not make disparaging remarks about women as they communicated with each other—and her—on their radios. She too worked individually with her boss, Hussein, asking him how he would feel if it were one of his daughters (to whom he was devoted) being described in the way he heard drivers speak. Hussein got the point and issued a written directive to all drivers: No disrespectful language tolerated. Hussein put in a penalty, a three-strikes-and-you're-out (of a job) clause. It was effective, and Sandy finds her work environment dramatically more comfortable.

Sometimes men themselves initiate actions to change male opinion. Charles Hall, an ad executive from Los Angeles, is an example. After a woman attended a party at his house and was raped by her date later in the evening, he made a decision to raise male awareness about rape. Using his advertising skills, Hall created a series of stickers and posters that challenge men to reconsider their attitudes. One states:

Rape.
In a recent UCLA study 65%
of college educated males
said they would rape a
woman if they thought they
could get away with it.
What % are you?

Why, he was asked in a *USA TODAY* interview, this costly leap—Hall spent $5,000 on the campaign—from thinking to doing the right thing?

"After the rape happened," Hall told his interviewer, Marco della Cava, "I just kept thinking of my mother, my girlfriend, my cousins, thinking, I don't want them to suffer from this, so what can I do?" Because men listen to other men, the ads are especially effective.

As for whether one man can make a difference, Hall commented, "This is the way we handled racism in the '60s. It wasn't corporations that got together, it was one person getting fed up, stepping on a bus and going to demonstrate." (It's good to be reminded that one person can spark a movement that sweeps a nation. We are indeed powerful creators of our environments. It's also critical to know that Rosa Parks was a skilled organizer and, as secretary of the Montgomery NAACP, a long-time member of an established network. After her action, a committee of one hundred women immediately organized carpools, providing the backbone of the bus boycott and enabling its success. Individuals matter—and so do groups.)

Hall is not alone in getting "fed up" with the conditions he sees women facing. There are hundreds of men's groups, like Men Against Violence Against Women, that are active allies to

Businesses committed to promoting minority and women workers had an average annualized return on investment of 18.3 percent over a five-year period, compared with only 7.9 percent for those with the most shatter-proof glass ceiling.

—Federal Glass Ceiling Commission Report, 1995.

women. One group recently formed at Morehouse College, where students started a group called Black Men for the Eradication of Sexism, which opposes "misogyny, date rape, sexual harassment, paternalism, and other affronts to women." Omar Freilla, the group's founder, told *Ms.*, "In my involvement in liberation movements, sexism wasn't dealt with, issues that did not directly affect men weren't recognized. We saw how women were objectified, just really treated as sexual objects... being called 'ho' and 'bitch.' We have discussion groups and talk about what it is, what it means to be a man, and how we were brought up. We're really trying to deprogram ourselves." Yes!

Men act publicly to support women in a variety of ways. One man at a rally held a sign proclaiming him to be an "Angry White Male for Affirmative Action." Others, like the interracial group of men at the Oakland Men's Project in Oakland, California, work in teams to support men to unlearn their training to treat women violently.

Nina, an organizational consultant, experienced an unexpected ally intervention in a situation where she didn't expect to need one. She was invited to a major conference of business leaders to speak on a plenary panel. Yet, after the initial brief presentations, the moderator referred all questions to her colleagues, Samuel and Boris. The moderator repeated, "How would you handle that, Samuel?" so often that the refrain became almost humorous to Nina. When a woman in the audience commented on this apparent silencing of women's voices, she was accused by the male moderator of "making mountains out of mole hills." Furthermore, he said, he wanted to reserve the remainder of the session for "serious questions." His referral of questions to the male experts had appeared so normal that it was invisible to most of the observers. Yet one of the men in attendance rose, at some professional risk, to state that, now that it was pointed out to him, he realized it was true: the moderator's behavior did slight the female panelist, to an alarming extent. She, an expert in the field of organizational behavior and author of a briskly selling text, was asked to comment once; the men, a dozen times each. This was too lop-sided for chance. He wanted an explanation.

Confronted by a man asking that question, the moderator wasn't so quick to respond with an accusation of exaggeration or oversensitivity. He hemmed and hawed and allowed as to how yes, but he hadn't noticed anything amiss, and maybe it was because Samuel and Boris were so renowned. He went on to recount their professional credentials as justification for deflecting so many questions to them. But in the end, he offered a tepid apology, and asked Nina to speak. She chose to use the scene they had all just witnessed as a teachable moment, framing it as a case study of unintended impacts created by unaware actions, demonstrating the organizational chaos and ill will that can result from business-as-usual, in which "newcomers" maintain their historical invisibility. She received a standing ovation.

This was a situation in which a male ally made a stunning difference.

Other men find more private, individual ways to express their determination to break the cycle of male supremacy. Some men, for instance, have noticed that in mixed gender conversation, other men often direct comments and attention to each other, not the women present, even when women asked the questions, or are clearly the experts on the topic under discussion. These men consciously direct eye contact to a woman when another man is inappropriately responding to a woman's question while looking at a man. They thereby force the speaker to follow suit, so that he shifts his attention to her. It works. Suggest it as a tactic to male colleagues if someone is making you invisible.

Other men act as allies by sharing equal responsibilities for the home. Often women have to ask. A woman wrote to Dear Abby: "Two years ago I accepted a full-time job after working part time for ten years and juggling all the household chores and cooking. When I accepted full-time employment, I sat

In the knowledge-based economy of the future, the real value of an organization will lie in its people's ability to think, to process information, to evolve creative solutions to complex problems.

—Sally Helgesen, author, business consultant

down with my husband and told him that I would be working until 5:30 P.M. every weekday, and by the time I finally got home it would be too late to start cooking dinner. My husband agreed to do the cooking every weeknight, and I would do the dishes. On weekends, I would cook and he would do the dishes." This man didn't offer to become an ally, but upon request—and who knows how firmly it was made?—he became one.

Some men act as allies by bringing babies to work. As well as giving the fathers a chance to enjoy their children, and providing needed child care, they contribute to breaking the stereotype that it is women, and only women, who can nurture. Representative Bill Orton, a first-time father from Utah, brings his three month old to work two days a week—not because of day care problems, but simply because he wants to spend as much time with his son as he can.

Orton shows up at Congressional meetings pushing his infant son, Will, in a stroller and, according to a *San Francisco Chronicle* report, he wears a Mickey Mouse pacifier clipped to his lapel. He takes the baby onto the House floor for votes, feeds Will a bottle while talking on the phone, burps him while meeting with constituents, and changes diapers between appointments. Orton knows that he can get away with flouting tradition in a way that a new mother in his position would probably find more challenging, since her presence with an infant at work could reinforce the image of women as casual workers, more concerned with home and hearth. But as more men jump into the role, the culture will change. As Orton, a three-term member, says, "I think we're catching up with what the rest of the country is doing. We're recognizing the importance of parenting, and we're putting a priority on that." Real family values.

For the vast majority of working women (most of whom earn under $25,000 a year) stress from attempting to balance home and work is the number one problem. Women (and ultimately, men) need more responsive, family-friendly workplace cultures. Men can serve a powerful ally role by helping create more flexible workplaces.

Surprisingly, some companies that allow employees to bring infants to work on a part-time basis have discovered that not only is this a useful management technique for keeping a happy parent-employee, but a baby in the office lifts morale in astonishing ways. It turns out it's impossible to be stressed when a radiant spirit is looking at you with total delight and chortling as he drools on your finger.

At Equity Institute, one staffer brings her infant to work two days a week, planning (to the dismay of colleagues) to cut back to Fridays-only when he is eight months old. We all look forward to Ryan-days. His playful spirit is infectious and the whole workday is more fun when he's around. Watching our formerly harried staff members stop by to play for a few minutes with him, I realized we couldn't pay to have this kind of morale booster—and fun. Some corporations hire comedians for an hour or two to bring this kind of joy to employees. We have Ryan sixteen hours a week.

Male allies play a critical role in creating work environments that support women, by using their influence to encourage family-friendly policies. All sorts of companies are considering them. Hillary Rodham Clinton, in her weekly news column, describes how "even at a place as hectic and workaholic as the White House, we have tried to offer some flexibility to working parents." She describes time off granted to fathers and mothers and the welcome extended to children coming to work with their parents. "We are hardly alone in this. Employers and organizations in the public and private sectors are beginning to recognize that family-friendly workplaces are not just good for morale, but also for the bottom line." She cites several examples:

- In San Francisco, a group of businesses, unions, and community groups established a twenty-four hour day-care center for airport employees.

I believe that you cannot go any further than you can think. I certainly believe if you don't desire a thing, you will never get it.

—**Rev. Charleszetta Waddles, founder, Detroit Perpetual Mission for Saving Souls of All Nations**

- In Boston, a school bus schedule was redesigned to make it easier for children to get to after-school programs.

- In Northern California, a consortium of law and consulting firms is establishing an 800 number that employees can call twenty-four hours a day, seven days a week, for prescreened, in-home emergency child and elder care.

- In New Jersey, a company with 3,000 employees is creating a pilot program offering compressed four-day work weeks, job sharing, part-time and flex-time options, and telecommuting for its work force.

Environments that respond to working parents are the workplace future. In late 1995, twenty-one of the nation's largest companies—including IBM, AT&T, Citicorp, Aetna, Bank of America, Chevron, and Hewlett-Packard—agreed to an unprecedented $100 million six-year effort to improve child and elder care for their employees. The new funding will expand existing programs, and will be used to develop special projects such as a voice-mail service in ten cities, to help parents keep up on their children's school assignments and activities.

Women don't need to make these changes on our own. We need to assist—and insist—that the men in our lives co-create environments that allow us to succeed. It's not an easy process; it involves colossal change. But it's one we're all in the middle of. And by remaining firmly grounded in our understanding of who we really are, we can negotiate the complications of supporting men in their struggles, without the old, insincere, flattery we all learned so well—while at the same time insisting that they support us too. As equals, not victims in need of rescue.

It's often easier for women to give—to be advocates for others—than to ask for and receive support. Used to acting as midwives to other lives, women are not accustomed to strategizing for support from our allies. As we go forward, part of taking charge is planning how to enlarge that aid, rather than simply waiting and hoping—for Prince Charming, for our lucky day, or for champions to magically arrive.

Believing that we are entitled to such attention, that we qualify for assistance, implies that we deserve to grow and to lead. We haven't had female Presidents or famous playwrights not because we aren't worthy or smart. It's that we haven't been given the spotlight. In fact, it's often been grabbed from us. But still, like all targeted groups, we are used to blaming ourselves: "Maybe if I didn't speak so forcefully at the meeting I would be in a better spot now." Or, "Maybe if I had spoken up more. . . ." However we play it, when we delve deeply enough, we often find that we believe our lack of power is somehow due to our own mis-deeds.

One characteristic of self-blame is a habit of giving up, before we get to our destination. Or—its flip side—blaming others. Especially men. They're so powerful, we believe. And this thought comes with a corollary: We're so weak.

Blaming ourselves/blaming others are two sides of the same coin. When we stop devaluing ourselves—and blaming that "opposite sex" (a phrase designed to emphasize difference)—we will be able to strategize effectively for ally development.

We don't have to feel like imposters, furtively seeking undeserved authority. Women are absolutely entitled to the networks, support, and resources we need to succeed. Whether our dream is going to school, having that ideal job, organizing the community, or being financially supported to stay at home for two years to raise a child—or paint—we get to choose, and then strategize about how to implement the dream.

How do we find the resources to turn our hopes and fantasies to reality? By taking ourselves seriously, allowing our dreams to become choices; setting goals, and planning how to reach them. Women are entitled to strategize for supporters who see our potential and want us to succeed—just as we plan for anything else (school for the kids, vacations for the family).

So, for example, to attract the help we desire, we may have to consciously showcase skills and position ourselves to shine.

A woman provides background information before she recommends an idea. A man gets to the bottom line quickly. The man perceives the woman as talkative and wasting time; the woman perceives the man as pushy and aggressive.

—Pat Heim and Susan K. Golant, authors and consultants

This often doesn't come easily to women, who have been instructed early and well to put others first. We're not used to bragging about our talents and achievements, especially work-related ones. We're more used to showcasing our children's or partner's accomplishments, finding many opportunities to tell about their moments in the sun.

"My daughter got high honors in French," we beam.

"My partner got promoted to supervisor of the construction crew where he's only worked six months. He's making $22 an hour," we enthuse.

It's a wonderful capability to be able to delight in others' successes. Now we simply need to add a little self-centeredness to our emotional repertoire, learning to refocus the light of recognition on ourselves as well.

If we're embarrassed on center stage, let us notice that as we gain more power, we're better advocates for others. Who, after all, needs a weak ally? With greater resources, strengths, skills, and networks, we can help other women more effectively—as well as ourselves.

As we look for allies, we have to be specific about our requirements, and let potential allies know what we want: visibility, support when we get harassed, a mentor, or some other form of assistance. It's also helpful, in gaining male allies, to demonstrate how they will benefit by acting upon our needs— and lose out if they don't. One powerful example is cited by Judy Rosener in *America's Competitive Secret: Utilizing Women as a Management Strategy.* When Jill Kerr Conway, the former President of Smith College, became Nike's first female corporate board member, she thought the company's understanding of the female market was limited, and suggested that Nike create a women's division. At first, her idea was completely rejected. Rosener quotes Nike president Richard Donahue recalling, "Our habit was to take a male product, color it pink and sell it." But Conway kept arguing for a separate division run by women, targeting female customers. Finally, her fellow board members agreed with her projection of profits, and created a women's division. Within just a few years, after a major advertising campaign, 20 percent of Nike's domestic revenues came from its women's division.

What if Jill Kerr Conway didn't have a seat on the board? What if she hadn't spoken up? And what if the men on the board had not listened to her? Nike, and female consumers, would be worse off.

Men in business and in academia are discovering that it makes good bottom-line sense to be allies to women. One top East Coast medical school recently calculated that it costs a quarter of a million dollars to recruit, train and set up one basic science faculty member. If she doesn't make it after a few years (as so many women don't), the school—or the corporation—has lost a sizable investment. Multiply that turn-over by even a small number—say, five losses in a year—and the institutional waste is staggering.

The Federal Glass Ceiling Commission reported in late 1995 on its research into the profitability of firms with a range of women-friendly policies: businesses supportive of women (and men of color) had an average rate of return on investments over twice that of more discriminatory companies. Such research is a powerful tool as you make the case that male allies, and institutions, have much to gain by doing the right thing.

Think of the reasons your potential male allies should help actualize your potential. Whether you're a taxi dispatcher or a bank analyst, a bus driver or a faculty member, your employer has made an investment in finding and training you. The firm doesn't want to lose you. And doesn't want you to only give 50% to the company. Your employers want your maximum effort. Let them know what you need in order to deliver it.

As we take the wheel and accelerate into the future, let us remember: We are not alone. We do have allies, people who want and need us to succeed. We can work in partnership with men, and still be women taking charge of our lives!

American business increasingly understands that there's no place to get the talent from anymore. This understanding may, ultimately, do as much to liberate women and blacks as the antidiscrimination measures. The need for their talent in a country where birthrates are declining and talent needs accelerating is irresistible.

—Eleanor Holmes Norton, Congresswoman

The Tool Kit: Strategies for Developing Male Allies

 Identify your needs for allies. Be specific. What gaps do you have? Where do you need assistance? What would help you meet goals at your present job, or long-term career goals?

 What are your strengths? Ask your ally to remind you of them, and assist in building on them.

 Identify allies in your past. Think of times you've had helpers. These may have been mentors, friends, or others who intervened to see that things went well for you. They championed your cause and cared about your success. They watched your back. Mentally replay your allies' actions in slow motion, so you can understand what was helpful. What, exactly, did they do? (If you can't think of a time you had an ally—imagine one. What would you have wanted an ally to do? Create a fantasy ally, and picture him, or her, saying and doing the perfect things.)

How did you recognize your allies, or did they find you? Develop a personal ally history, so you'll recognize how these serendipitous connections came to pass. Your personal history gives you baseline data. Perhaps you'll choose to recreate circumstances in which allies were helpful in the past. Or, based on your ally history, you may determine that you want to try new strategies.

 Identify people already in your life who are potential champions. Are they people you know well? What is their proximity to you? Are they at your job or in your professional network, are they members of your family or friendship circle? Spend some time thinking about who your potential allies are, and then:

Develop a plan. Put your goal-setting skills to work. Be bold enough to decide you are worth strategizing for. Select one or more potential allies and plan steps to develop them in the role. How will you maneuver time with him or her? Will you openly talk about what you need to succeed, and the role you hope this person will play, or will you be more subtle? Either way may be appropriate, depending on your prior relationship and current circumstances. Be deliberate, plan, create a timeline with next steps . . . and allow room for flexibility and spontaneity. Then go for it!

Surround yourself with people who are invested in your doing well. Identify them—men and women—and put energy into forming or further developing these relationships. Notice how you feel during and after each of your interactions. Who helps you feel refreshed, supported, and centered? Foster those people as friends and allies.

Ask for help. Don't be afraid to ask. You can do it powerfully. You don't have to pretend that you know everything and can do everything alone.

Put yourself into situations where you can shine by demonstrating leadership and successes. Strategize, plan ahead, and take charge of showcasing your skills. Sometimes life will effortlessly transition you into a new position; other times, you need to move your feet.

Encourage male allies to learn how to listen to you. Men are often used to being attended to by women, and not reciprocating with the same kind of careful attention. Select one man and decide that you will teach him to listen attentively to your thinking, analysis, and reflection. You will make a commitment to his growth, and insist that he be a better ally to you. Pick a man who will succeed. Start by talking about your ideas (or needs); if his

If folk can learn to be racist, then they can learn to be antiracist. If being a sexist ain't genetic, then, dad gum, people can learn about gender equality.

—Johnnetta B. Cole, President, Spelman College

195

attention wanders, remind him, "Weren't we talking about me?" If you notice a disproportionate amount of your joint attention goes to his concerns, point that out, as blamelessly as possible. It really isn't his fault—that was his conditioning—and he's probably unaware of the disparity. Nonetheless, you can be clear, and unyielding, about your expectations.

 Don't give up on your allies. There will be inevitable moments of disappointment. But there are many males who care about women's empowerment in general and yours in particular. Use your remembering-self and centering techniques—your anchor points—to focus on this reality. Think about the success stories in this book, and others you've heard of; ponder your own ally history, and ask your friends about theirs. Much as the news is filled with stories of crime and short on stories of good deeds, we often tell each other horror stories about men ("He did what?!"), while the ally anecdotes—the man who promoted us, mentored us, made sure we were in the loop—don't make the rounds with the same frequency.

As in other areas, we need balance when we're thinking about our male allies. We don't want to sugarcoat reality, and the truth is that there is vast discrimination and backlash against women, at work and at home. It's important that we notice it, and tell each other about it as part of our learning to cope, survive, and overcome. Simultaneously, we need to hear stories about the support we've each been given, rounding out our picture to give us an accurate understanding of current circumstances and possible future assistance.

It took sheer determination to be able to run a hundred yards and remember all of the mechanics that go along with it. It takes steady nerves and being a fighter to stay out there.

—Wilma Rudolph, athlete

Using Your Action Team to Develop Male Allies

Tell about successes with male allies and use the group to discuss disappointments. (Such success stories could be the check-in question at one gathering.) Even if you've had experiences that point you in an opposite direction, do a memory scan, looking for situations to help you remember that men and boys are capable of—and often practice—superb support. Reread the ally anecdotes in this chapter, ask friends and group members for stories, research your family past.

Strategize with group members about how to insist, and assist, men to do whatever they need in order to be there for us. Do some concrete planning with the team. Ask each other where you struggle when you get close to a man. Typical responses, from women of every sexual orientation and preference, are:

"I want to know what they're thinking, so I don't have to guess why they're upset."

"My expectation gets too big, so anything can pop it."

"I try hard. It's like talking to a wall."

"I don't trust that they'll come through with commitments, to finish a project or show up on time."

"It's hard to get men to open up about feelings. I feel helpless when they don't."

We can use the group to identify our own parts of these communication difficulties. What are our urgencies when we meet that kind of "wall"? What debris from the past gets thrown up, and how can we remove it?

We can remind each other not to take those stony male faces personally. It's really not about us. We just need to continue being grounded and centered, so we don't waver in remembering who we are (intelligent and thoughtful women), and what we are entitled to, no matter what responses we encounter.

As the group supports us in remaining centered, we can keep moving along on the road to full empowerment,

One of the things women bring to the situation in terms of sharing power is new styles of leadership. I am no less the bishop. I know where the buck stops and who is responsible. But that doesn't mean that I have to exert power in such a way that other people feel they are less than who they are because of who I am.

—Leontine T.C. Kelly, bishop

In my country, fathers receive one-month compulsory paternity leave. We passed that measure to support men's participation in family life.

—Mona Sahlin, Deputy Prime Minister and Minister for Equality of Sweden

knowing that men are right there beside us. Sometimes we have to fasten our seat belts when they're around, now and then they take us on detours, and occasionally they seem like traffic barriers themselves—but in actuality, most men want to be driving on the road to power with us, taking turns driving the car.

Strategize with your Action Team about the steps you can undertake to acquire male allies, and how to mature relationships you already have. Use the Tool Kit interventions above for discussion questions.

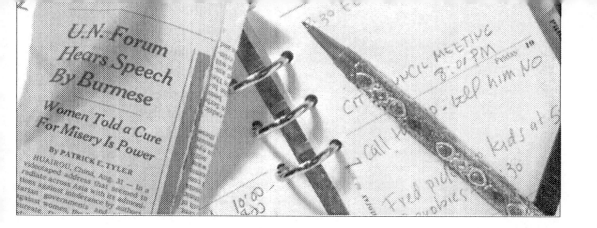

Highway Four:
Creating a Vision

●

Mile Marker Ten:
Envision a New World

Envisioning the future we want
expands our sense of the possible; we set our
goals higher and further out than we might have
if we hadn't allowed ourselves the luxury of a
"vision." We make our plans based
on the expanded goals.

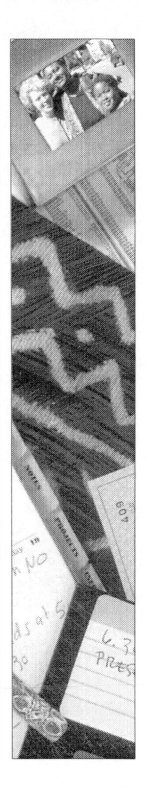

Mile Marker Ten:
Envision a New World

The beginning of the achievement of women's liberation may be the symbolic shift from consciousness-raising to fund-raising.

—Patricia Aburdene and John Naisbitt, authors

Imagine a world in which only women had been presidents of the United States. And vice presidents. A world in which, a few years ago, during the Year of the Man, men made unprecedented gains in political and business life. Today—a first—women retain just over 90% of the nation's highest elective offices.

In this mythical country, women hold 96% of corporate director and CEO slots. The entire layer of senior corporate positions, at the vice presidential level and above, is female-dominated, numerically and culturally. Cars and desks are designed with a spot for purses; rhythms of menstruation, birth and menopause define the work month and provide business metaphors. Managers are often described as midwives to the process of birthing new products. When men speak of the thrust of seminal ideas, they are frequently admonished to "play the games father never taught you" if they want to get ahead. They are instructed to learn the language of female power: webs, collaboration, communication, circles. And to mistress the lingo of PMS, pregnancy, and child care.

In this land, women give the news—and make it. School superintendents, police and fire chiefs, as well as beat cops and firefighters: overwhelmingly female. Women run publishing houses, control international finance, and make national and international policy decisions. Men who work outside the home for pay are clustered in a small range of occupations: clerical, secretarial, teaching, and low-paying social service jobs. Seventy-five percent of working men still earn less than $25,000 a year. Most old men are poor.

In this imaginary world, women frequently take advantage of their superior positions to harass or belittle men, who are socially valued primarily for their bodies, often used as bait in bathing suits to sell everything from cars to exotic vacations. Objectified this way, and with low status, they are subject to constant verbal and physical abuse. The leading cause of death worldwide among men ages fourteen to forty-four is the violence they are subjected to in their own homes.

Every ten years, men gather together under sponsorship of the United Nations, for a major international conference, focusing on how to change their limiting circumstances. A U.N. statistic embroiders a popular postcard: while men do 90% of the world's work, they own less than 1% of its resources.

That mythical land isn't a fair world. But the simple gender reversal highlights today's inequities.

What would an equitable world look like? Can we even imagine a just distribution of power, roughly proportional to population?

In this fair world, there is approximate gender balance (and proportionate ethnic representation) in powerful spots, with a slight preponderance of females, due to their greater numbers in the population. Election tickets, in this just environment, typically have female/male teams, with females heading slates only slightly more than half the time. Because the distribution of power is so even, and so pervasive, little is made of gender or ethnicity. Religion and sexual preference aren't news. They're simply part of the inevitable diversity of all life on the planet.

Nor is it news that in male/female households, tasks are evenly distributed. Women and men both are concerned with their work—and with dinner, laundry, and child care. In some homes men take more responsibility for maintaining personal relationships and networks, remembering the in-laws' birthdays, making sure a card or gift is given, celebrating special times in the lives of friends, and remembering the holiday recipes; in other homes, women continue to tell the stories of family life. They remember and recount stories of the grandmother clearing brush well into her '90s, stories of the little ones being born, and the power of giving birth. These stories may be exchanged around the cars where women sometimes congregate, talking shop about motors and new car design.

We haven't written the conclusion yet, but I think the future of Chinese women in the communities (in the U.S.) is very bright, much brighter than it could have been for first generation women or women who lived before 1950 . . . among the women we have interviewed the sky's the limit . . .

—Judy Yung, Director of The Chinese Women of America 1848–1982 pictorial exhibit

Men who carry community histories often find themselves sit-ting around the coffee pot in the kitchen, tired but satisfied after creating a good dinner for friends and family.

Taking the lead from same-sex couples, heterosexuals also sort out tasks according to temperament. Who sews (if anyone does), who takes out the garbage, balances the check-book, or runs when the child cries—all of these threads in the tapestry of everyday life are no longer gender-specific.

Since there are all kinds of people designing products we use every day, they suit the needs of a variety of consumers. Lecterns are made with easily adjustable heights—no one ever again has to carry a personal foot stool to news conferences to be seen above the podium. Chairs are also normed for different body sizes, with many types of seating available in public places: conference rooms, lecture halls, bus and rail stations, theaters. There are large chairs and small ones, and always spaces designed to accommodate wheelchairs.

Women's public bathrooms are regularly twice the size of men's, since time-studies show that women (with more cum-bersome clothing) need double the time men do.

In this equitable world, sports teams are gender-integrated. There is some concern that women seem to be "taking over" ice hockey, with their numbers getting slightly higher than their demographic representation, but most analysts see this as a current statistical blip without real meaning or consequence.

In this time to come, even Cinderella liberates herself. The fairy tale told to children now goes this way:

Once upon a time there was a young woman who had to do all the housework for her family. Cinderella was brought up to believe in fairy godmothers, so she kept waiting for one to appear and put everything right. One day in a blinding flash she understood that was a fantasy; she had to take charge of her own life, get over accommodating everybody else's needs, and set some goals.

"To hell with this," she said. She called her family together, sat them down and told them how dissatisfied she was with her life. She had set herself a goal, she said, to change her living conditions. From now on she wasn't going to do all the household labor, but only her equitable share: one-fifth. "Furthermore," she continued, "you all look pretty unhappy too. Let's form a Family Action Team to plan a change for all of us."

After initially getting furious at Cinderella ("Have you lost your mind?" they shouted, "Who's been influencing you? What have you been reading?"), her family settled down and began to acknowledge that their lives were indeed rather empty. In spite of living together, they each felt pretty isolated and often, lonesome. In the end, after much storming, they agreed to form a support group for family change.

At the first Action Team meeting, Cinderella led a lively discussion about the ways sexism works to keep women (and men) apart. She had carefully planned a brief non-confrontational presentation, and lobbied her sisters and parents individually before the meeting, helping them understand how they were each long-term losers in such a negative, distrustful environment. At the meeting, they initiated cooperative housework, with each family member choosing tasks, and telling each other the kinds of support they'd like. Cindy's sister Aggie made a list of jobs, with assignments, and posted it next to their favorite gathering spot, the fireplace.

At the second Action Team meeting, they decided every person in the family should get a paying job. Within a few months, each of them found interesting part-time work, and, pooling their resources, they all lived more creatively ever after.

This is the world we are creating, where even Cinderella, that symbol of woman-as-trophy-bride, takes charge of her life. And it is coming into being. It's startling to realize that the world we envisioned twenty-five years ago, at the beginning of this wave of the women's movement, is actually upon us.

Who thought, for instance, at the 1985 U.N. Conference on Women in Nairobi, that sexual rights for women would ever be discussed at such a forum? Yet, ten years later, at the U.N. Women's Conference in Beijing, delegates agreed on an

> *Our spiritual path is with each other, helping each other to be who we were meant to be in the world. I think we are beginning to see that the Women's Movement is one of the most important spiritual revolutions of our time.*
>
> **—Coeleen Kiebert, artist, therapist and teacher**

unprecedented statement asserting the right for women everywhere to make decisions about sexuality, free of coercion.

Women are on a roll, taking on everything from international finance—with Women's World Bank start-up loans—to the last bastions of male privilege: the Senate, The Citadel. And the home. The culture is changing so fast it's astonishing, as we can see if we step back for a moment (and many are trying to step back for more than a moment).

This is the future we are making, with places that fit us all. And if we remember who we are, if we use our Action Teams well and truly take charge everywhere, if we build bridges across all the chasms history has driven between us, we'll find one day that we have arrived in a marvelous land. So fasten your seat belts, get out your maps, and full speed ahead!

> *When I look at the future, it's so bright it burns my eyes.*
>
> —Oprah Winfrey, talk show host

Strategies for Making Your Visions Come True

 Imagine your life exactly as you'd like it. How, in your ideal world, do you spend your time? How much money do you have, and what friends? What does your family look like and what are the relationships within it? What gives you the deepest satisfaction? How do you proportion work and play—and how do you define them?

Your vision for yourself is the beginning of your vision for the world, because it's impossible to have one woman's life be exactly right without altering its context.

 Dedicate a portion of your time to visioning. If you are an entrepreneur, build visioning time into your annual work plan. Structure such time, either alone or with a key colleague—in a quiet place before the business day starts, or away from the office during a work day—to reflect on your business. How has it evolved, and where is it headed? Look beyond your customers' needs now and ahead to what they might require in the future. Using your imagination this way helps you transform your role from run-of-the-mill service provider to visionary leader.

No matter what your job is, your visionary skills will assist both you and your entire workplace. If you are a short-order chef, or a hotel clerk, how might your job be structured to be more efficient and interesting? How could the restaurant or hotel be better run? What foods, or room amenities, will people likely be requesting next year? Next decade? Even though you are only responsible for one segment of the whole operation, your envisioning of the whole, as well as your part, will make it all run more smoothly.

Imagine your town or city precisely as you want it. How is the town government organized and who is in it? What are the policies and rules that govern community life? What is the justice system, rewards, media? Assume it can all be just the way you'd feel most comfortable. What is going to enhance your life and that of others you cherish? That is how it can be. You don't have to take responsibility for changing it all, but having some image of a rationally organized and just society will inform many small decisions you make, and conversations in which you participate.

Imagine the planet as it would suit you best, in every detail. It's your world. You get to have to be right for you. And you can assume that as it becomes most suitable for you, so will it be right for others.

Most women that have to fight for survival get a special strength sooner or later.

—**Elizabeth Catlett, sculptor**

When people ask me why I am running as a woman, I always answer, "What choice do I have?" I have a brain and a uterus, and I use both.

—Patricia Schroeder, veteran Colorado congresswoman

Action Team Visioning

Take time with your group to envision the world precisely as you desire it and think would work well for all. Composing a group vision can illuminate current reality—how is the vision at variance with life today?—and give you a sense of how to shape your goals and your map. Envisioning the future we want also expands our sense of the possible; we set our goals higher and further out than we might have if we hadn't allowed ourselves the luxury of a "vision." We allow fresh ideas of possibilities into our minds; as glimmers of the new ways begin to show themselves, we have a better chance of recognizing them. And our plans can be based on expanded goals.

Be concrete. What does this world you want smell like, how does it appear, and what are your places in it? How is work structured? Family life? Individual life? Group life? Money? Who does what?

In order to get your creative juices flowing, freeing you to imagine existence as significantly different, use Brainstorming. As its name implies, this is a technique that stimulates rushes of energy; it's highly effective for generating fresh ideas. The group records, for a designated period of time (five or ten minutes), all the thoughts people produce. There is no judgment, discussion, or evaluation at this point. Just inspiration.

"I want a world in which everyone, regardless of job status, gets a paid sabbatical every six years for three months."

"Women-only slates in the next two Presidential elections, just to break the ice and get everyone used to the idea of women in the highest offices. And as remedy for past exclusion."

"Day-care centers on every block."

"Lesbian partnerships legally equal to heterosexual ones."

"The language has changed so much we don't even have distinctions based on social categories."

"A thirty-hour work week for everyone."

"Legislation assuring equal sharing of household responsibilities."

"Completely automated homes for everyone."

"Homes for everyone, period."

At this stage of brainstorming, no idea is deemed too outrageous to be recorded. In a very short time creativity blooms in remarkable ways. Imagination seems to be like those wire snakes concealed in jars of fake "Nuts" or "Jam." It can remain bottled up indefinitely; but take the lid off and it springs right out. When you brainstorm together you benefit from group synergy, stimulating each others' reserves of genius.

At the conclusion of the brainstorm, select several ideas to examine more closely. Some of them will become the basis of goals—hopes we begin to take seriously. This in turn sets into motion a planning process, however subtle it may be: ideas from the brainstorm will provide a basis for future choices. Once an idea has been put into the air, it begins to take on life. The next time you hear it or speak it, the notion won't be so unfamiliar; soon it may become a friend, one you want to spend more time with.

In the group you may also create individual visions. Take time to carefully think about what you want. What you picture is the world you are making. It is the destination of your highway.

It's impossible to live and be unauthentic. You can't be someone else. There's a parallel with what happens to women when we realize being good girls doesn't work— so we might as well be whoever the hell we are.

—Gloria Steinem, author, founder, Ms.

Every Woman's Action Guide Map for Success

Every Woman's Action Guide
Map for Success

The future belongs to those who believe in the beauty of their dreams.

—Eleanor Roosevelt (1884–1962) U.N. delegate, journalist, First Lady

As you finish this book, take some time to assess your own profile in relation to *Taking Charge*. Where do you need to go next? As you reflect on that question, you'll create your individual map for success.

What areas do you find most difficult, and which are more comfortable? For some women, getting over the training to be cookie-cutter "nice" is a constant struggle ("Am I acting mean if I say what I want?") and strategizing for allies seems too cold and calculating. But making thoughtful, aware choices and setting goals is second nature. For other women, building alliances comes easily, while making themselves central presents a major challenge. "Getting over the guilt I feel as a mother is my big task," said Tamyra when she reflected on her relationship to power and leadership. "Being central sounds like an impossible, totally selfish—though enviable—state. But I've always had good male and female allies, and once I put my mind to it, I meet my goals. I need to make a goal to get over guilt, I guess, and strategize about how to do it."

Your mix might be: "'Taking charge'—no problem. Developing male allies? That's hopeless."

And as for being a member of a group, you may have started an Action Team that is already changing your life—or still be wondering how to get one off the ground.

The checklist below is designed to give you insight into your own profile, helping you identify where you're already revved up to high gear, and where you want to make a conscious choice to accelerate.

Whatever your route, have a wonderful ride. Enjoy it, and may you arrive at your goals refreshed, ready to go exploring.

Every Woman's Action Guide Checklist

____ I put myself in environments that strengthen me.

____ I rely on strong women who are my predecessors.

____ I am in a supportive Action Team or other group that supports my growth.

____ I know that I am the center of my universe.

____ I don't worry about being "nice."

____ I know what I want—then plan to get it.

____ I ask questions, or observe, until I get all the data I need to make informed decisions.

____ I know what my top three life goals are.

____ I make choices that move me toward my goals.

____ I choose laughter, whenever possible.

____ I know I'm in charge of my life, all the time.

____ I never "settle" for less than I deserve.

____ I am comfortable in my body.

____ I support other women, remembering that a chain is only as strong as its weakest link.

____ I am in life-long learning mode about the differences, as well as similarities, between women.

____ I am an ally to all other women—and men.

____ I insist that men treat me, and my ideas, respectfully.

____ I expect men to be my champions.

____ I see myself as a powerful woman.

____ I anticipate, and envision, a future of equality.

ACKNOWLEDGMENTS

It is surprising how a book authored by one can rely on so many: women who shared stories from their lives, readers of drafts whose thoughtful comments deepened my thinking, friends whose love nurtured me, and leaders who developed expansive insights.

A heartfelt thanks to those who gave me your stories, encouragement, and ideas for inclusion, and to my reader-critics: Andrea Ayvazian, Hilary Cairns, Mary Ann Cofrin, Kerry Dietz, Nancy Duff, Susan Freundlich, Ronnie Gilbert, Diane Goldstein, Nina Grayson, Carole Johnson, Chandra Kendrix, Donna Korones, Malcolm Lester, Barbara Love, Mercedes Martin, Laura Menard, Elizabeth Seja Min, Twila Mullenix, Yeshi Sherover Neumann, Elouise Oliver, Betty Powell, Alean Saunders, Theresa Smith, Cullen Stanley, Barbara Steinau, Mardi Steinau, Morton Steinau, Virna Tintiangco, Léonie Walker, Tamyra Walz, Akaya Windwood, and Cynthia Wood-Tara.

My appreciation also goes to the staff and Board of Directors at Equity Institute whose enthusiastic support for Equity Institute's Media Project and for me personally helped make this book a reality. Thanks to Board members Rosemary Baker, Ann DeGroot, John Eastman, Carl Griffin, Betsy Koffman, Melissa Kohner, Barbara Love, Cynthia Mayeda, Maureen Phillips, Betty Powell, Linda Randall, Santiago Rodriguez, Elaine Seiler, and Hazaiah Williams; to East and West Coast Media Project Ad Hoc Committee members Sharon Blair, Joanie Bronfman, Joshua Green, Jim Hormel, Jay Hughes, Donna Korones, Betsy Koffman, Tracey Lake, Josh Mailman, Elaine Seiler, Laurie and Mare Wallace, and Lynn Wenzel; and to Equity Program Think Tank members Joshua Green, Carole Johnson, Yeshi Sherover Neumann, Anthony Ramsey, Alean Saunders, and Akaya Windwood. And to Equity East Coast Senior Consultants Loel Greene and Jamie Washington, who are thinking with us even when they can't be

To love what you do and feel that it matters—how could anything be more fun?

—Katherine Graham, publisher of *The Washington Post*

Almost everything I do—more and more as the years go by has an element of joy for me, and if it doesn't, I generally don't do it.

—Alice Walker, Pulitzer Prize-winning author

on site in the California office for Think Tank meetings.

I am also grateful to Equity Institute's clients, who inspire me with their persistence and growth; and to Equity Institute's many loyal donors, who sustain our national training and non-profit consulting services, which also inspire and continue to instruct me. My hat is off to Valerie Taylor, consultant extraordinaire, who has helped keep Equity Institute—and me as its Executive Director—on track during reorganization and transformation into a twenty-first century firm. And to Tamyra Walz for assisting me through every stage of the manuscript. Thank you all.

During the writing of this book I came to cherish my "Women, Money, and Power" Support Group. They provided flesh on the bones of my thinking about the sustaining nature of women's teams. My great appreciations to group leaders Susan Freundlich and Maria Franco-Morse, and to members Rita Alfred, Sue Korbel, Kathy Fong, Barbara Hazard, Carole Johnson, Michelle Ku, Elizabeth Seja Min, Yeshi Sherover Neumann, Veronica Obodo-Eckblad, Léonie Walker, and Akaya Windwood.

My thinking about women has also been stretched by the work of Diane Balser, Barbara Love, and Nancy Lemon, as I've watched them lead groups and listened to their analysis. Thank you for being out in front. And thanks to Pam Carrington for her creative adaptation of the Cinderella story, providing a jumping off point for my own reworking of the tale, as well as to W, whose anonymous story in *Sisters,* "Requiring Respect," gave me an outline for adaptation.

My gratitude to Eleanor Holmes Norton, who graciously agreed to use precious hours to read the manuscript and write a foreword for *Taking Charge.* Sharing a book cover with such an old friend is an enormous gift; it makes me deeply happy. Thank you for the honor.

And appreciations to my dear friend Jim Hormel, whose constant encouragement over five years of monthly lunches at Zuni Cafe has been invaluable. Thank you also to my sister artists, adventurers, and writers, whose friendship inspires and informs me: Ronnie Gilbert, Susan Griffin, Ruth King, Donna Korones, Mary Watkins, and Helen Zia.

Thank you to Eric Jansen and Lynn Ludlow for your superb editing of my radio and newspaper commentaries. Your skill has taught me much about writing.

A book would be little without its publisher. Deep thanks to Mary Jane Ryan, Conari Press co-founder and an editor upon whom I have come to rely; Emily Miles, director of publicity and a wonderful ally; Will Glennon, Conari Press co-founder; Ame Beanland, a brilliant artist; and to all the women and men of Conari Press. Mary Jane and Will had a vision of a publishing house that empowers women—and they made it a reality. I value our collaborative relationship.

I have also been sustained by the unwavering support of my parents, Barbara and Morton Steinau. Their careful reading of an early draft was helpful, as was their willingness to allow me to share challenging portions of their lives in the text. I am a lucky daughter to have such allies on life's journey—as well as the good fortune of a mother who models continual growth.

And my everlasting gratitude to the woman who holds up a vision of me as a leader when I lose it, the co-founder of Equity Institute and the person whose conversations generated many of the ideas which found their way into this book: my business and life-partner, Carole Johnson, who after all these years continues to astonish me with her thinking, expand me with her creative courage, and nourish me with the constancy of her love.

BIBLIOGRAPHY

Aburdene, Patricia and Naisbitt, John, *Megatrends for Women,* Villard Books, 1992.

Ackelsberg, Martha A., *Free Women of Spain,* Indiana University Press, 1991.

Allison, Dorothy, *Two or Three Things I Know for Sure,* Dutton, 1995.

Anonymous, "Thinking and Oppression," Ovifat, Belgium, report in *Sisters* No. 7, Rational Island Publishers, Seattle, Washington, 1985.

Anzaldua, Gloria, and Moraga, Cherrie, eds. *This Bridge Called My Back,* Kitchen Table/Women of Color Press, 1983.

Angier, Natalie, "Why Science Loses Women in the Ranks," *The New York Times,* May 14, 1995.

Applegate, Jane, "Business Women Say They Get No Respect," *Los Angeles Times,* October 22, 1994.

Aptheker, Bettina, *Woman's Legacy, Essays on Race, Sex and Class in American History,* University of Massachusetts Press, Amherst, MA, 1982.

_____, *Tapestries of Life: Women's Work, Women's Consciousness, and the Meaning of Daily Experience,* University of Massachusetts Press, Amherst, MA, 1989

Bateson, Mary Catherine, *Composing a Life,* Plume, 1990.

Beilenson, Joan and Jackson, Heidi, *Voices of Struggle, Voices of Pride: A Collection of Quotes of Great African-Americans,* Peter Pauper Press, Inc., 1992.

Bernstein, Nina, "Equal Opportunity Recedes for Most Female Lawyers," *The New York Times,* January 8, 1996.

Berry, Kathy, "Women and Physical Power Calendar," 5356 Nebraska, Toledo, Ohio, 1994.

Bilimoria, Diana and Piderit, Sandy Kristin, "Sexism on High: Corporate Boards," *The New York Times,* February 5, 1995.

Binder, David, "Odd Bond: Hijacker and Officer's Widow," *The New York Times,* December 19, 1994.

Blank, Renee and Slipss, Sandra, *Voices of Diversity: Real People Talk about Problems and Solutions in a Workplace Where Everyone Is Not Alike,* Amacon, American Management Association, 1994.

Bolen, Jean Shinoda, *Ring of Power: The Abandoned Child, the Authoritarian Father, and the Disempowered Feminine,* HarperCollins, 1992.

Bray, Rosemary L., "Rosa Parks: A Legendary Moment, a Lifetime of Activism," *Ms.,* Volume VI, Number 3.

Breggin, Peter R., *Talking Back to Prozac,* St. Martin's Paperbacks, 1994.

Browne, Susan E.; Connors, Debra; and Stern, Nanci, eds., *With the Power of Each Breath: A Disabled Women's Anthology,* Cleis Press, 1985.

Broyles, Yolanda Julia, "Women in El Teatro Campesino: '¿Apoco Estaba Molacha La Virgen de Guadalupe?'" in *Chicana Voices, Intersections of Class, Race and Culture,* National Association for Chicano Studies, Department of Sociology, Colorado College, Colorado Springs, CO., 1990.

Butler, Sandra, and Rosenblum, Barbara, *Cancer in Two Voices,* Spinsters Book Company, 1991.

Cantwell, Mary, "The Women in Their Ranks: Learning Not to be Nice," *The New York Times Magazine,* November 19, 1995.

Carrington, Pam, "Cindella's Liberation," *Sisters* No. 7, Rational Island Publishers, Seattle, Washington, 1985.

Carroll, Rebecca, *I Know What the Red Clay Looks Like: The Voice and Vision of Black Women Writers,* Crown Trade Paperbacks, 1994.

Chira, Susan, "Custody Fight in Capital: A Working Mother Loses," *The New York Times,* September 20, 1994.

Chodorow, Nancy, *The Reproduction of Mothering,* University of California Press, 1978.

Clinton, Hillary Rodham, "Help for Stressed-out Working Mothers," *San Francisco Examiner,* September 25, 1995.

Córdova, Teresa, et al, *Chicana Voices: Intersections of Class, Race and Gender,* National Association for Chicano Studies, 1990.

Davis, Eisa, "Sexism and the Art of Feminist Hip-Hop Maintenance," *To Be Real: Telling the Truth and Changing the Face of Feminism,* ed. by Rebecca Walker, Anchor, 1995.

Crow Dog, Mary, with Richard Erdoes, *Lakota Woman,* Grove Weidenfeld, 1990.

della Cava, Marco R., "Righting Rape is One Man's Crusade," *USA Today,* March 28, 1995.

Dobrzynski, Judith, "Way Beyond the Glass Ceiling," *The New York Times,* May 5, 1995.

Douglas, Susan, "Sitcom Women: We've Come a Long Way. Maybe." *Ms.,* November/December, 1995.

Duff, Carolyn, *When Women Work Together,* Conari Press, 1993.

Elber, Lynn, "'Alice's Lavin, MTM Team Up," *San Francisco Chronicle,* January 5, 1996.

el Saadawi, Nawal, *Two Women in One,* Seal Press, 1986.

Faludi, Susan, *Backlash, The Undeclared War Against American Women,* Crown Publishers, 1991.

Federal Glass Ceiling Commission, *A Solid Investment,* U.S. Government Printing Office, Washington, D.C., 1995.

_____, *Good For Business: Making Full Use of the Nation's Human Capital, A Fact-Finding Report,* U.S. Government Printing Office, Washington, D.C. 1995.

Fernandez, Elizabeth, "Women Rooted to the Workplace," *San Francisco Examiner,* May 11, 1995.

Fletcher, Connie, *Breaking and Entering: Women Cops Talk About Life in the Ultimate Men's Club,* HarperCollins, 1995

Gabor, Andrea, "Crashing the 'Old Boy' Party," *The New York Times,* January 8, 1995.

Genasci, Lisa, "Firms Vow to Boost Family Care," Associated Press Report, *San Francisco Examiner,* September 14, 1995.

Giddings, Paula, *When and Where I Enter: The Impact of Black Women on Race and Sex in America,* Bantam Books, 1984.

Gilligan, Carol, *In a Different Voice: Psychological Theory and Women's Development,* Harvard University Press, 1982.

Gilbert, Ronnie, *Ronnie Gilbert on Mother Jones: Face to Face With the Most Dangerous Woman in America,* Conari Press, 1993.

Glamour, "Women of the Year," December, 1995.

Goldberg, Carey, "Acting Like Men, Getting in Trouble," *The New York Times,* June 18, 1995.

Gray, Jerry, "Junior Senators Prevent a Vote on Budget Cuts," *The New York Times,* July 1, 1995.

Grove, Lloyd, "The Sermon on the Amount, Eleanor Holmes Norton, Preaching the Fiscal Gospel," *The Washington Post,* December 27, 1994.

Hammer, Michael and Champy, James, *Reengineering the Corporation, A Manifesto for Business Revolution,* HarperCollins Publishers, 1993.

Hancock, Emily, *The Girl Within,* Fawcett Columbine, 1989.

Harley, Sharon and Terborg-Penn, Rosalyn, *The Afro-American Woman,* Kennikat Press, 1978.

Harragan, Betty Lehan, *Games Mother Never Taught You: Corporate Gamesmanship for Women,* Warner Books, 1977.

Helgesen, Sally, *The Female Advantage, Women's Ways of Leadership,* Doubleday, 1990.

Heilbrun, Carolyn G., *Writing a Woman's Life,* Ballantine, 1989.

Heim, Pat and Susan K. Golant, *Smashing the Glass Ceiling, Tactics for Women Who Want to Win in Business,* Simon and Schuster, 1993.

Hendrik, Bill, "Exploring 'New Age' Healing Therapies," *San Francisco Chronicle,* November 25, 1995.

Herrera, Hayden, *Frida: A Biography of Frida Kahlo,* Harper & Row, 1983.

herrup, mocha jean, "Virtual Identity," *To Be Real,* ed. Rebecca Walker, Anchor, 1995.

Hernández, Antonia, "A Latina's Experience of the Nonprofit Sector," *Women and Power in the Nonprofit Sector,* ed. by Teresa Odendahl and Micahel O'Neill, Jossey-Bass Publishers, 1994.

hooks, bell, *Sisters of the Yam,* South End Press, 1993.

_____, "Tough Talk for Tough Times," *On the Issues,* Winter, 1996.

Hochschild, Arlie, and Maching, Anne, *The Second Shift,* Avon Books, 1989.

Hong, Maria, ed., *Growing Up Asian American,* Avon Books, 1993.

Horner, Matina S., "Toward an Understanding of Achievement-related Conflicts in Women," *Journal of Social Issues 8,* no. 2, (1972).

Hosler, Karen, "House Parents are Symbols of New Era," *Baltimore Sun,* July 30, 1995.

Hull, Gloria T.; Scott, Patricia Bell; Smith, Barbara; eds. *All the Women Are White, All the Blacks Are Men, But Some of Us Are Brave,* Feminist Press, 1982.

Hutchison, Susan, "Pick a Sport, Any Sport!", Women Leaders Workshop Materials, Northern California Re-evaluation

Counseling Communities, San Francisco State University, July, 1994.

Ibarruri, Dolores, *They Shall Not Pass, The Autobiography of La Pasionaria,* International Publishers, 1966.

Ivins, Molly, "In the Wake of Abigail and Sojourner," *San Francisco Chronicle,* August 29, 1995.

Jetter, Alexis, "The Roseanne of Literature," *The New York Times Magazine,* December 17, 1995.

Jewell, Teri L., *The Black Women's Gumbo Ya-Ya,* Crossing Press, 1993.

Johnson, Carole L., "Dismantling Classism Workshop Exercises," Dismantling Classism Program, Equity Institute, 1995.

_____, *"Sticks, Stones and Stereotypes; Palos, Piedras y Estereotipos,"* Video and Workbook Curriculum, Equity Institute, 1987.

Johnson, Diane J, *Proud Sisters: The Wit and Wisdom of African-American Women,* Peter Pauper Press, 1995.

Kalogerakis, George, "The Brainy Bombshell," *Vogue,* May, 1994.

Kaminer, Wendy, "Feminism's Third Wave: What Do Young Women Want?" *The New York Times Book Review,* June 4, 1995.

Kanter, Rosabeth Moss, *Men and Women of the Corporation,* Basic Books, 1977.

Kaye/Kantrowitz, Melanie, *The Issue is Power,* Aunt Lute Books, 1992.

_____, and Klepfisz, Irena, eds., *The Tribe of Dina, A Jewish Women's Anthology,* Sinister Wisdom Books, 1986.

Kennedy, Flo, *Color Me Flo, My Hard Life and Good Times,* Prentice-Hall, 1976.

Kenny, Mary (Mary Kenney O'Sullivan), manuscript autobiography, Radcliffe College, Cambridge, Mass.

Kingston, Maxine Hong, *The Woman Warrior: Memoirs of a Girlhood Among Ghosts,* Knopf, 1976.

Klepfisz, Irena, *Dreams of an Insomniac: Jewish Feminist Essays, Speeches and Diatribes,* The Eight Mountain Press, 1990.

Kuhn, Maggie, *No Stone Unturned,* Ballantine Books, 1991.

Lanker, Brian, *I Dream A World: Portraits of Black Women Who Changed America,* Stewart, Tabori & Chang, 1989.

Lerner, Harriet G., *The Dance of Deception: Pretending and Truth-Telling in Women's Lives,* Harper Collins, 1993.

_____, *The Dance of Intimacy: A Woman's Guide to Courageous Acts of Change in Key Relationships,* Harper & Row, 1989.

Lester, Joan Steinau, *The Future of White Men and Other Diversity Dilemmas,* Conari Press, 1994.

Levi, Jan Heller ed., *A Muriel Rukeyser Reader,* W.W. Norton & Co., 1994.

Lewin, Tamar, "Men Whose Wives Work Earn Less, Studies Show," *The New York Times,* October 12, 1994.

_____, "Women Earn Half of Families' Incomes," *The New York Times,* May 11, 1995.

Library of Congress, *Women Who Dare,* 1995 Calendar, Catalog No. 95061.

Longman, Jere, "As Parents Squirm, Women Happily Scrum," *The New York Times,* May 8, 1995.

Lorde, Audre, *Sister Outsider: Essays and Speeches,* Crossing Press, 1984.

Louie, Elaine, "The Cars Supply the Drive," *The New York Times,* February 23, 1995.

Matsui-Estrella, Julia Keiko and Wenh-In Ng, Greer Anne, "Culture, Theology, and Leadership," *Women of Power, A Magazine of Feminism, Spirituality, and Politics,* Issue 24 (1995).

McMillan, Terry, *Waiting to Exhale,* Pocket Books, Simon and Schuster, 1992.

Menchú, Rigoberta, *I...Rigoberta Menchú, an Indian Woman in Guatemala,* edited by Elisabeth Burgos-Debray, translated by Ann Wright, Verso, 1984.

Miller, Jean Baker, *Toward a New Psychology of Women,* Beacon Press, 1976.

Mitchell, Elizabeth, "An Odd Break with the Human Heart," *To Be Real,* ed. by Rebecca Walker, Anchor Books, 1995.

Moore, Teresa, "A Literary Forum for Black Sisterhood," *San Francisco Chronicle,* September 27, 1995.

Morgan, Robin, ed., *Sisterhood is Powerful, An Anthology of Writings from the Women's Liberation Movement,* Random House, 1970.

Morrison, Ann M., *The New Leaders, Guidelines on Leadership Diversity in America,* Jossey-Bass Publishers, 1992.

Mukherjee, Bharati, *Jasmine,* Fawcett Crest, Ballantine Books, 1989.

Navratilova, Martina, with Vecsey, George, *Martina,* Knopf, 1985.

Ness, Carol and Gorden, Rachel, "Beating the Rap," *San Francisco Examiner,* August 13, 1995.

"News in Brief," *Ms.,* July/August, 1995.

Nunez, Sigrid, "Chang," in Hong, Maria, ed. *Growing up Asian American,* Avon Books, 1998.

Odendahl, Teresa and O'Neill, Michael, *Women and Power in the Nonprofit Sector,* Jossey-Bass Publishers, 1994.

Olsen, Tillie, *Silences,* Delacorte, 1979.

Partnoy, Alicia, ed., *You Can't Drown the Fire: Latin American Women Writing in Exile,* Cleis Press, 1988.

Peavey, Fran, *By Life's Grace: Musings on the Essence of Social Change,* New Society Publishers, 1994.

Pender, Kathleen, ed., "Through the Glass Ceiling," *San Francisco Chronicle,* September 18, 1995.

Piercy, Marge, *The Moon is Always Female,* Knopf, 1980.

Pollon, Zélie, "That Diva Jocelyn Taylor Is at It Again," *Deneuve,* December, 1995.

Preston, Anne E., "Women in the Nonprofit Labor Market," *Women and Power in the Nonprofit Sector,* ed. by Teresa Odendahl and Michael O'Neill, Jossey-Bass Publishers, 1994.

Rapping, Elayne, "Power Babes & Victim Feminists," *On the Issues,* Summer, 1995.

Rich, Adrienne, *Of Woman Born: Motherhood as Experience and Institution,* W. W. Norton & Co., 1976.

Rimer, Sara, "Nation Analyzes and Agonizes Over Citadel Dropout," *The New York Times,* August 21, 1995.

Roberts, Sam, "Women's Work: What's New, What Isn't," *The New York Times,* April 27, 1995.

Roscoe, Will, *Living the Spirit: A Gay American Indian Anthology,* St. Martin's Press, 1988.

Judy B. Rosener, *America's Competitve Secret: Utilizing Women as a Management Strategy,* Oxford University Press, 1995.

_____, Interview, Forum (Michael Krasney Show), KQED, San Francisco, July 6, 1995.

Rosenwasser, Penny, *Voices From a "Promised Land": Palestinian and Israeli Peace Activists Speak Their Hearts,* Curbstone Press, 1992.

Rountree, Cathleen, *On Women Turning 50: Celebrating Mid-Life Discoveries,* HarperSan Francisco, 1993.

Russell, Julia D., "Smoke and Mirrors," *Sojourner: The Women's Forum,* June, 1995.

Schaef, Anne Wilson, *Native Wisdom for White Minds: Daily Reflections Inspired by the Native Peoples of the World,* Ballantine Books, 1995.

Schwartz, Felice, *Breaking With Tradition: Women and Work, The New Facts of Life,* Warner Books, 1992.

Sheanin, Wendy, "Women Builders Breaking New Ground," *San Francisco Examiner,* April 16, 1995.

Sheehy, Gail, *New Passages: Mapping Your Life Across Time,* Random House, 1995.

Simon, Joel, "Mexican Senators Wary of 'La Tigresa,'" *San Francisco Chronicle,* January 23, 1995.

Simons, George F. and Wissman, G. Deborah, *Men and Women, Partners at Work,* Crisp Publications, 1990.

Sinton, Peter, "How Women CEOS Climbed to Top," *San Francisco Chronicle,* December 18, 1995.

Smith, Barbara, ed., *Home Girls, A Black Feminist Anthology,* Kitchen Table: Women of Color Press, 1983.

Snortland, Ellen, "Bitch, Bitch, Bitch," *On The Issues,* Spring, 1995.

Steinem, Gloria, *Moving Beyond Words,* Simon and Schuster, 1994.

_____, *Revolution From Within, A Book of Self-Esteem,* Little, Brown and Co., 1992.

Stephens, Autumn, *Untamed Tongues, Wild Words From Wild Women,* Conari Press, 1993.

Stevens, Mark, "How Am I Doing? Four Ways to Ask Your Customers," *Executive Female,* July/August, 1995.

Susman, Tina, "Female Ship's Captain—She's the Only One in Africa," *San Francisco Chronicle,* January 24, 1996.

Taylor, Susan L., *Lessons in Living,* Anchor Books, Doubleday, 1995.

Tax, Meredith, *"The Rising of the Women,"* Monthly Review Press, NY, 1980.

Thoele, Sue Patton, *The Courage to Be Yourself: A Woman's Guide to Growing Beyond Emotional Dependence,* Conari Press, 1991.

Tousignant, Maylou, "'Superwoman' Losing Hero Status," *The Washington Post,* January 3, 1995.

Trask, Haunani-Kay, *From a Native Daughter: Colonialism and Sovereignty in Hawai'i,* Common Courage Press, 1993.

Trask, Mililani B., "Decolonizing Hearts and Minds," *Woman of Power: A Magazine of Feminism, Spirituality, and Politics,* Issue 24, (1995).

Tyler, Patrick E., "U.N. Forum Hears Speech by Burmese," *The New York Times,* September 1, 1995.

W. (Anonymous), "Requiring Respect," *Sisters,* No. 9, Rational Island Publishers, Seattle, Washington, 1991.

Walker, Alice, ed., *I Love Myself When I am Laughing...and Then Again When I am Looking Mean and Impressive: A Zora Neale Hurston Reader,* The Feminist Press, 1979.

_____, *The Same River Twice: Honoring the Difficult, A Meditation on Life, Spirit, Art, and the Making of the Film The Color Purple Ten Years Later,* Scribner, 1996.

_____, *The Temple of My Familiar,* Harcourt Brace Jovanovich, 1989.

Walker, Rebecca, ed., *To Be Real: Telling the Truth and Changing the Face of Feminism,* Anchor, 1995

Warner, Carolyn, *The Last Word: A Treasury of Women's Quotes,* Prentice-Hall, 1992.

Wheatley, Margaret J., *Leadership and the New Science: Learning About Organization from an Orderly Universe,* Berrett-Koehler Publishers, 1992.

White, Evelyn C. , "Sisterly Support for Accused," *San Francisco Chronicle,* February 20, 1995.

Williams, Patricia J., *The Alchemy of Race and Rights,* Harvard University Press, 1991.

Wolf, Naomi, *Fire With Fire: The New Female Power and How to Use It,* Fawcett Columbine, 1993.

Wockner, Rex, "A Critical Mass," *The Advocate,* October 17, 1995.

Zepernick, Mary, "A Picture Distorted by Exclusion," *Cape Cod Times,* December 8, 1995.

Zook, Kristal Brent, "A Manifesto of Sorts for a Black Feminist Movement," *The New York Times Magazine,* November 12, 1995.

INDEX

C

D

E

I

J

K

L

T

U

V

W

Conari Press, established in 1987, publishes books on topics ranging from spirituality and women's history to sexuality and personal growth. Our main goal is to publish quality books that will make a difference in people's lives—both how we feel about ourselves and how we relate to one another.

Our readers are our most important resource, and we value your input, suggestions, and ideas. We'd love to hear from you—after all, we are publishing books for you!

For a complete catalog or to get on our mailing list, please contact us at:

CONARI PRESS

2550 Ninth Street, Suite 101
Berkeley, CA 94710

(800) 685-9595 • Fax (510) 649-7190
e-mail: Conaripub@aol.com